WYLYE VALLEY
IN OLD PHOTOGRAPHS

THE WYLYE VALLEY IN OLD PHOTOGRAPHS

COLLECTED BY
DANNY HOWELL

ALAN SUTTON
1988
Published in collaboration with
Wiltshire County Council
Library & Museum Service

Alan Sutton Publishing Limited
Brunswick Road · Gloucester

First published 1988

British Library Cataloguing in Publication Data

The Wylye Valley in old photographs.
1. Wiltshire. Wylye Valley, history
I. Howell, Danny, *1956–*
942.3′1

ISBN 0-86299-573-6

Typesetting and origination by
Alan Sutton Publishing Limited.
Printed in Great Britain by
WBC Print Limited.

CONTENTS

ACKNOWLEDGEMENTS

I am indebted to the following individuals and groups, without whom compilation of this book would not have been possible:

For the loan of photographs and postcards:
Mr N. Barnard; Mr G. Beach; Mr R. Bryant; Mrs B. Bull; Miss N. Bull; Mr R. Burgess; Mr P. Cole; Mr A. Dawkins; Mr C. Dawson; Miss L. Dredge; Mr R. Fear; Mr J. Fleming; Mr A. Ford; Mrs A. Gilbert; Mr T. Gillingham; Mrs J. Grace; Mr and Mrs L. Hallett; Mr R.P. Harvey; Mrs E. Hibbs; Mrs G. Howell; Mr E.F. Huntley; Mr R. Kiddle; Mr A. Moulding; Mrs K. Pearce; S. Petty; Mr and Mrs L. Phelps; Mrs C.E. Reeves; Miss M. Ryall; Mr G. Sims; I. Smith; Mr W. Symes; Warminster Dewey Museum; Warminster History Society; Mr P. White; Mrs B. Williams; Wiltshire Library & Museum Service; Mrs R. Wyeth.

For help with production and research:
Dr J. Chandler; the County Record Office, Trowbridge; Mr J. Field; F. Gilmour; the Local Studies Library, Trowbridge; Mr M. Marshman; Mr R. Pybus; Col. M. Randall; Warminster Library.

And, last but not least, for encouragement and support throughout:
My parents, Mr and Mrs B. Howell.

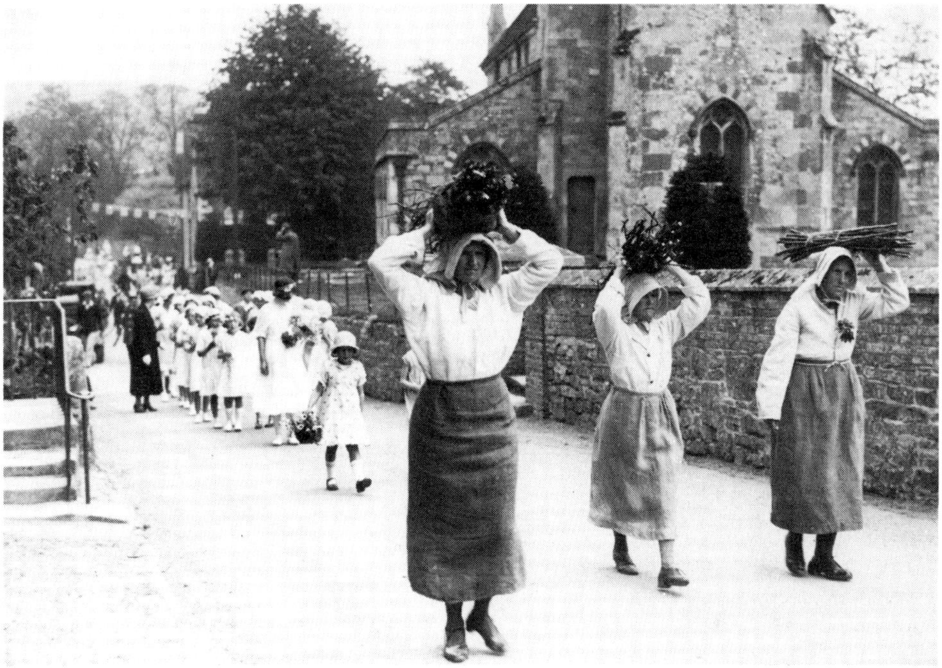

INTRODUCTION

I am proud to say that I was born in the Wylye Valley. My birthplace, on the eastern outskirts of Warminster, was within half a mile of the River Wylye and, except for a short stay in a Bath hospital when I was a child, my grammar school days in Frome and the occasional business trip or holiday away, I have spent every day of my life so far living and working in the Wylye Valley.

On leaving school I fulfilled my first ambition, farming, by working on local farms, where I immediately felt at one with the landscape. Through the changing seasons I was able to glimpse, at close quarters, much of the local wildlife. Up before dawn milking cows and afield late at night, particularly during harvest time, life on the land was a strange contradiction of hard work and simple enjoyment. I made many friends in the local farming community and it was partly through them that I came to appreciate the beauty and the charm of the Wylye Valley.

In May 1984, realising my other ambition, writing, I launched a community magazine for the area, called *The Wylye Valley Life*, which proved popular with readers; through this I was able to renew old acquaintances and make new friends. One of the features most looked forward to in the magazine was the inclusion, each issue, of an old photograph. Pictures of the villages as they used to be and photographs of local people in days gone by jogged many memories. Sometimes, just the mention of someone's name or the recognition of an apparently forgotten face was enough for people to put pen to paper and write to me. During my time as editor of the magazine I had the pleasure of meeting many of the Valley's 'characters'. Through talking to people, particularly the older generation, I came to appreciate their thinking, which has helped me to shape my own personal philosophy.

When I was asked to compile this book of old photographs of the Wylye Valley, as part of a nationwide series, I readily agreed. I had wanted to do something like it for a long time, not only for the sake of providing a pictorial record of how things used to be, but also as a 'thank you' to everyone in the Valley who has been a friend or offered kindness to me during the past few years. It is to them that I dedicate this book and I hope everyone, residents and visitors, will enjoy looking at the pictures. I was, of course, spoilt for choice when it came to making the final selection and it was more a case of what to leave out, than what to include. Warminster and Wilton are, of course, an integral part of the Wylye Valley, but I have deliberately omitted any photographs of these two towns as it was my intention from the beginning to make this book a truly rural celebration. Sadly, for some villages, particularly the smaller ones, photographs seem scarce and my search was hindered by the fact that 'genuine' born and bred villagers are becoming few and far between. In one village I discovered only one person, an elderly gentleman in his 90s, who could rightfully claim to have been born in the place! The immigrant population now taking up residence in the Valley may bring new blood and new ways to the villages, but they do not have, amongst other things, old photographs of the area they have chosen for buying their homes. Hopefully, this book will help more old pictures to come to light and I dare say there are hundreds of photographs and postcards at this moment, half-forgotten in drawers and cupboards, or gathering dust in attics. If shared, they could form the basis of a second collection for publication in the near future.

Danny Howell
October 1988.

SECTION ONE

River and Vale

The word 'Wylye' is believed to be a derivation of the Celtic word 'gwili', meaning 'twisting, turning or tricky stream'; a phrase which aptly describes the river Wylye in places.

The Wylye rises west of Kilmington, near the Wiltshire/Somerset border. For the first part of its journey it is barely a trickle during the summer months, resembling a 'winterborne' though it is also fed by the rivulets from Long Knoll which is reputed to be the highest point in Wiltshire (974ft.). In particularly dry times, the first glimpse of the Wylye is at Blackwell Spring, a pond-like feature next to the B3092 Frome–Mere road, near the turning for Kilmington village. From here, the water takes a north-east course, passing under the little tarmac road that leads to Coombe Barn, Norton Ferris. Then, along the ditch and going underground, it greets daylight again at another spring (some say the main spring) west of Kingston Deverill.

From this point the stream is known as the Deverill, giving its name to the valley in the lea of Cold Kitchen Hill. The name has also been adopted as the suffix to the villages it passes peacefully through: Kingston Deverill, Monkton Deverill, Brixton Deverill, Hill Deverill and Longbridge Deverill. By the time it leaves Longbridge Deverill the stream has grown into a river, the River Wylye, which heads north, past Crockerton, curving in a loop just south of Warminster below Salisbury Plain, before making eastward down the Wylye Valley.

The river meanders about the vale, through villages, many of which originated because of their feasibility as crossing places, hence the use of the word 'ford' so often in the Valley's place names: Codford, Hanging Langford, Little Langford, Steeple Langford, Stapleford, Stoford, and Wishford. At Codford, the waters of the Chitterne Brook flow into the Wylye and further on, at Stapleford, the Wylye is joined by another 'winterborne', the Till which, during wet winters, rises as far upstream as the village of Tilshead on Salisbury Plain.

The Wylye ends its journey of nearly 30 miles at Wilton, the ancient capital of Wessex. The town was, in fact, the capital of the shire by the eighth century and gave its name to the county – Wiltshire being a shortened version of the former Wiltonshire. The village of Wylye, the town of Wilton and the county of Wiltshire, all, therefore, take their names from the river. Beyond Wilton the Wylye joins the waters of the Nadder, the Avon, the Ebble and the Bourne, forming the Salisbury Avon which finally meets the sea at Christchurch in Hampshire.

For the first section of this book I have included a few glimpses of the Wylye on its diverse journey, together with one or two scenes showing man's involvement in the surrounding landscape. Hopefully, these pictures will portray something of the essence of what is still, perhaps, the most beautiful countryside in Wiltshire.

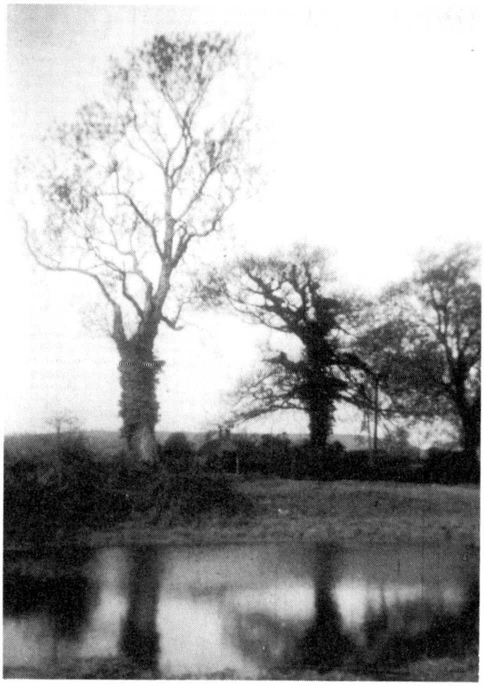

BLACKWELL SPRING, at Norton Ferris, pictured during the late 1940s. This was considered for a long time to be the birth of the River Wylye. It is during exceptionally dry periods, but the 'true' source of the Wylye is west of Kilmington.

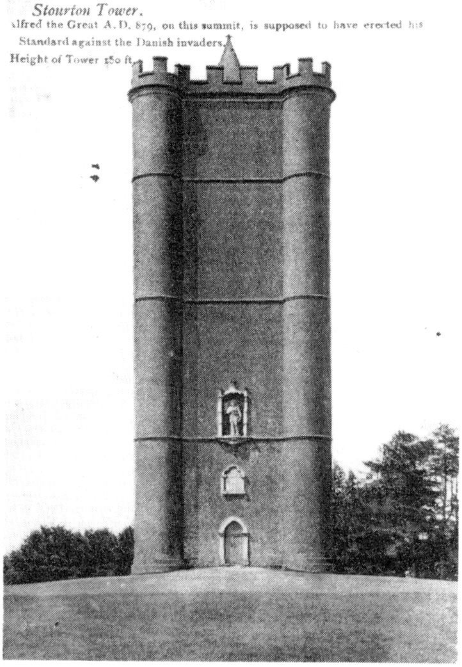

ALFRED'S TOWER on Kingsettle Hill, near Kilmington, before 1907. The site is traditionally regarded as the place where Alfred the Great assembled his army of 4,000 men to do battle with the invading Danes at Ethandune. The tower was conceived in 1762 by Henry Hoare after he read of Alfred's valiant exploits in Voltaire's *Histoire Generale*. Designed by Henry Flitcroft, it is triangular in shape to give less resistance to wind, is 150ft. high and comprises a million red bricks. The last brick was laid in 1772.

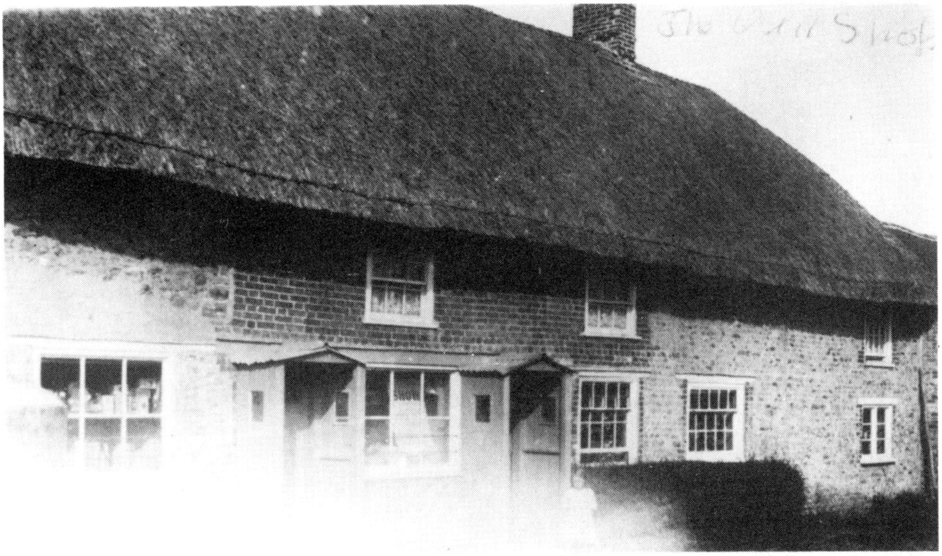

THE THENFORD STORES at Kilmington during the 1920s, when Granny Curtis was the proprietor. The poster in the window advertises a show, possibly the annual one at Gillingham or Shaftesbury or maybe Frome Cheese Show. The shop has just re-opened (1988) after being closed for several years.

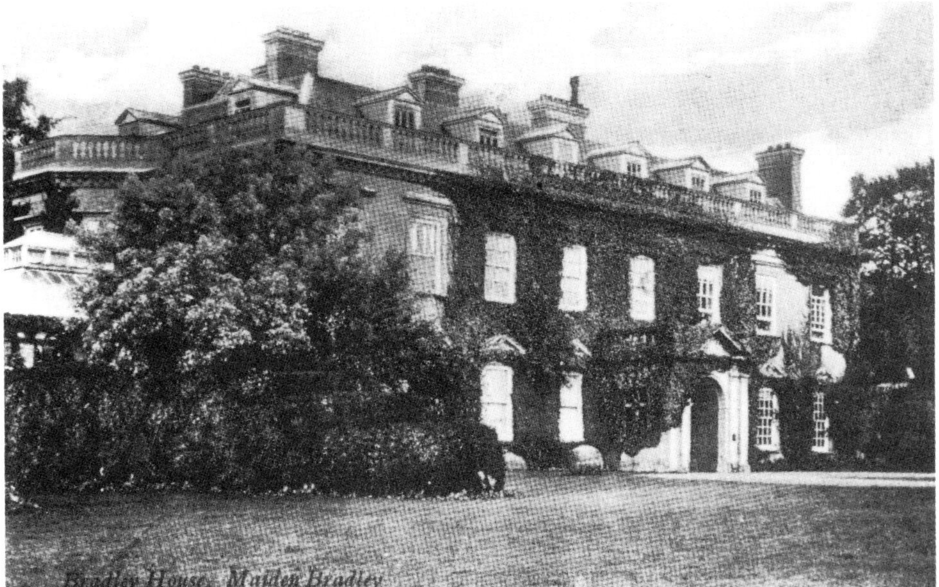

MAIDEN BRADLEY HOUSE, the home of the Dukes of Somerset, pictured during the 1920s.

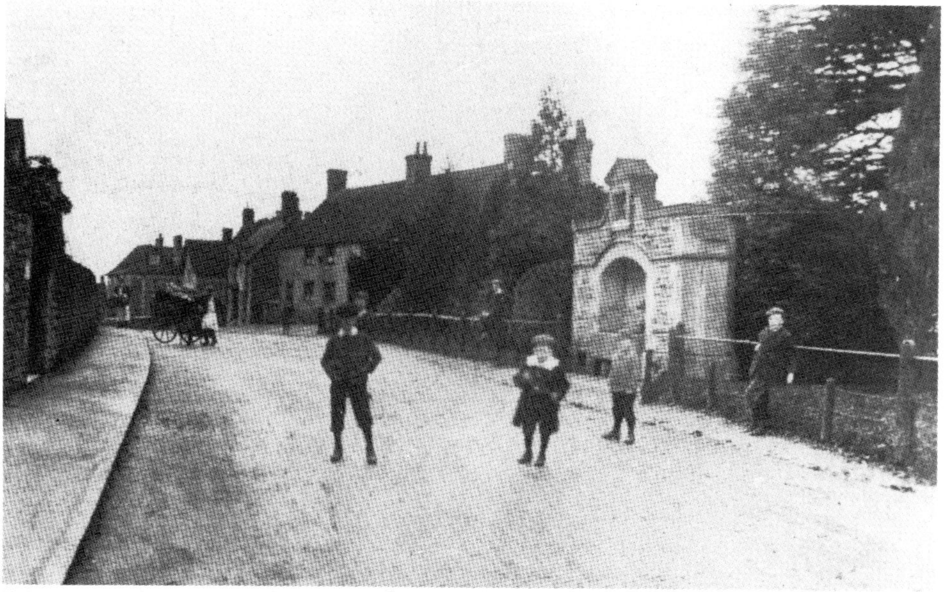

THE VILLAGE STREET AT MAIDEN BRADLEY features this ornamental drinking trough for horses. It was presented to the village by Algernon, 14th Duke of Somerset, in 1891. A plaque above the trough reads 'Drink Travellers Drink, of Bradley's Purest Rill, Which, strange to say, runs quite a mile up hill; Then to your panting Steed let all attend, An Honest Horse is Surely Man's Best Friend'.

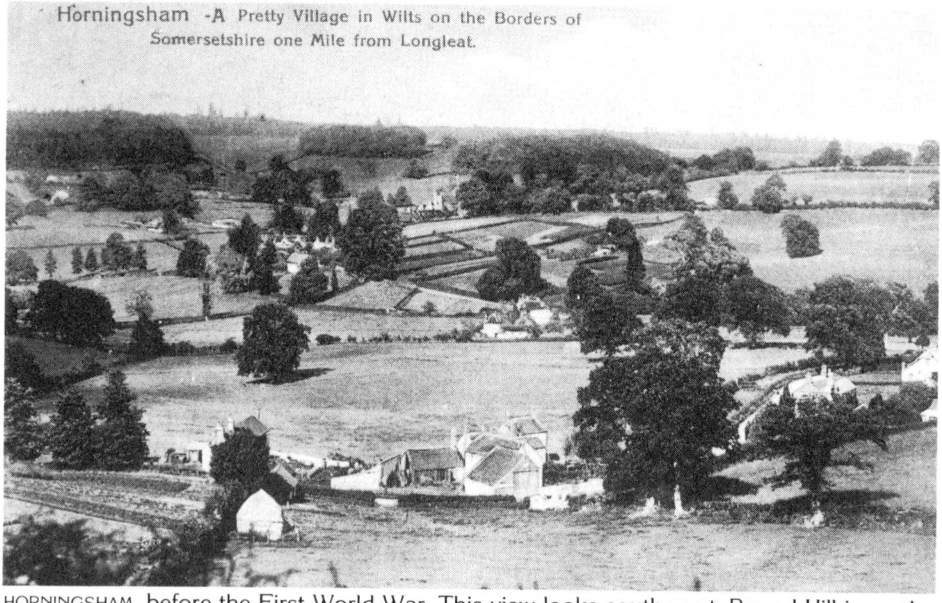

HORNINGSHAM, before the First World War. This view looks south-west. Round Hill is on the distant horizon.

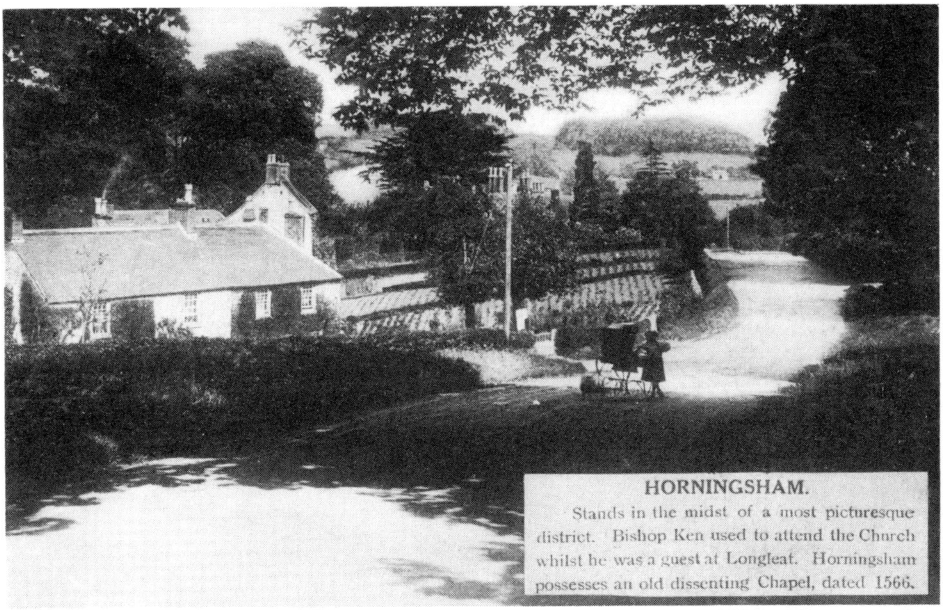

THE VILLAGE OF HORNINGSHAM on the Longleat Estate, during the mid-1920s. This scene has changed little over the years.

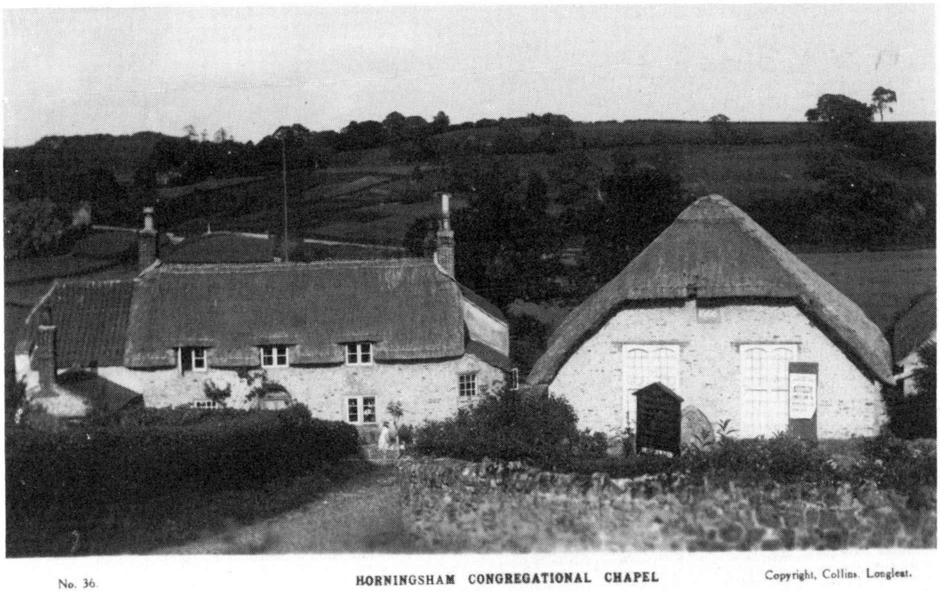

HORNINGSHAM CONGREGATIONAL CHAPEL, pictured here in the 1930s. It is reputed to be the oldest nonconformist chapel in the country. The south wall features the date '1566' and a plaque recording a death from hydrophobia.

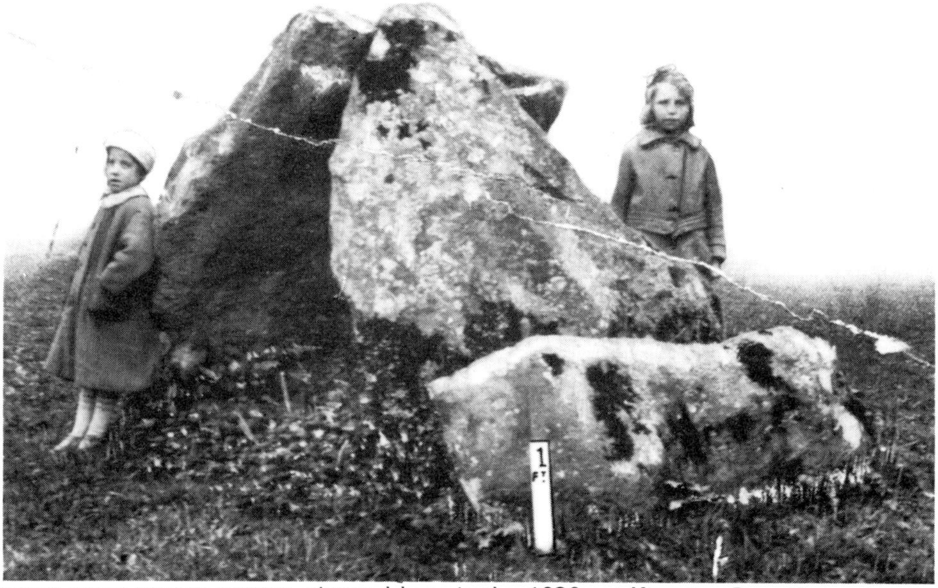

THESE THREE SARSEN STONES, pictured here in the 1920s at Kingston Deverill, are known locally as the Egbert Stones. Before 1877 they were removed by a farmer from King's Court Hill nearby, where it is said King Egbert once held his court. Following their use as stepping stones to a barn, they were moved again by the rector to the Rectory garden. Two of the stones can be seen today in the paddock east of St Mary's Church.

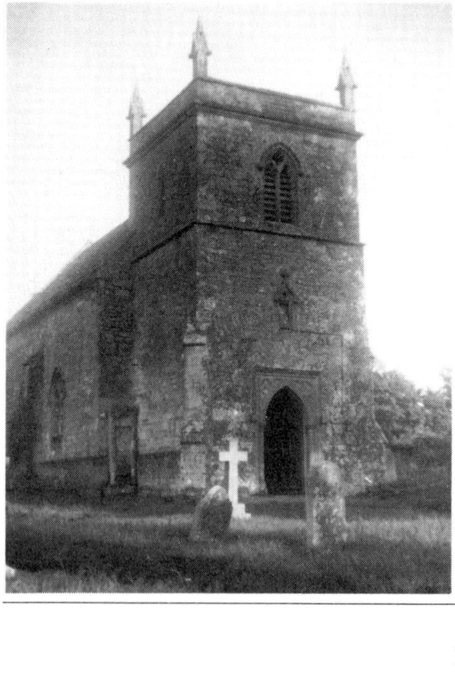

ST MICHAEL'S CHURCH at Brixton Deverill, pictured in 1948. The lower part of the tower is believed to be thirteenth century, while the upper part containing the belfry was added much later. An inscription on the exterior wall at the top reads 'Of that which God gave, this spire was erected and the tower adorned by the Rector, A.D. MDCCCLII'. A stone coffin, resting against the northern wall and visible in this photograph, can still be seen in the same place today.

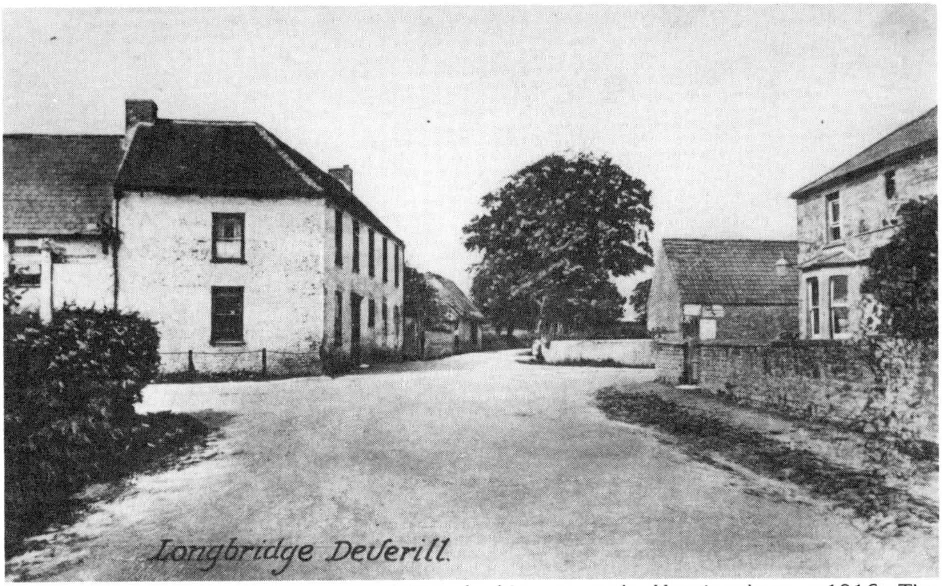

THE CROSSROADS AT LONGBRIDGE DEVERILL, looking towards Horningsham c.1916. The George Inn is on the left. The landlord at this time was Alfred James Perry. Avery's village shop and bakery, on the right, has long since been demolished, making way for road improvements.

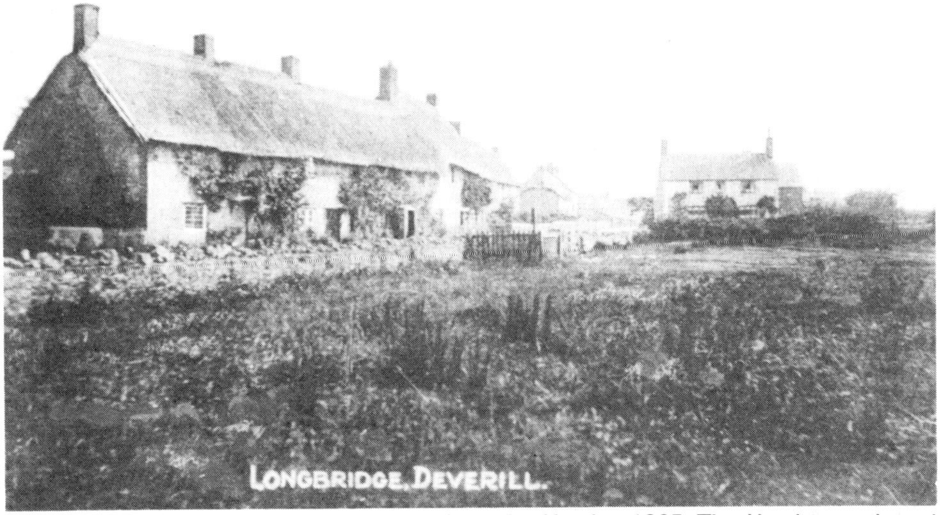

SAND STREET, Longbridge Deverill, viewed from the Marsh c.1905. The Marsh was planted with withy trees by the Marquis of Bath in 1910 and these grew into a dense forest. A gale blew down most of the trees in 1941 and, because the undergrowth would have given possible cover to German paratroopers, the trees were cleared. After the Second World War the present Lord Bath had the Marsh re-planted with Lombardy poplars and bamboo.

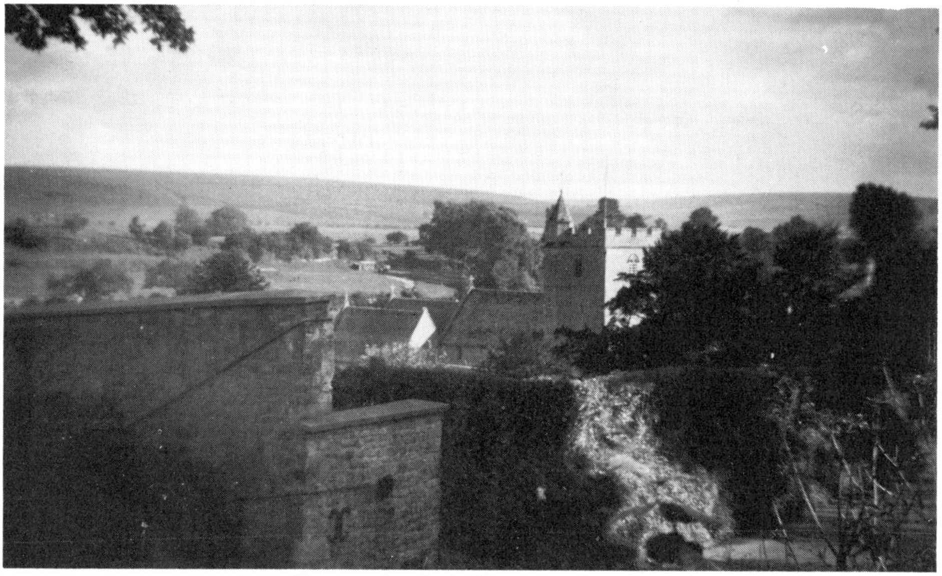

THE OLD MANOR HOUSE of the Thynne family (of Longleat fame) stood north of the church at Longbridge Deverill (now the new churchyard). The only part remaining is a wall of the house, seen here on the left, which is known locally as the Jew's Wall. A local legend recalls a Jew who was murdered at Lord's Hill and buried there. Folklore says that when the wall falls the male line of the Thynnes will die out. As you can see the wall is kept in good repair and is reinforced with iron struts.

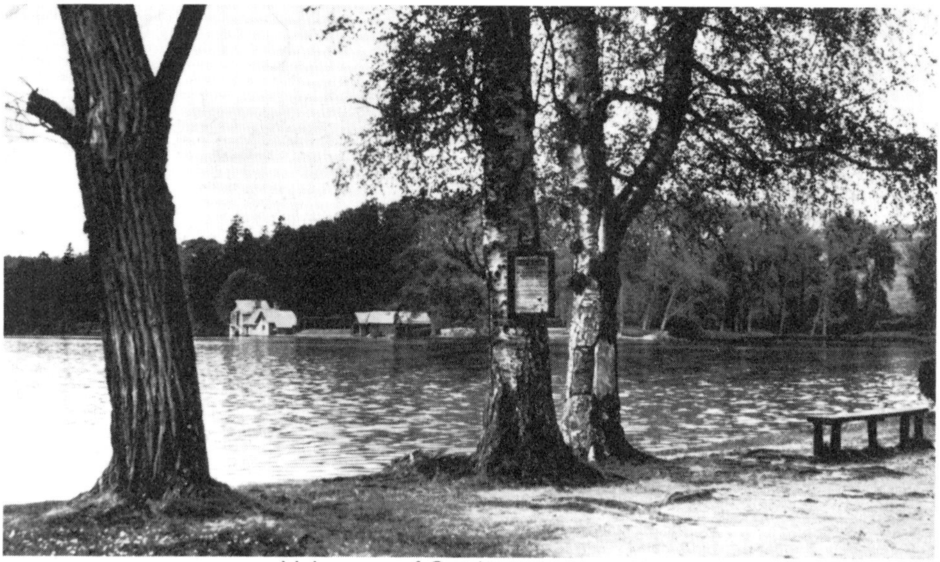

SHEARWATER, an ornamental lake west of Crockerton pictured here in 1930, was made for Lord Weymouth in 1792 by damming the stream which rises in the woods east of Longleat Park.

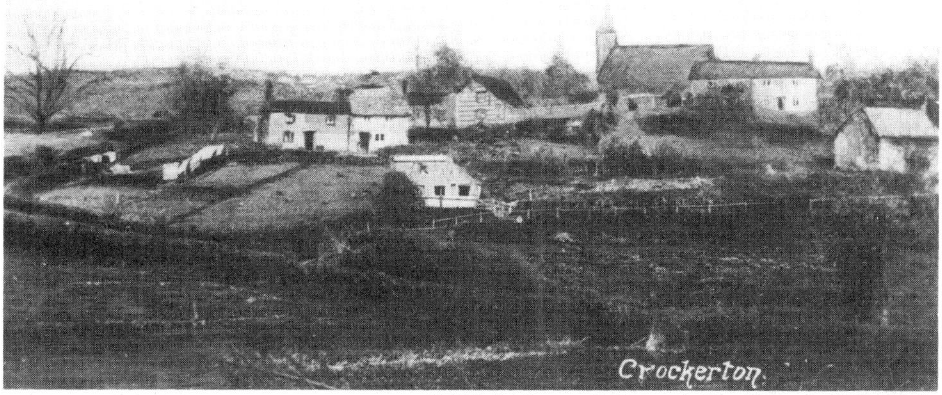

THIS RATHER BLEAK VIEW OF CROCKERTON, *c.*1900, looks north towards the Church of the Holy Trinity. Old cottages and untidy gardens contrast the Crockerton we know today with its much sought after cottages and bungalows.

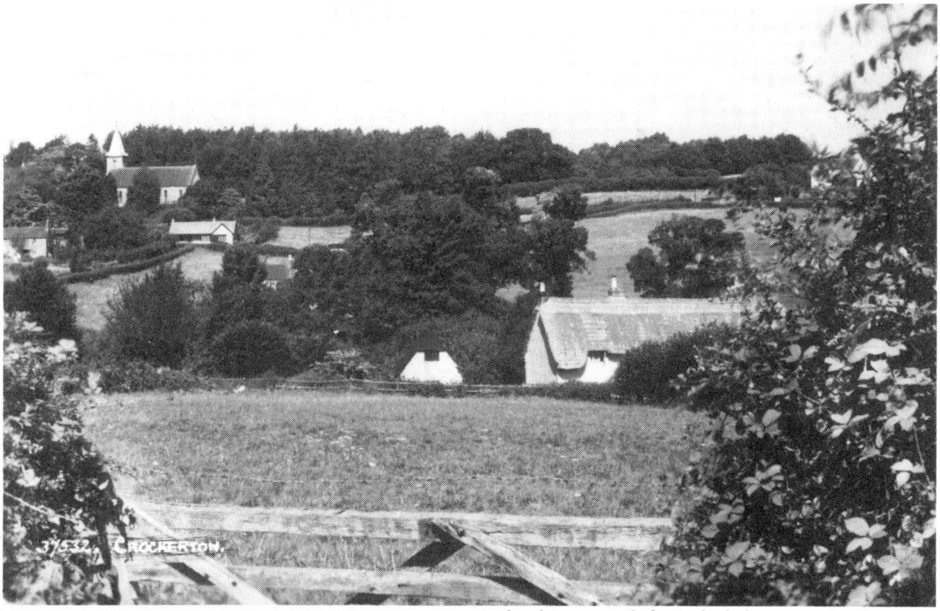

THIS IS A MORE RECENT VIEW OF CROCKERTON, again looking north but slightly more to the east of the previous photograph. The church was built in 1843 and closed in 1973. It has since been converted into a studio-house.

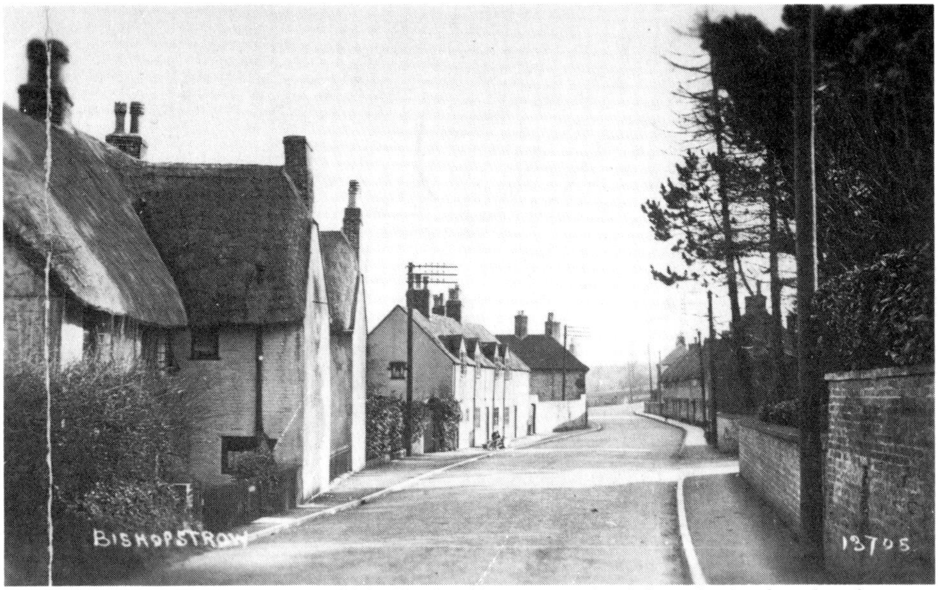

BISHOPSTROW, looking south, *c*.1920. Shirley House, on the left, is built of timber-framing with cross wings, north and south, around a central hall. Over the years it has been altered and added to. The south wall features some gothic-revival windows.

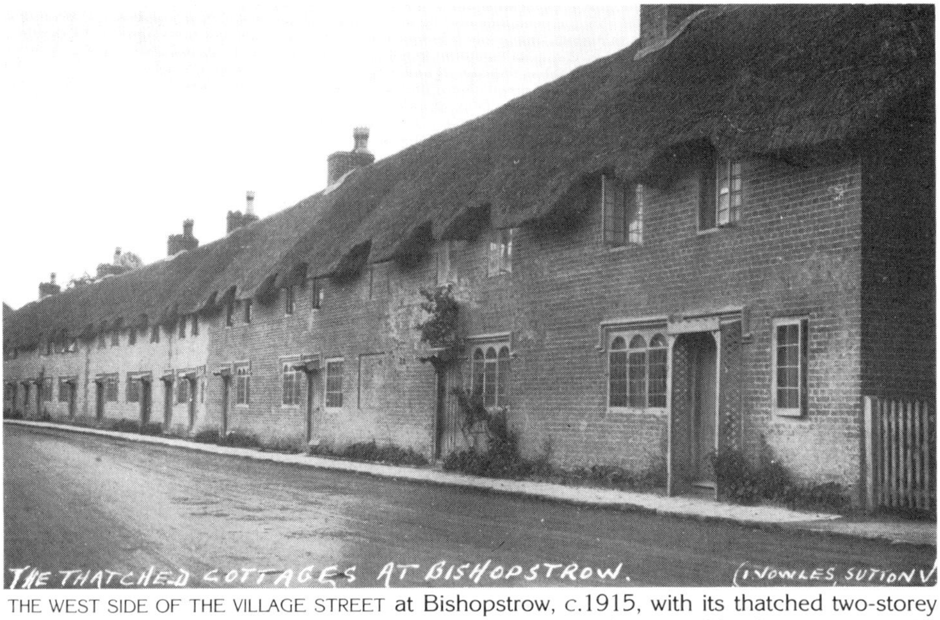

THE WEST SIDE OF THE VILLAGE STREET at Bishopstrow, *c*.1915, with its thatched two-storey cottages of rubble stone. The roofs have since been raised by several brick courses and the thatch replaced by tiles.

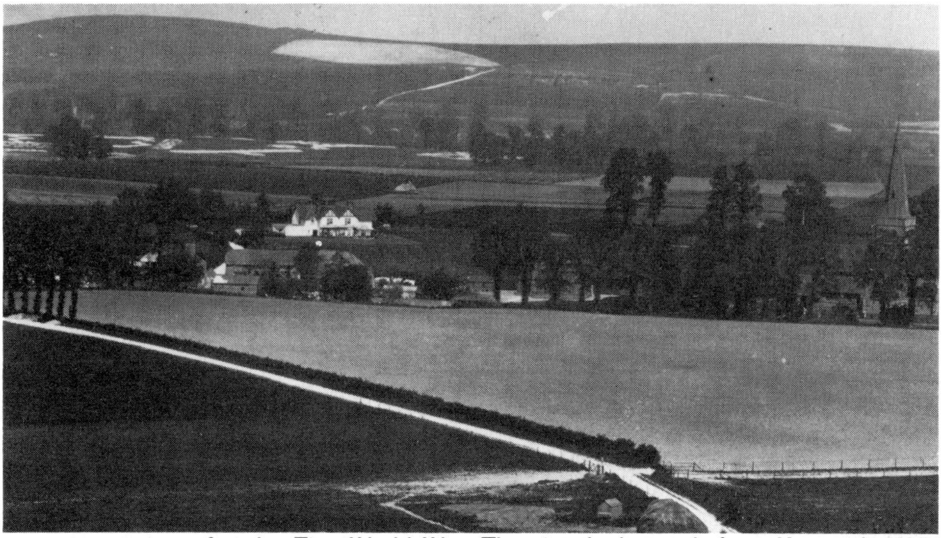

SUTTON VENY, just after the First World War. The view looks north from Haycombe Hill, across the village towards Norton Bavant, Scratchbury Camp and Cotley Hill. St John's Church is on the right. The imposing house, almost centre of the picture, is the Rectory (built 1913) at Best's Lane. The chalk-white markings in the field, near the top left, are where they have tidied up some of the practice trenches dug by soldiers in camp at Sutton Veny during the war years.

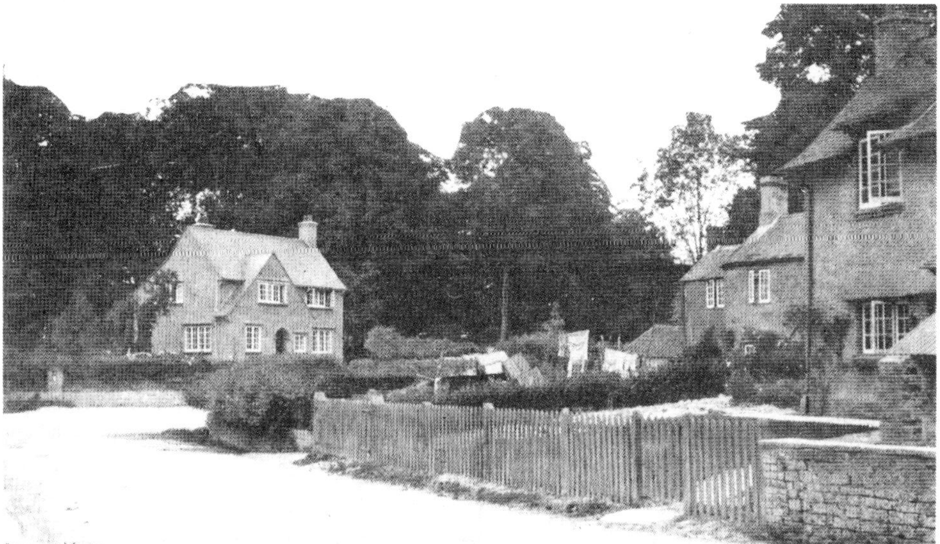

THE LOWER END OF SUTTON VENY, junction of High Street with Duck Street, probably before 1920. The house on the left of the picture is known as the Lodge and is at the entrance to the Old Manor House. The latter was the home of the rectors of the parish up until 1913. There is still a letterbox in the wall on the corner (now an 'ER' type).

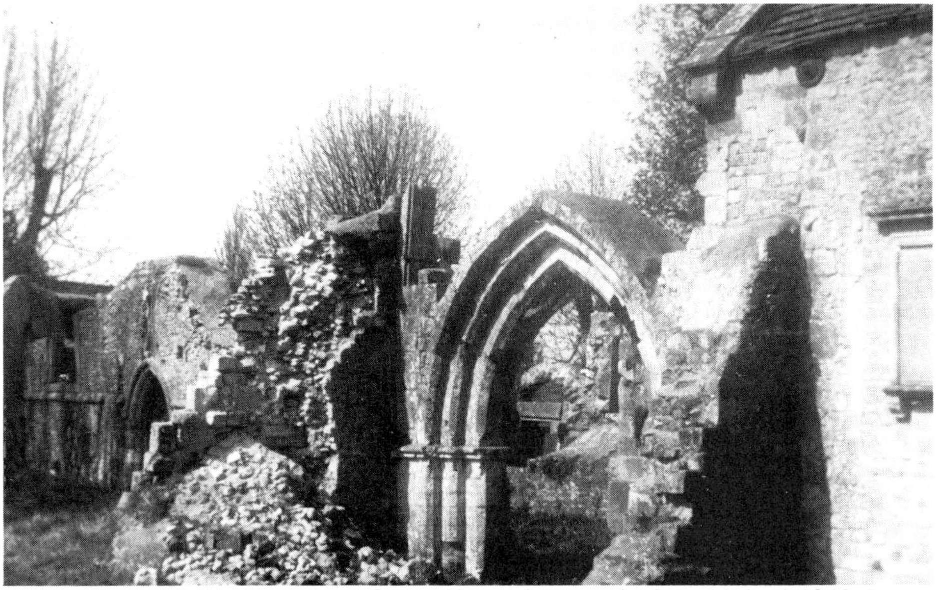

THE RUINS OF ST LEONARD'S CHURCH, Sutton Veny, photographed on 11 April 1948. Dating from the thirteenth century, it was abandoned in 1868 and declared redundant in 1968. It is now in the care of the Redundant Churches Restoration Fund and is well worth a visit.

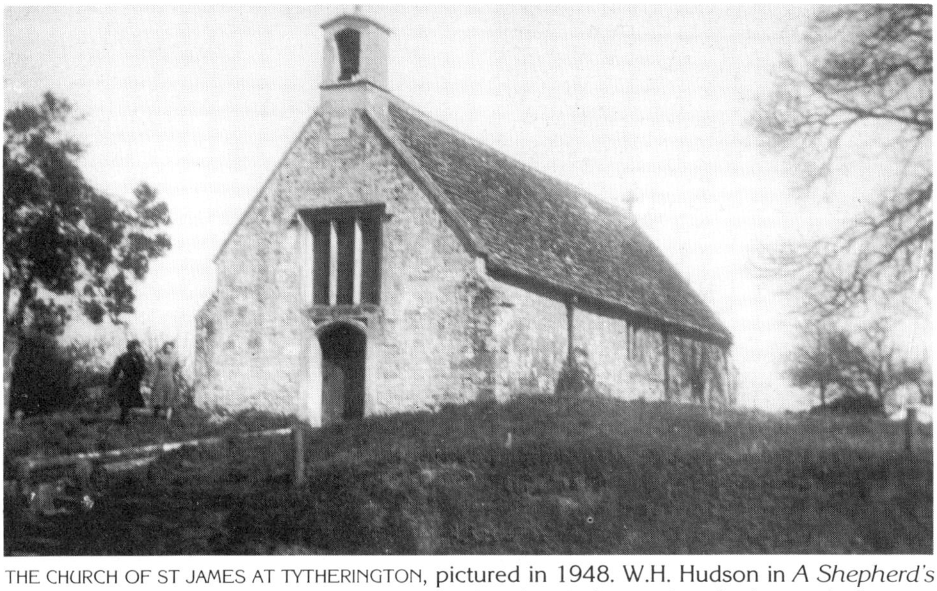

THE CHURCH OF ST JAMES AT TYTHERINGTON, pictured in 1948. W.H. Hudson in *A Shepherd's Life*, written in 1910, tells a tale concerning the church from a hundred years before – a terrier dog, accidentally locked in the church for three months, was found alive and looking like a 'skelington'. Apparently, it had survived the ordeal by licking the condensation from the walls inside, but died not long after its deliverance from the church.

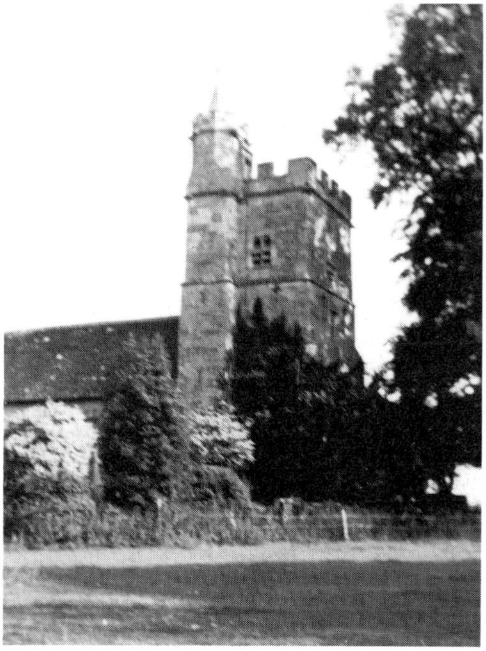

ALL SAINTS PARISH CHURCH, NORTON BAVANT. The photo was taken on 31 November 1948. Originally a twelfth-century building, it was completely rebuilt except for the west tower (fourteenth century), by William Walker of Shaftesbury in 1840. Restoration of the main part took place in 1863 and the tower was attended to in 1894.

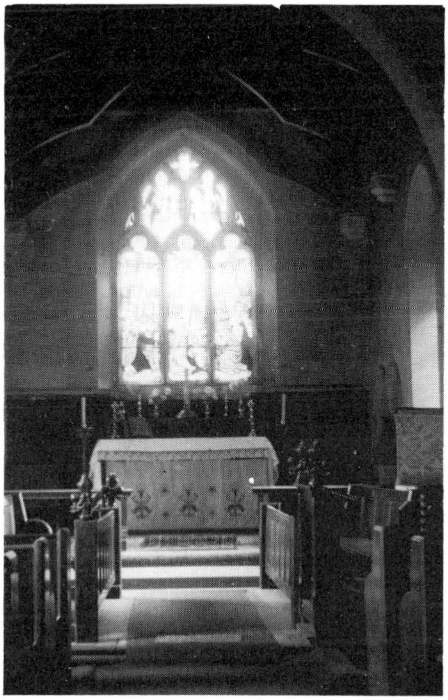

INSIDE ALL SAINTS PARISH CHURCH, Norton Bavant, again on 31 November 1948. The church is usually locked but the key may be obtained from No. 6 Norton Bavant. The churchyard is cloaked in yew trees which give a dark, eerie feeling to the place.

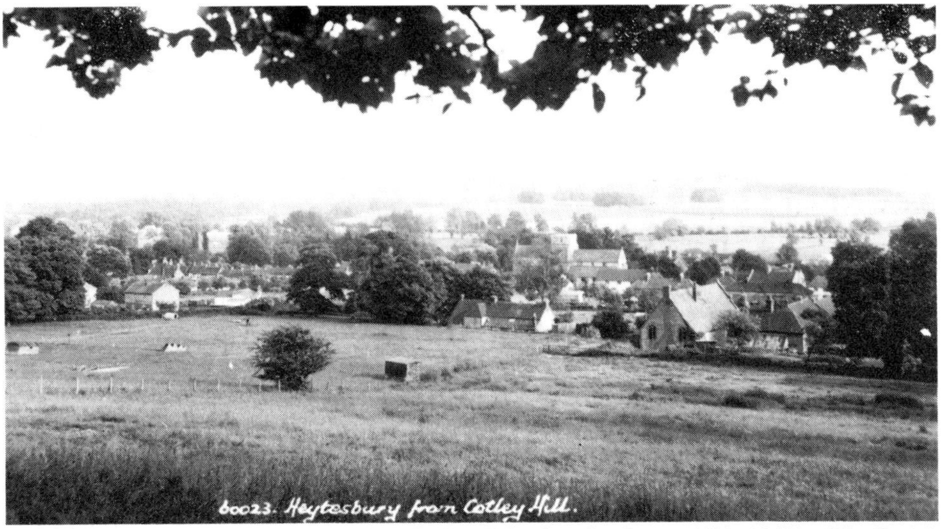

HEYTESBURY, looking south from below Cotley Hill, after the Second World War. The Parish Church of St Peter and St Paul, which Sir John Betjeman described as 'noble', is visible near the centre of the picture. The fields in the foreground are now crossed by the Heytesbury Bypass (constructed 1986), which has removed nearly all of the traffic from the village street.

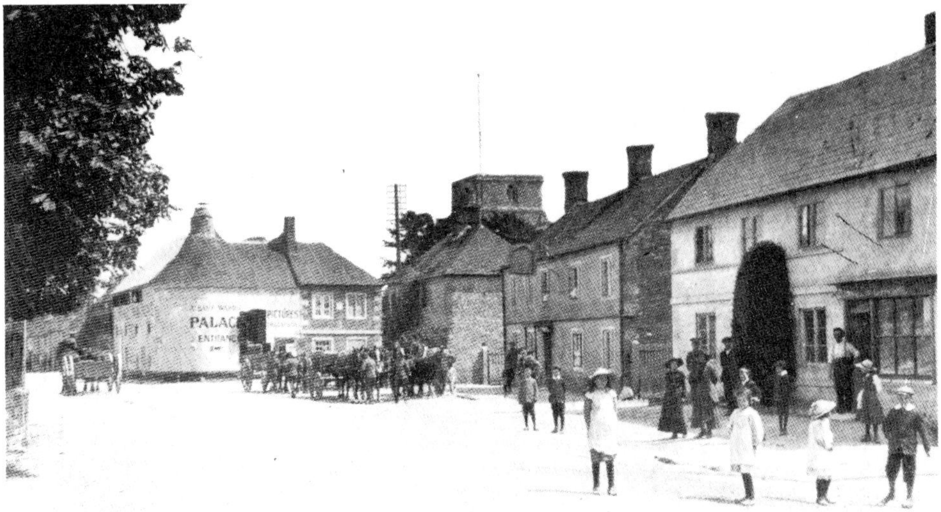

OUTSIDE THE RED LION at Heytesbury, during the First World War. The old malthouse, north of the church, was converted by Albany Ward into a cinema called the Palace. The paintwork on the wall advertises 'Pictures, twice nightly'. The Revd J. Raymond later purchased the building from the Heytesbury Estate and it was handed over to the village in 1936 by his widow in perpetuity for all denominations and for Knook and Tytherington. Henceforth it was known as the Raymond Hall. The chestnut tree just visible on the left, under which the farmworkers used to hold their union meetings, was felled in the summer of 1988.

THE LOCK-UP AT HEYTESBURY, in 1914. This is one of several in Wiltshire. During the eighteenth century lock-ups were used as temporary prisons for drunks and wrong-doers, who were usually incarcerated overnight while waiting to appear in front of a magistrate. These purpose-built buildings are sometimes called blind-houses, because of their lack of windows. The thought of a night in one of these dark, cold places was often enough to keep people on the right side of the law.

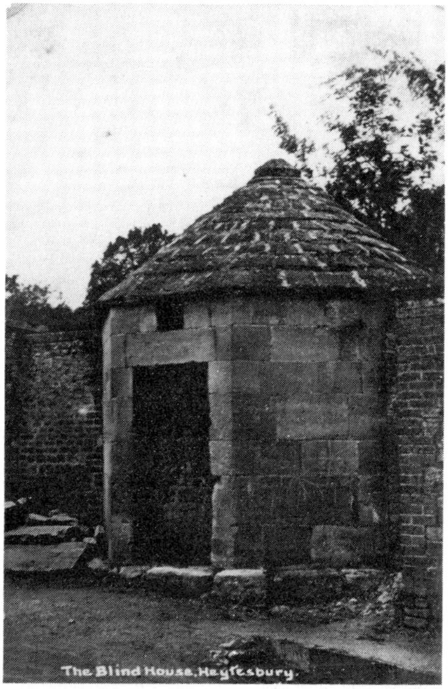

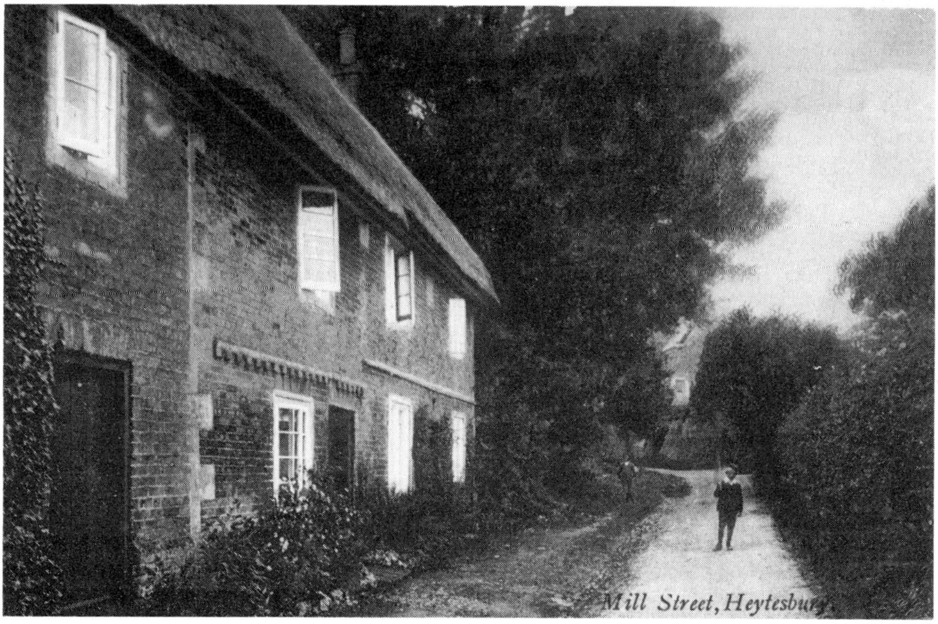

MILL STREET, Heytesbury, in 1905. The thatched cottage, seen here, has a datestone on its north-facing wall, beneath the eaves, which reads 'R. Dann 1726'.

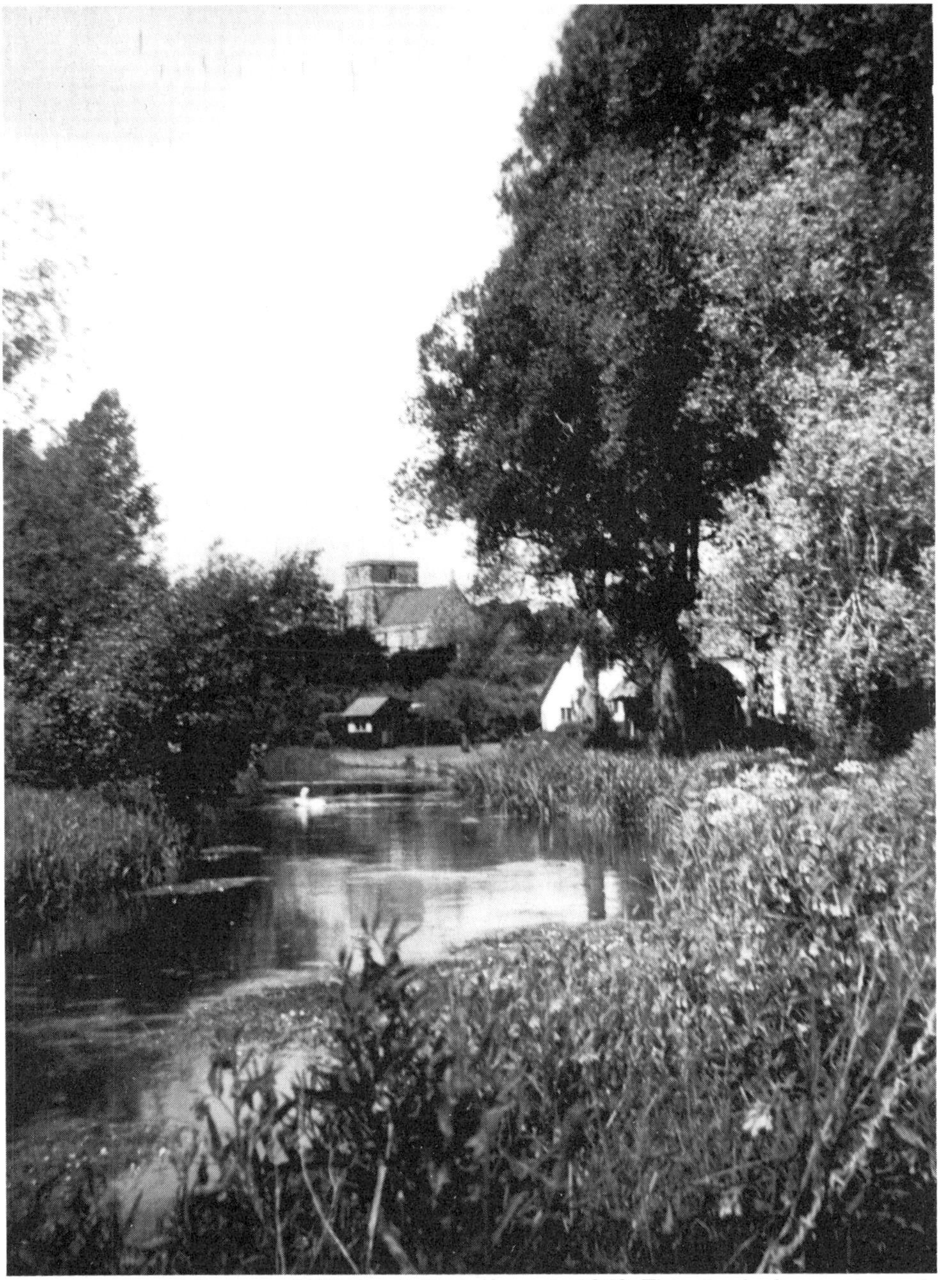

THE RIVER WYLYE at the rear of Mill Street, Heytesbury, in 1949. This view looks west towards the parish church. A lone swan appears to have this idyllic scene all to itself.

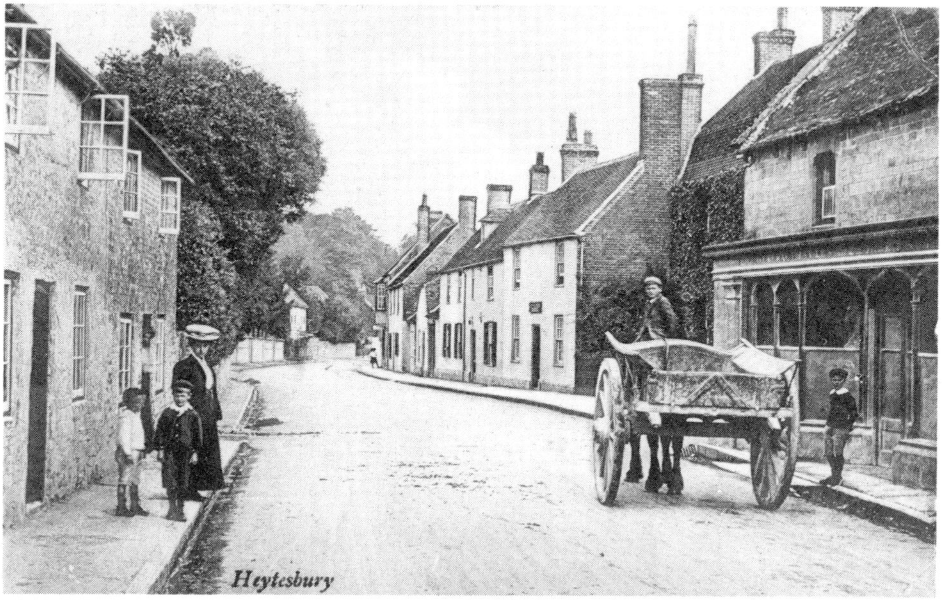

LOOKING EAST ALONG HEYTESBURY HIGH STREET in 1900, showing how the church was hidden from the main road by a line of buildings including a shop, an old reading room and a caretaker's house. In 1907, Margaret, Lady Heytesbury, had the whole block demolished by the Heytesbury Estate staff with the idea of improving the street and bringing the church into view. The churchyard now extends to the pavement and part of this 'new' area includes the village war memorial.

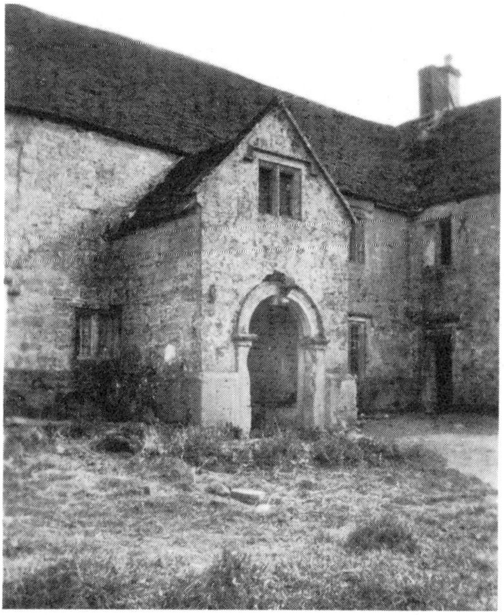

KNOOK MANOR HOUSE, during the 1920s. It stands between St Margaret's Church and the River Wylye.

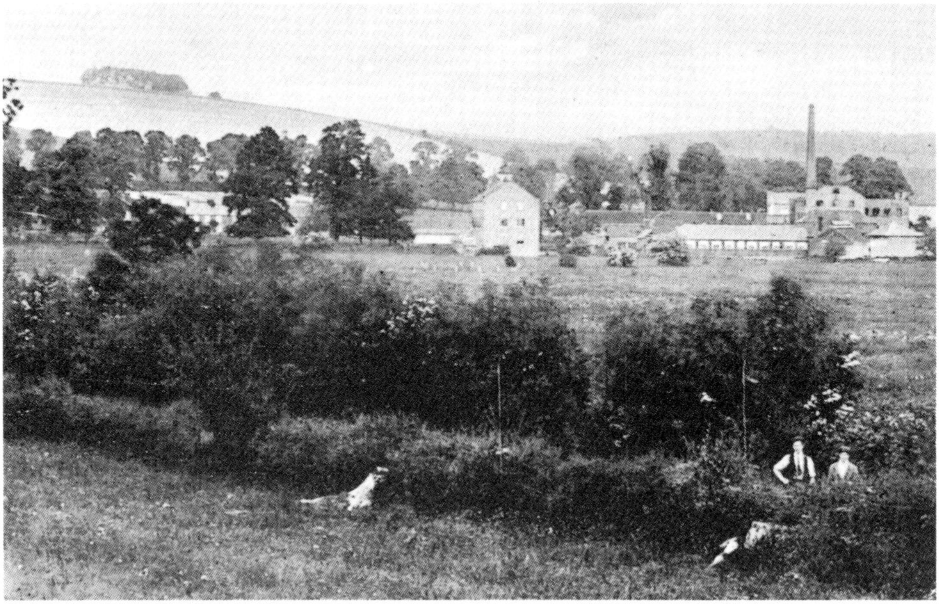

LOOKING NORTH-EAST FROM CORTON TO UPTON LOVELL c.1900, where the chimney and the buildings of the cloth factory dominate the scene. Several Corton people were employed at the factory in days gone by. A footpath connected Corton with the factory gates on the other side of the River Wylye. A 79-year-old weaver, who used to walk daily from Corton to the factory for work, fell in the river on his way home one night and was drowned.

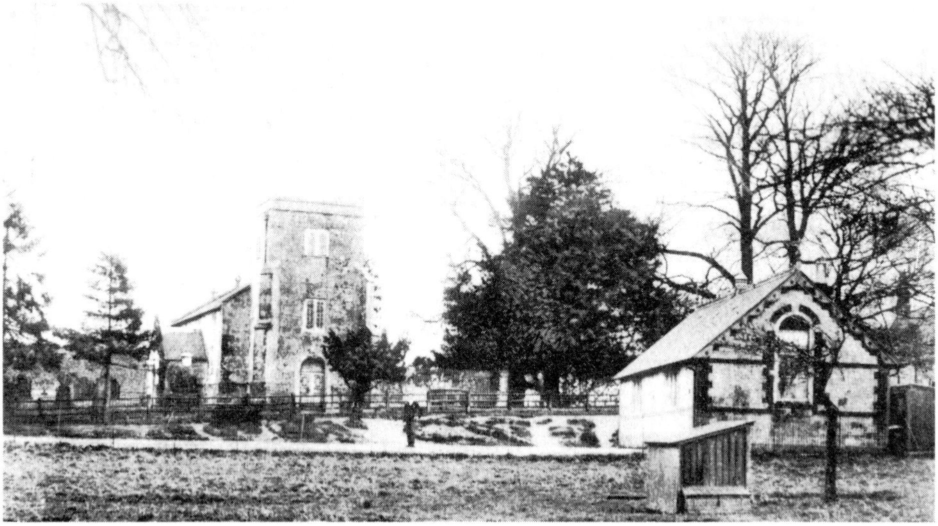

UPTON LOVELL CHURCH, from a postcard franked 1903.

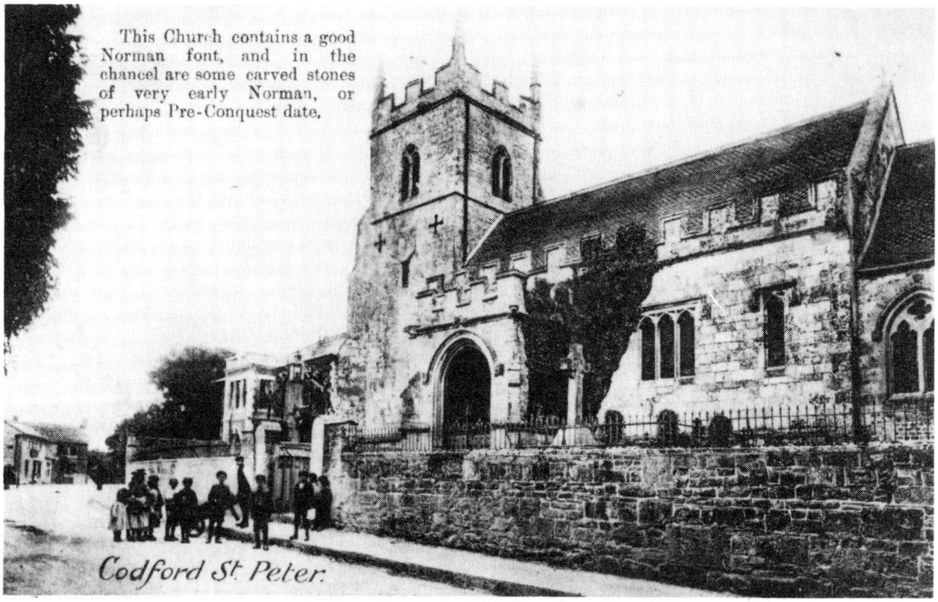

ST PETER'S CHURCH, CODFORD, during the early 1900s, when Revd Douglas Macleane MA was the vicar. The church features a ninth-century carved stone cross.

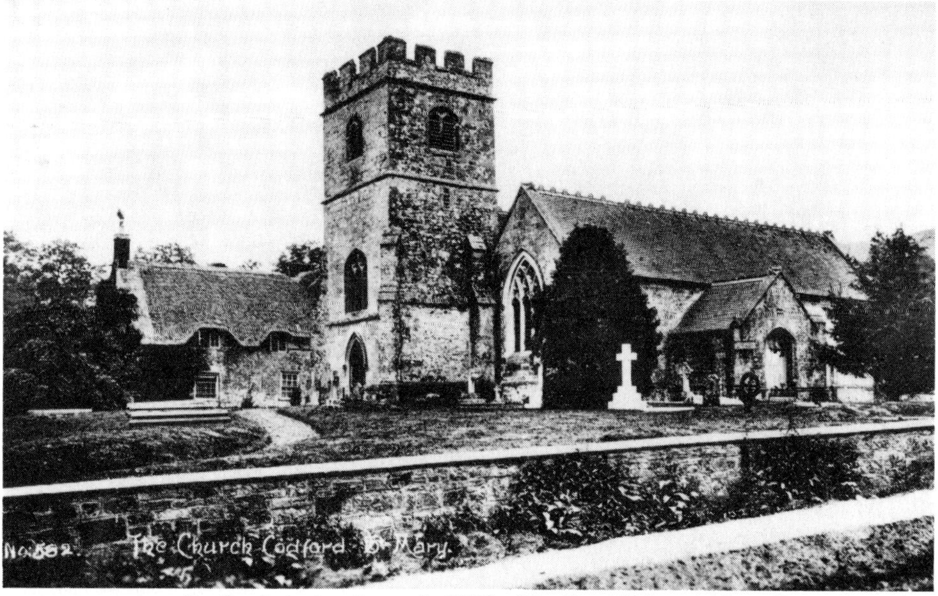

ST MARY'S CHURCH, Codford, during the early 1900s. The Revd Edward Albert Henry Aston MA was vicar here from 1892. The church was restored, first by T.H. Wyatt in 1843 and then in 1879 at a cost of £1,200.

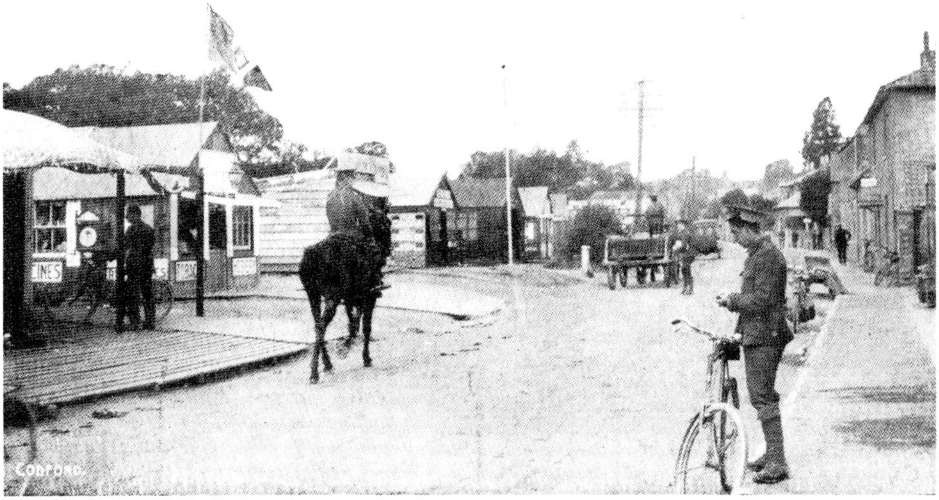

HIGH STREET, Codford, during the First World War. The exact location can be ascertained by the Carson & Miller milepost, left of the wagon, near the centre of the picture. This milepost survives to this day, just east of what is now the Central Garage. The hut with the flag flying, on the left, is the YMCA. Outside is a weighing machine where, for a penny, the troops could find out how much weight they were putting on or losing. No doubt the villagers used it too.

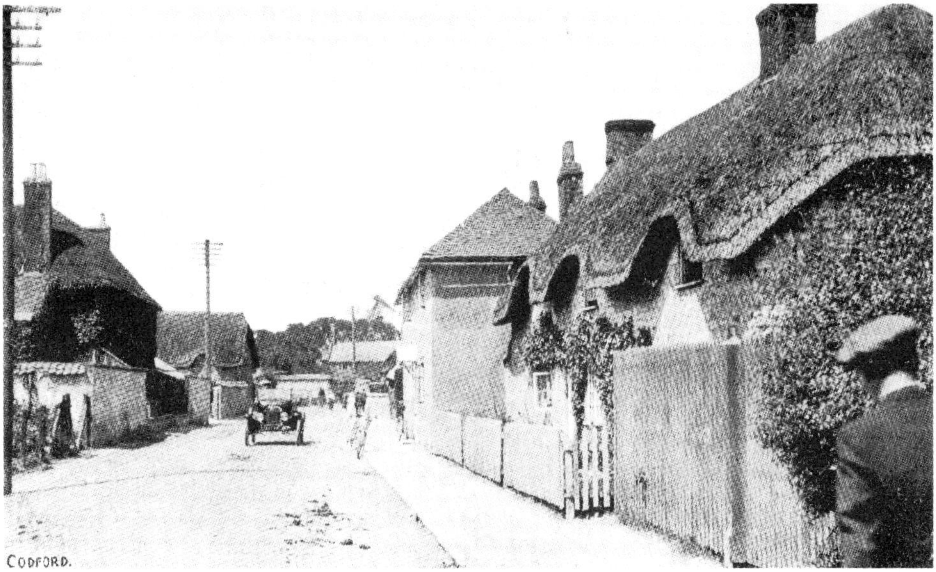

A RATHER SPLENDID MOTOR CAR makes its way through Codford during the 1920s. The picture was taken just east of the turning for Chitterne. The thatched cottages, on the right, have since been renovated and their roofs are now tiled.

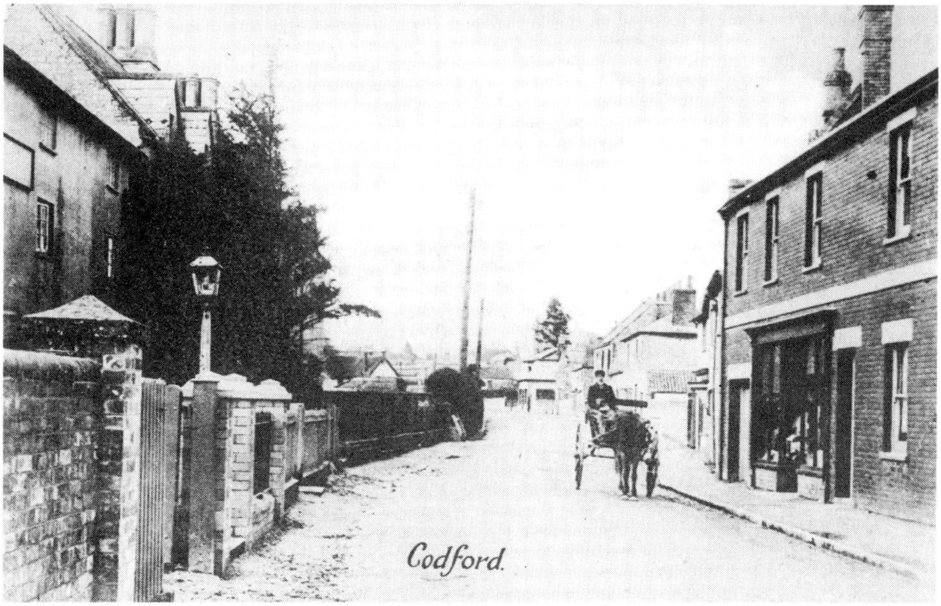

A DIFFERENT FORM OF TRANSPORT – a pony and trap – makes its way along Codford High Street during the 1920s. The shop on the right is used as the village post office today.

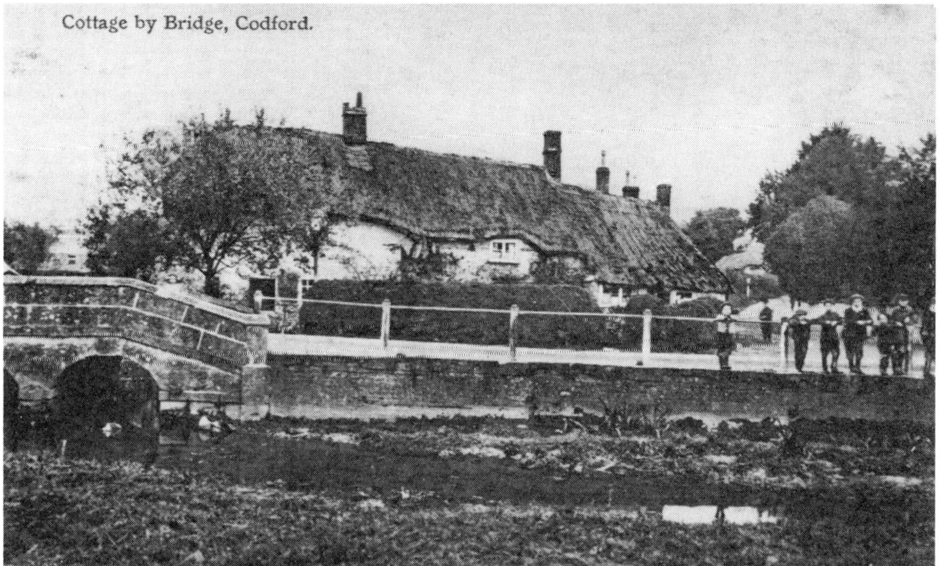

SCHOOLBOYS POSE FOR THE CAMERA near the bridge at the eastern end of Codford in 1917. The Chitterne Brook passes under the bridge here on its way to join the River Wylye. After stormy weather the water level rises considerably; in February it is a deep torrent, while in summer it returns to its usual, peaceful flow.

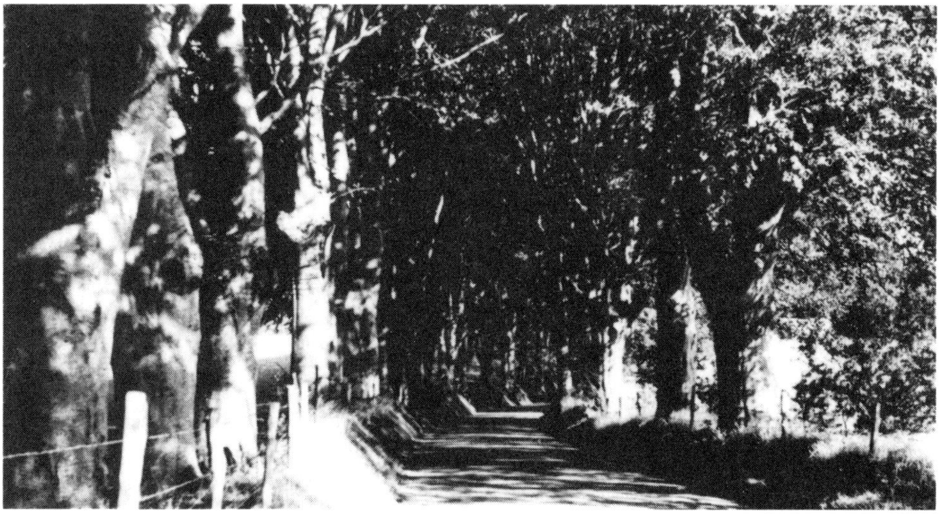

THE ROAD EAST OF TYTHERINGTON ascends a small hill before reaching Corton and is bordered by an avenue of splendid beech trees, known locally as Corton Wheatsheaf (sometimes referred to as Corton Whitesheet). A local yarn says a headless ghost pushes a wheelbarrow with his head in up and down the hill during the night! This photograph, looking east, was taken during the 1960s. Some of the beech trees have been felled recently for safety reasons.

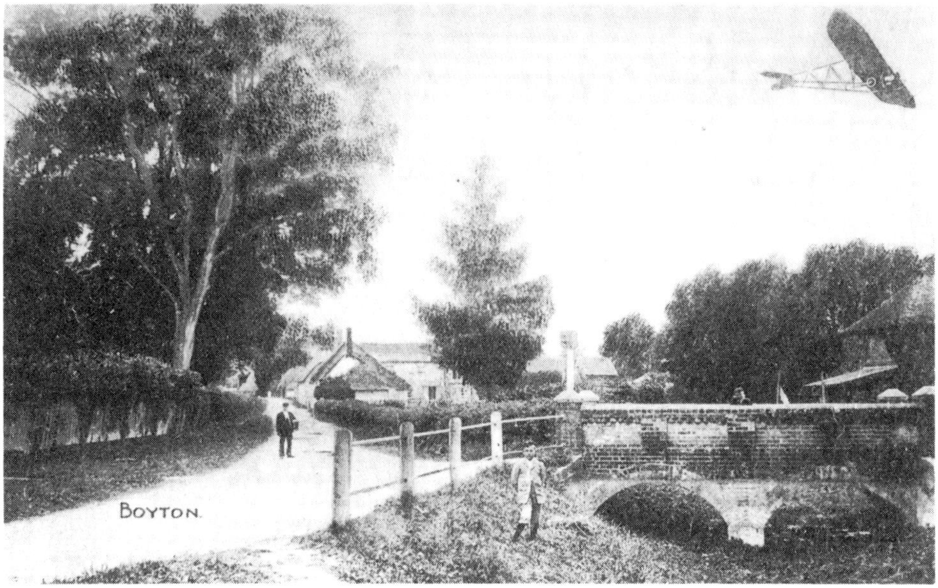

LOOKING WEST AT BOYTON, c.1915. The aeroplane in the top right corner of the picture is faked – the photographer, in an attempt to enhance his work, added it afterwards. The bridge at Boyton was rebuilt in 1949 by Wiltshire County Council. A plaque upon it records the name of the County Surveyor, H.S. Ganderton, OBE.

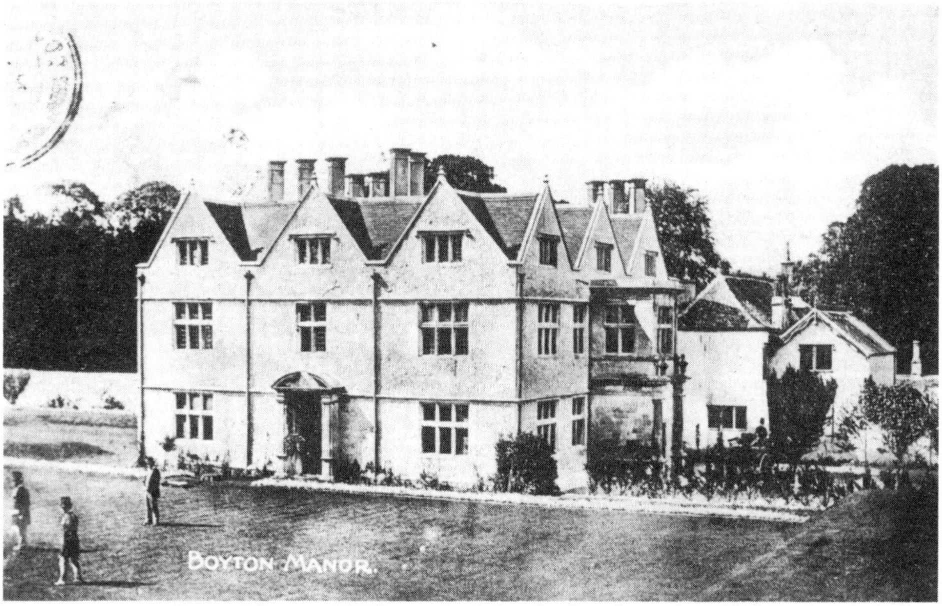

BOYTON MANOR, pictured here *c*.1910, was built by the Lamberts in 1618. During the latter part of the nineteenth century it was owned by Mr E.D. Fane; and Prince Leopold, Duke of Albany, lived in the house for several years. The Prince paid for the organ in Boyton Church. His name is preserved in the locality – the inn at Upton Lovell is called the Prince Leopold and Albany Cottages are situated at Sherrington.

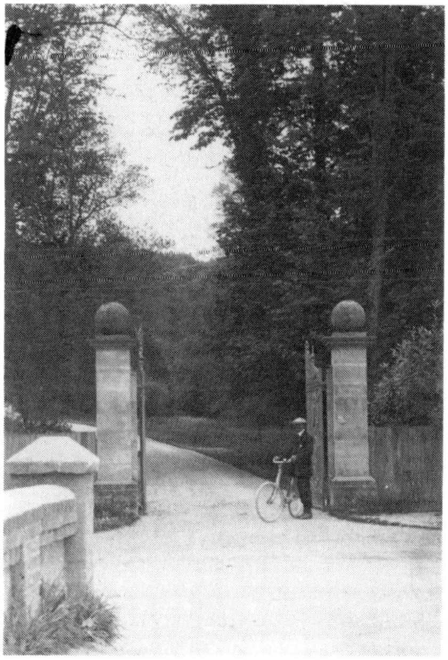

THE ENTRANCE TO BOYTON MANOR, between 1905/1908. The man with the bicycle is believed to be Mr Sims who was the head gardener at Boyton Manor.

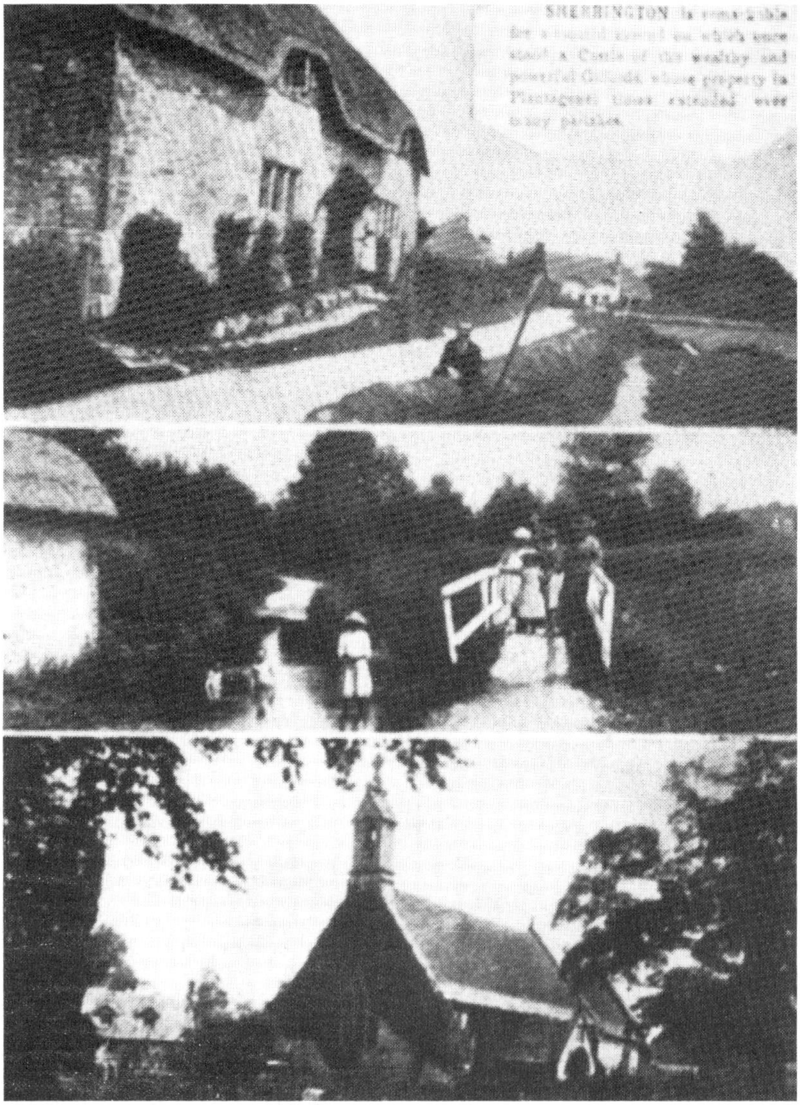

THREE VIEWS OF SHERRINGTON, *c.*1916. Top: a thatched cottage opposite the water-cress beds. Cress Cottage in the background. The crystal-clear spring water at Sherrington made for successful cress growing. A Mr Case managed the cress beds (for Major Fane of Boyton) in the latter part of the nineteenth century, and he cut the cress at a dinner to celebrate Queen Victoria's Jubilee (1887) at Broadchalke. The next owner was Mr Pond, followed by Mr Case whose family continued to grow cress at Sherrington until the Second World War. Mr Case was known as far afield as Bristol as 'the Watercress King'. Middle: the ford and the footbridge over the River Wylye. Bottom: the Church of St Cosmos and St Damian is one of only four in England dedicated to these Middle-Eastern saints. The others are two in Kent and one in Sussex.

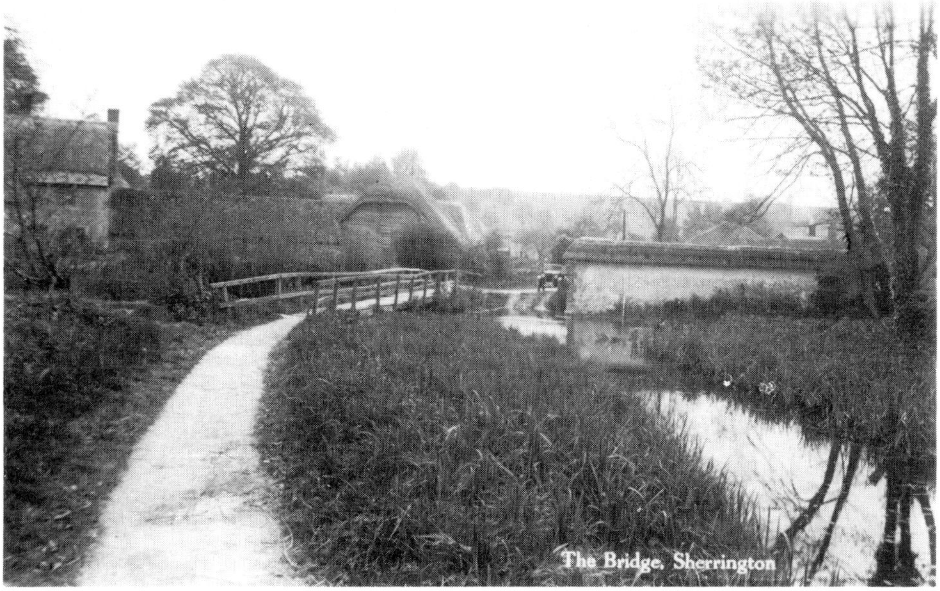

The footbridge over the River Wylye at Sherrington in the 1930s. The path leads past Sherrington Mill, crossing the railway line at Codford Station (now no more), emerging at Codford opposite New Road.

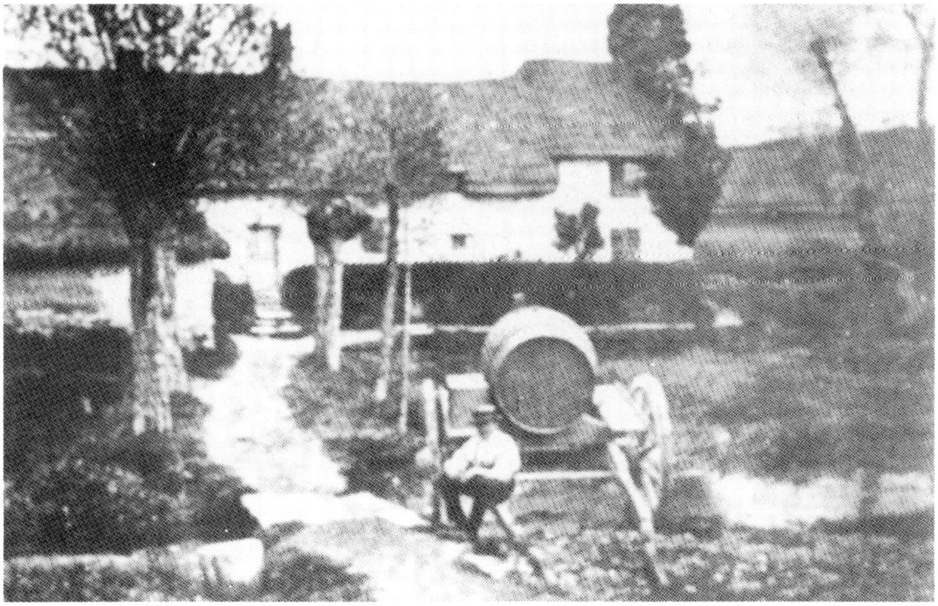

A SCENE AT SHERRINGTON which appeared on a postcard dated 1900. The sender of the card wrote on the back 'This is the house my mother was born in; it belonged to my great great grandfather, and was the oldest farmhouse in the West of England'.

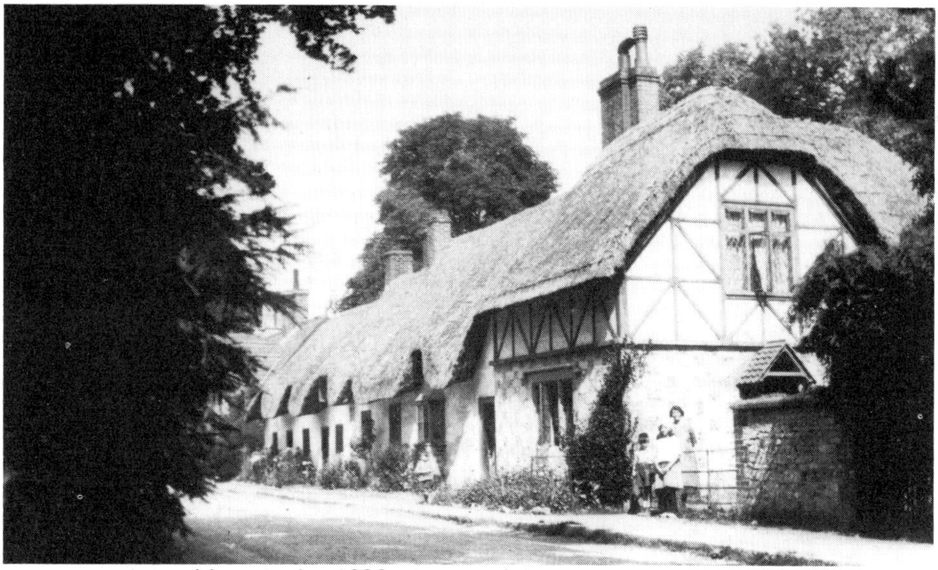

STOCKTON, pictured here in the 1920s, is one of the most attractive villages in the Wylye Valley with its thatched cottages both sides of the street. Every year, hundreds of house-martins nest under the eaves – they obviously think that Stockton is the best place for rearing a family!

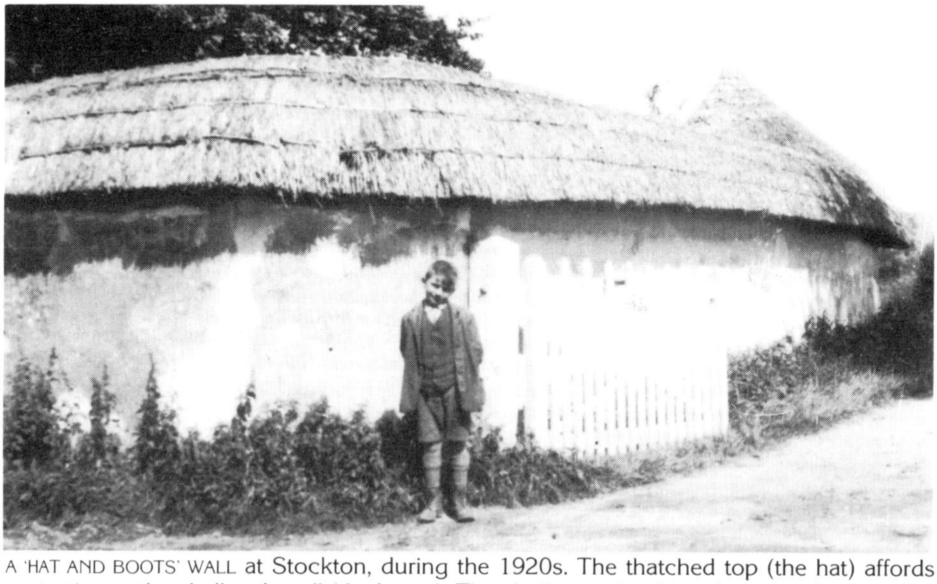

A 'HAT AND BOOTS' WALL at Stockton, during the 1920s. The thatched top (the hat) affords protection to the chalk cob wall (the boots). The chalk was dug from the subsoil and mixed with water, horsehair and chopped straw to make a paste which sets hard. There are several of these walls in the Wylye Valley. They were built c.1830, probably to define boundaries, at the time of the Machinery Riots when people were on the rampage through the Valley.

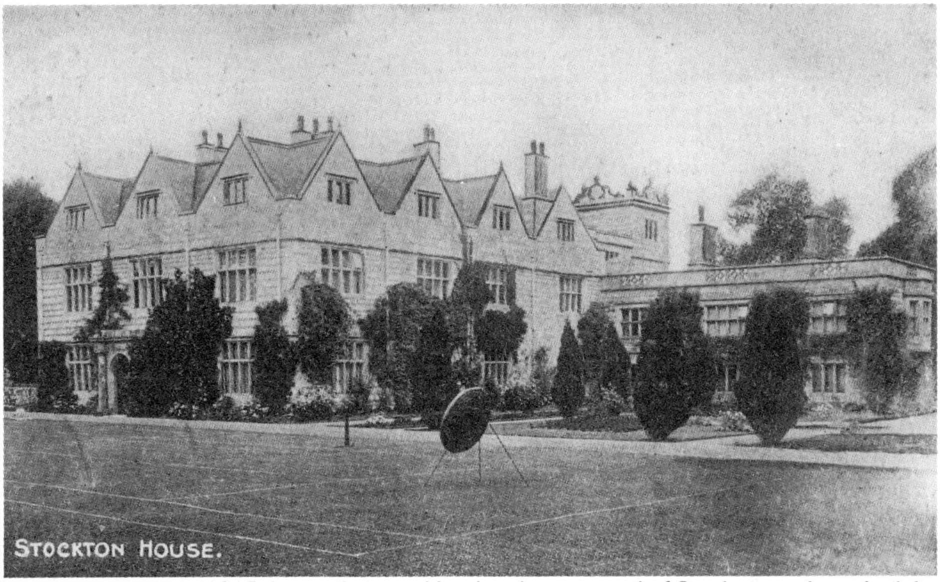

STOCKTON HOUSE, *c*.1915. It stands in parkland at the west end of Stockton and was built by the wealthy clothier John Topp, who also built the almshouses in the village in 1641. This photograph shows a tennis court marked out on the lawn and the archery target suggests that a toxophilite is in residence.

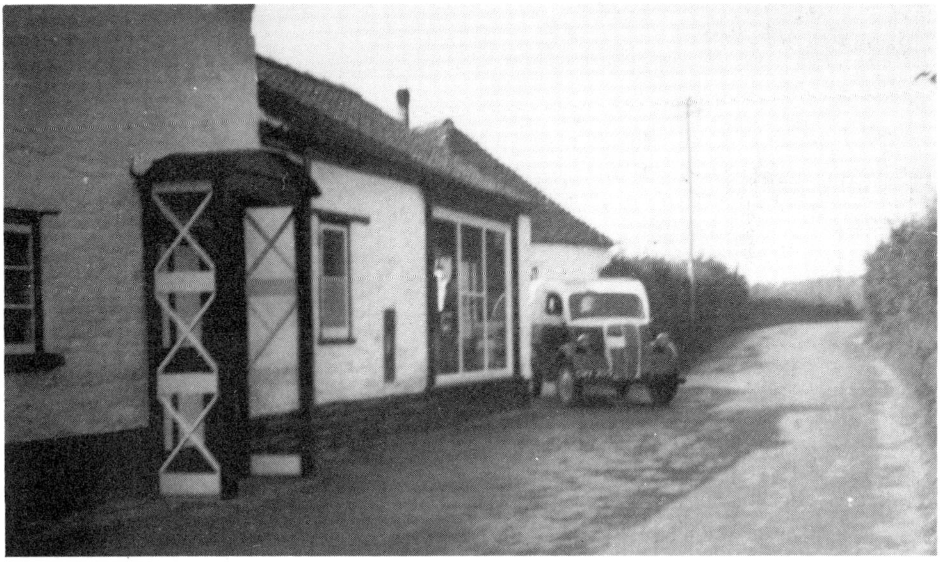

BRYANT'S STORES AT BAPTON during the 1950s, with a Bedford delivery van outside. The building is reputed to be 400 years old and the shop part was, supposedly, a chapel in days gone by. At one time the road here, which connects Wylye with Stockton, ran to the south of the building.

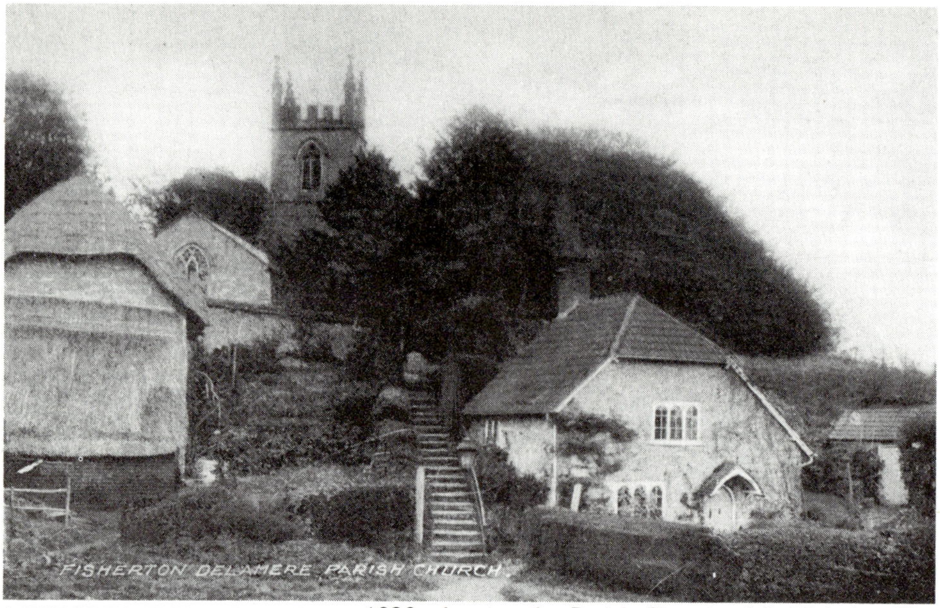

A VIEW OF FISHERTON DE LA MERE, c.1930, showing the Parish Church of St Nicholas. The church was re-built by 84 years-old John Davies Esq. of Bapton (he owned Bapton and Fisherton de la Mere) in 1833 and re-opened in June 1834.

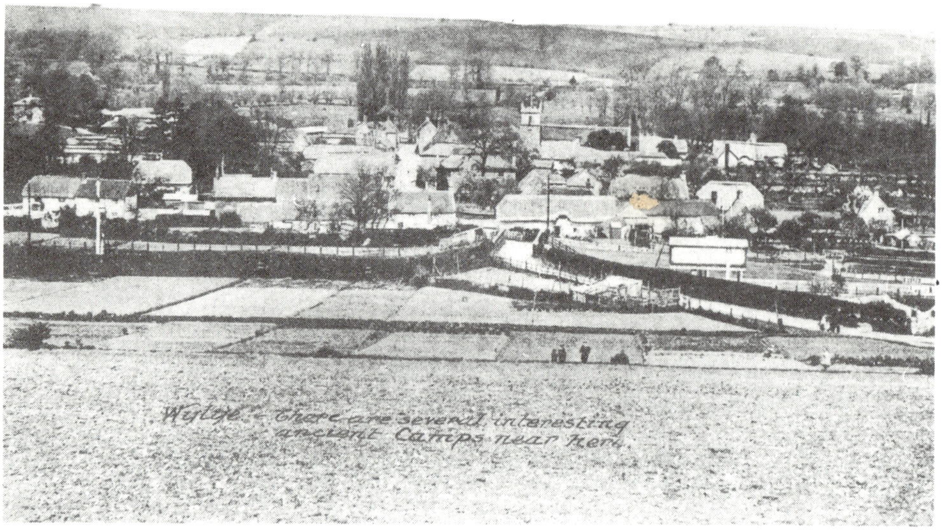

THIS VIEW LOOKS NORTH ACROSS WYLYE towards Yarnbury Castle (hill fort), before 1932. St Mary's Church is almost centre of the picture.

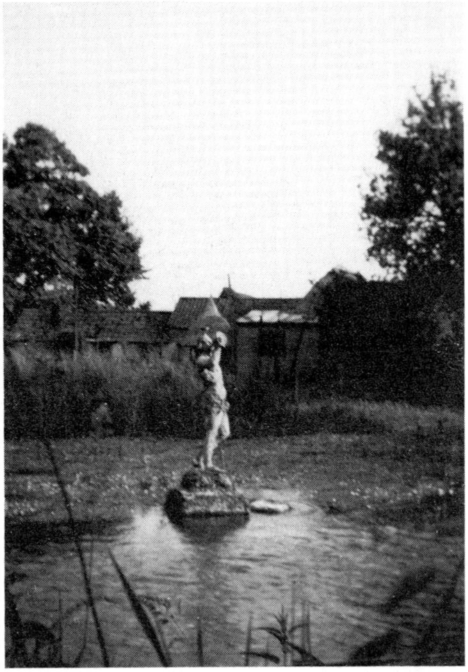

THE STATUE OF A POSTBOY BLOWING HIS HORN, which is situated in the river behind the Mill at Wylye. It is a reminder of an eighteenth-century coaching accident. The mail-coach was on route between London and Exeter, and was fording the river at Wylye, which was deeper than usual due to torrential rain, when it got into difficulties and turned over. A local story relates how a post-boy drowned while attempting to save members of the coach's crew. The statue, once visible from the bridge at Wylye but now hidden by a hedge, toppled in a gale in 1904 but was successfully reinstated. This photograph was taken in 1948.

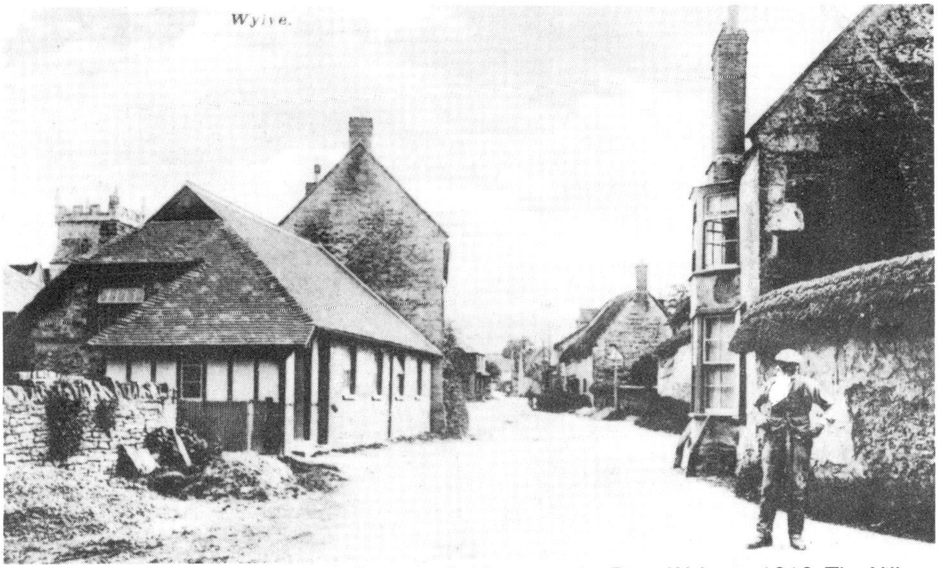

HIGH STREET, WYLYE, looking south from the bridge over the River Wylye in 1918. The Village Hall and the Bell Inn are centre of the picture and the tower of St Mary's Church is visible on the left.

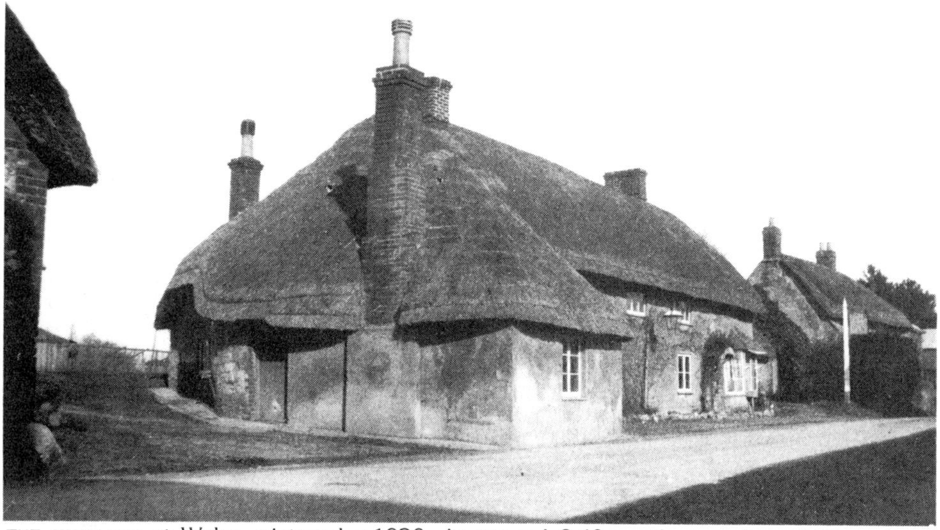

THE SWAN INN at Wylye, pictured *c*.1920. At around 8.40 on the evening of Thursday 6 December 1923, while the landlord, Frederick Johnson, and his customers were discussing the election held that day, a fire broke out in a spare bedroom above the kitchen. Salisbury Fire Brigade were delayed by thick fog and didn't arrive until 10.35 p.m., by which time it was too late. The building was burnt to the ground, although the wooden sign outside was not even singed. The building was the property of Messrs Mathews, brewers, of Gillingham and was valued at £3,000.

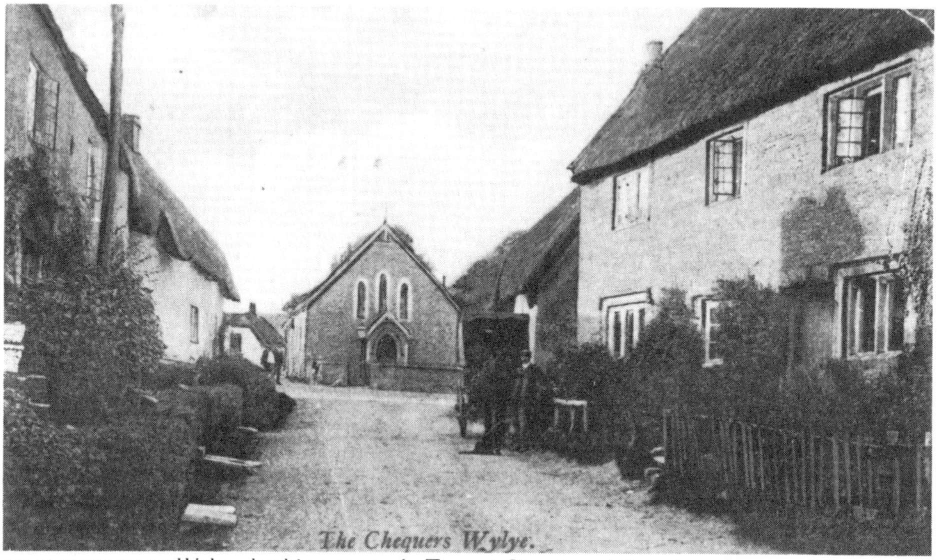

THE CHEQUERS at Wylye, looking towards Teapot Street and the chapel, around the turn of the century.

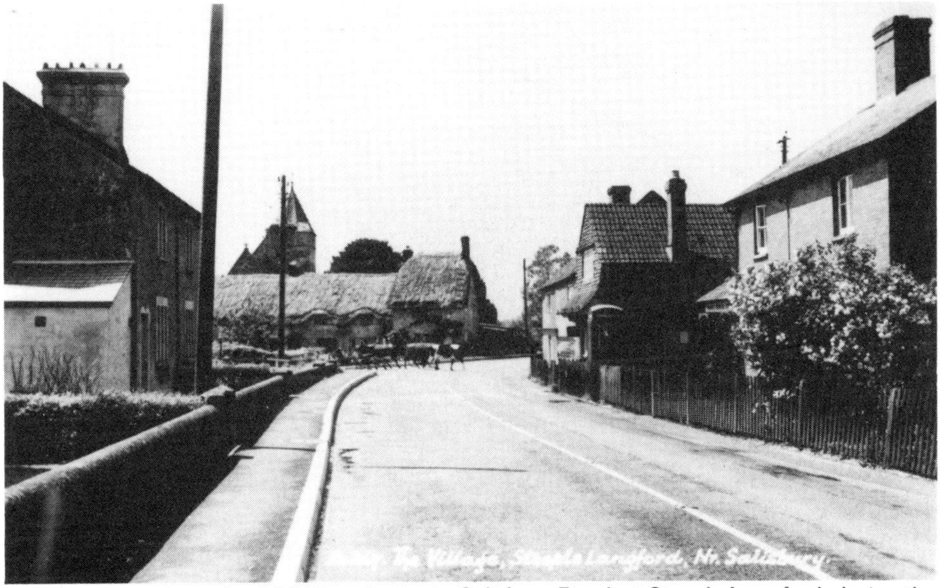

LOOKING WEST, along the A36 Warminster to Salisbury Road, at Steeple Langford, during the 1940s/1950s. Apart from the cattle crossing the road, the scene is almost deserted. Perhaps it will return to this again when the Steeple Langford Bypass (currently under construction – 1988) is completed. The telephone box, next to the village shop on the right, has recently been replaced by a new one further east, next to the turning into the Wirr.

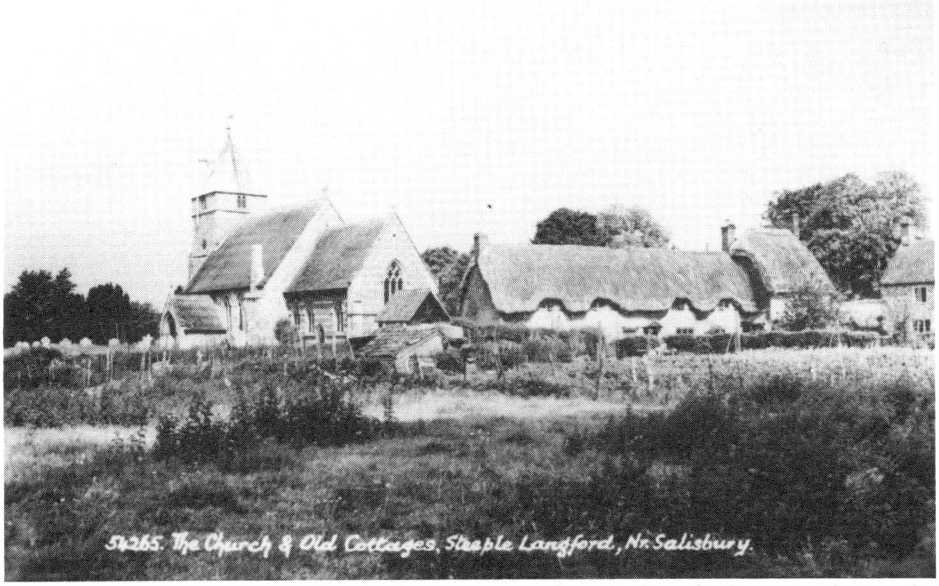

ALL SAINTS CHURCH and old thatched cottages at Steeple Langford, again during the 1940s/1950s.

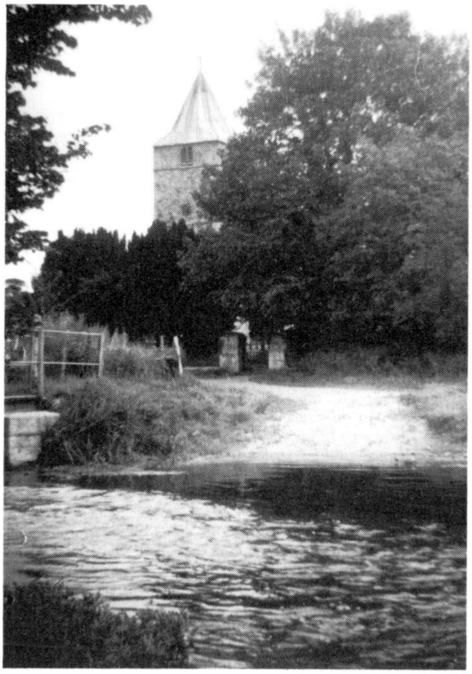

THE TOWER OF ALL SAINTS CHURCH at Steeple Langford, as seen from the River Wylye, 1948. The prefix 'Steeple' in the name of the village has nothing to do with a steeple on the church; it is derived from 'staple' and is a reminder of the area's association with the wool trade in years gone by.

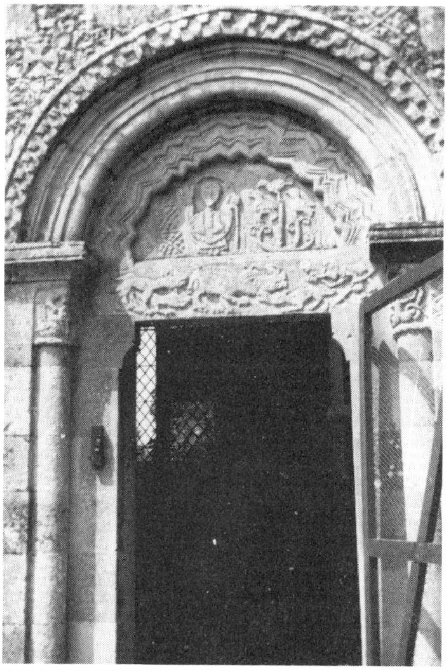

THE CHURCH OF ST NICHOLAS at Little Langford has a fine Norman doorway. This photograph was taken in 1948. The tympanum features a carving of a bishop raising his hand in blessing. At his side is a strange tree complete with three birds on the branches. Below, three dogs wearing spotted collars attack a wild boar, watched by a huntsman with spear and horn. The arch above has several worn figures – one of which resembles a mermaid, something hardly ever seen in church decoration. Perhaps this is the only church in Wiltshire with a mermaid!

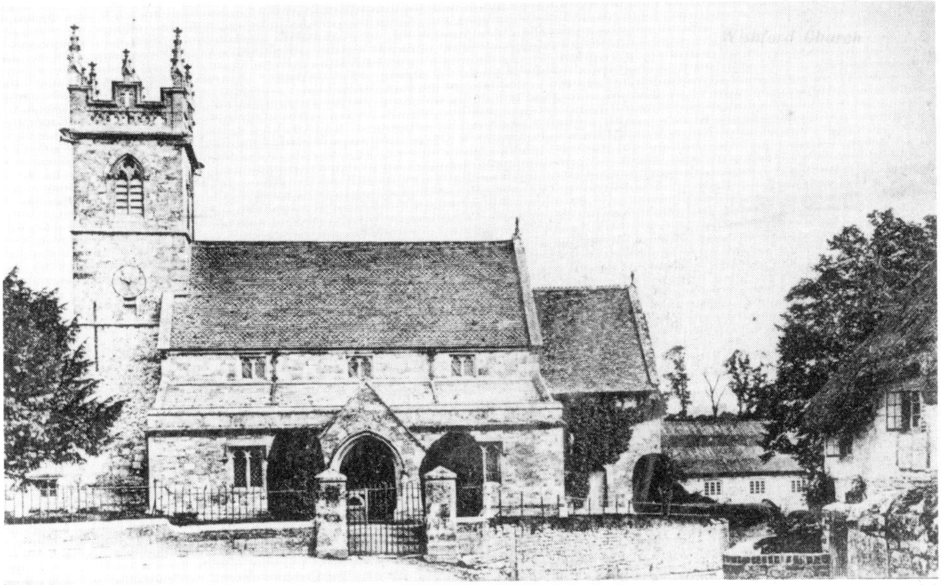

ST GILES' CHURCH, Wishford, *c*.1900. The rector from 1895 to 1924 was Frederick MacDonald who quarrelled with the founders of the Oak Apple Club. He died in 1928 and his grave in the churchyard is marked by a Celtic cross.

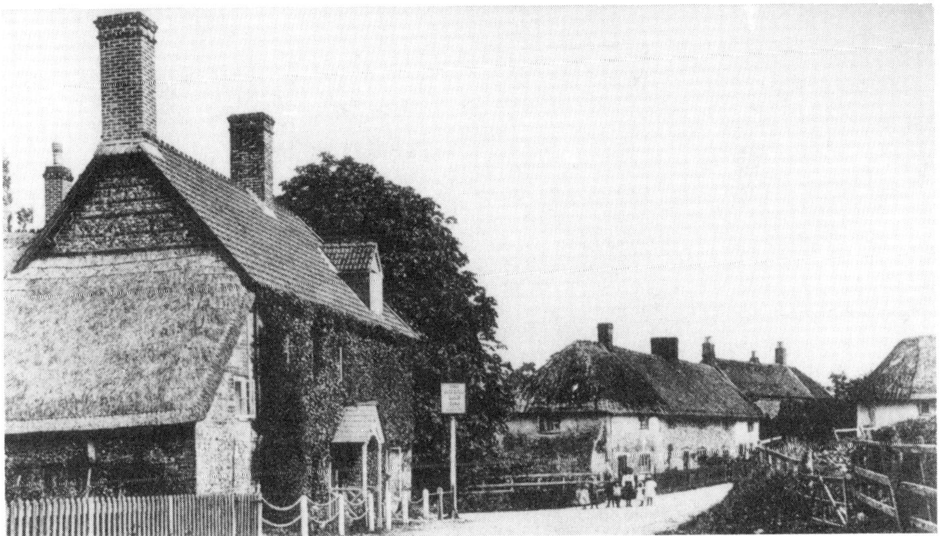

THE ROYAL OAK INN at Great Wishford, *c*.1907. The landlord at this time was Albert Fox. The cottages further up the street, towards Hanging Langford, have since been demolished. Their site is occupied today by the entrance to the Bonham Close housing estate.

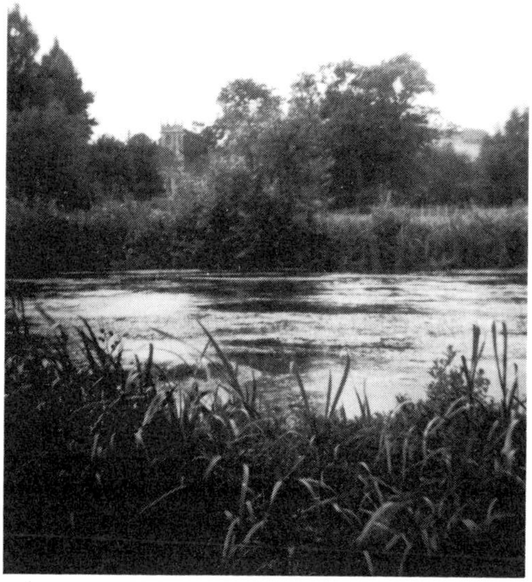

LOOKING SOUTH ACROSS THE RIVER WYLYE at Stoford towards St Giles Church, Wishford, in 1948.

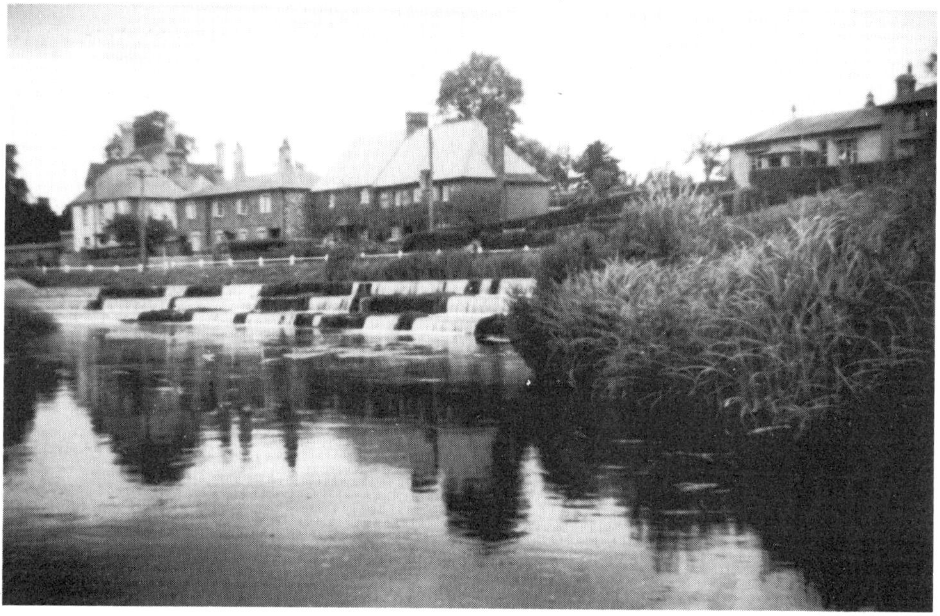

THE WEIR AT SOUTH NEWTON, pictured during the late 1940s. It no longer exists – it succumbed to a road-widening scheme.

SECTION TWO

Village Life

'A village could hold its own, years ago' is a phrase I have often heard said by older Wylye Valley residents. A glimpse at any page in the old trade directories shows just how true that statement is. Take Codford St Mary, for instance. In 1907 (population 277 in 1901) there were two bakers, three grocers, a draper, a saddler, a boot-maker, a cycle agent, a tobacconist, a laundress, a blacksmith and a resident doctor. At Codford St Peter, the immediately adjacent parish, there was a butcher, another grocer, a coal merchant, two more laundry ladies, a dressmaker and a beer retailer. Codford was therefore well provided for and that goes for just about any village in the Valley before the Second World War. Even places where there is no sign of a shop or trader today were not without facilities. Tytherington in 1907 boasted such erudite traders as grocer Augustus Ebenezer Dark, baker Edward Everley, shoe-maker William Hancock and butcher and poulterer Francis John Lines. Although the small shop/post office survives in some, but not all, Wylye Valley villages today, it has to be said that the majority of people shop in the big supermarkets at Salisbury or Warminster. That's a pity but quite a few villagers do support their local traders, not wanting to lose the facilities on their doorstep. How things have changed! Most villagers now have a car or cars, most commute to their workplaces, often miles from home, including London. Some residents are better described as 'visitors', their cottages bought as second and third homes for weekends and holidays away from the city. Recently, while wandering around one small village on a Sunday afternoon, I noticed the cars parked outside the cottages had Borough of London car-parking permits attached to the inside of their windscreens. We know where they are during the week!

The new immigrants, with their big money, are only part of the reason why village life has changed. The new affluence is not totally to blame; mechanisation on the farms has reduced the number of local jobs – a farmer's staff is minimal now, compared with years ago. Today's school-leaver, influenced by the media, particularly television, has a different attitude to life, and some I have spoken to care little for how their grandfathers and grandmothers lived. Sadly, young people who were born and bred in the villages cannot afford to buy a home where they spent their childhood, and are forced to move elsewhere when it comes to marriage and a family. The old feeling of continuity, and its associated stability, is lost. The photographs in this section glimpse village life as it was in the old days, when everyone knew everybody else, when people respected property and others, when every villager worked on the land or within a stone's throw of his or her home, and when the community spirit was far greater than it is today.

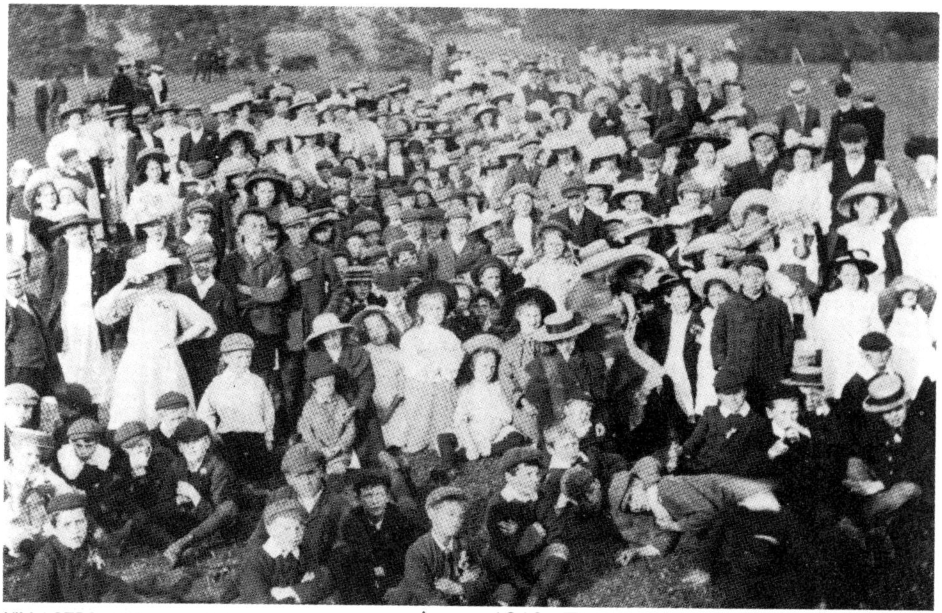

VILLAGERS AND VISITORS AT KILMINGTON FÊTE, *c.*1910. The well-known Warminster sweet maker, Benny Withey, and his bride-to-be, Kate Poddy, are standing near the back, on the right.

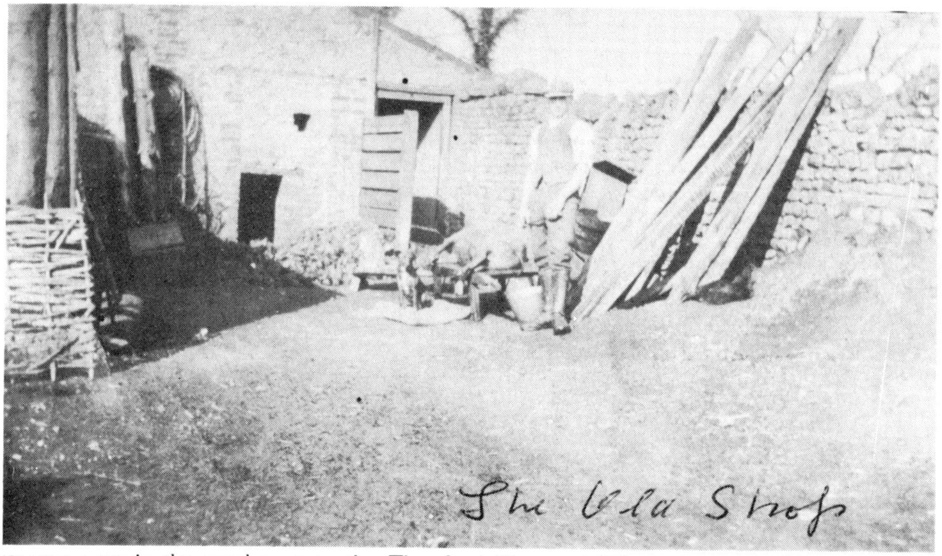

KILLING A PIG in the yard next to the Thenford Stores at Kilmington, possibly during the 1920s. The pig, as per the usual method, was stuck in the throat with a sharp knife and the blood was caught for black puddings. The pig was then laid upon a bench and the bristles burnt off, before butchering and curing.

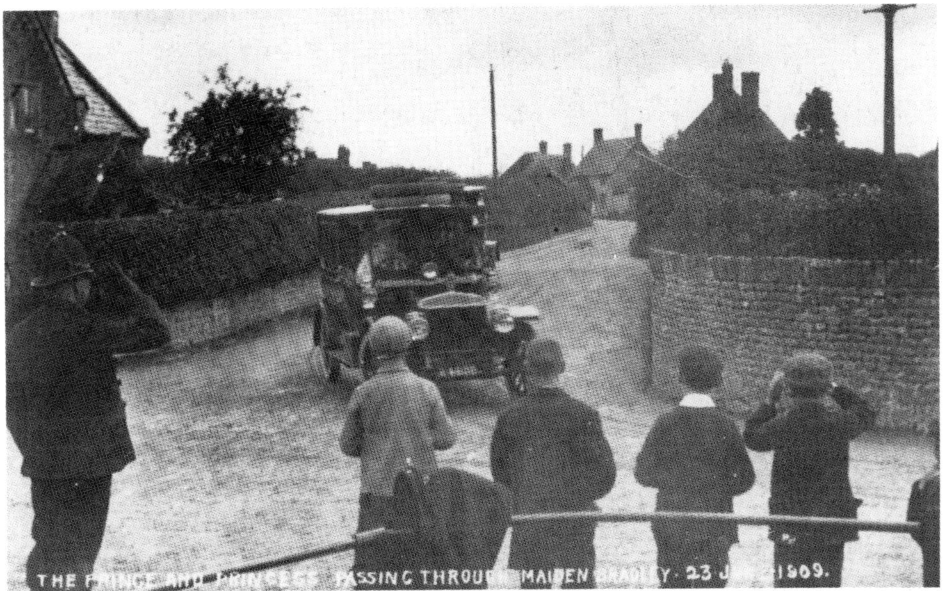

A POLICEMAN SALUTES and children watch as the Prince and Princess of Wales (later King George V and Queen Mary) pass through Maiden Bradley on 23 June 1909. They were travelling by car to catch the train at Gillingham, to return to London after a short stay as guests of the Marquis of Bath at Longleat.

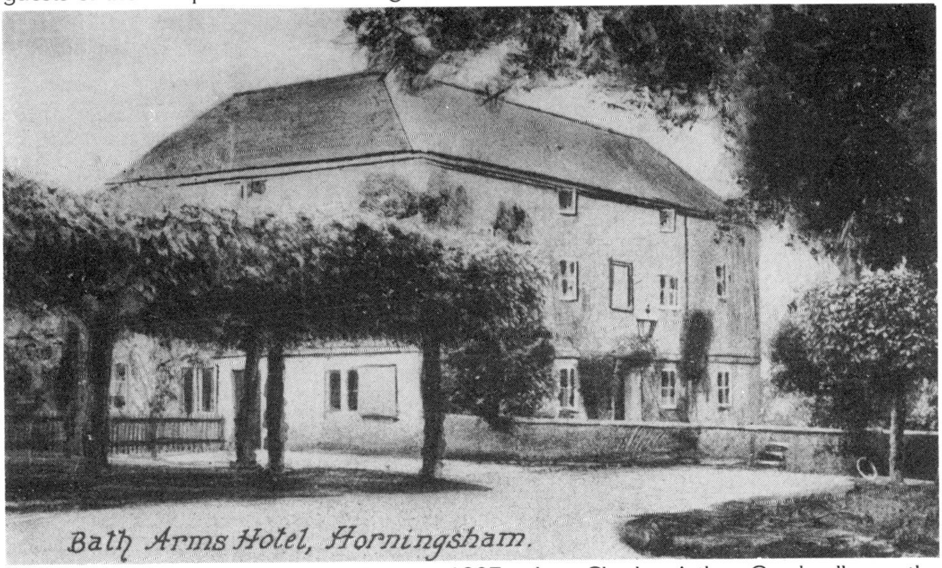

THE BATH ARMS HOTEL at Horningsham, c.1907, when Charles Arthur Cracknell was the hotelier. Outside is an unusual arrangement of old, pollarded lime trees. Four rows of three limes are known as 'The Twelve Apostles', while nearby is a smaller group called 'The Four Disciples'.

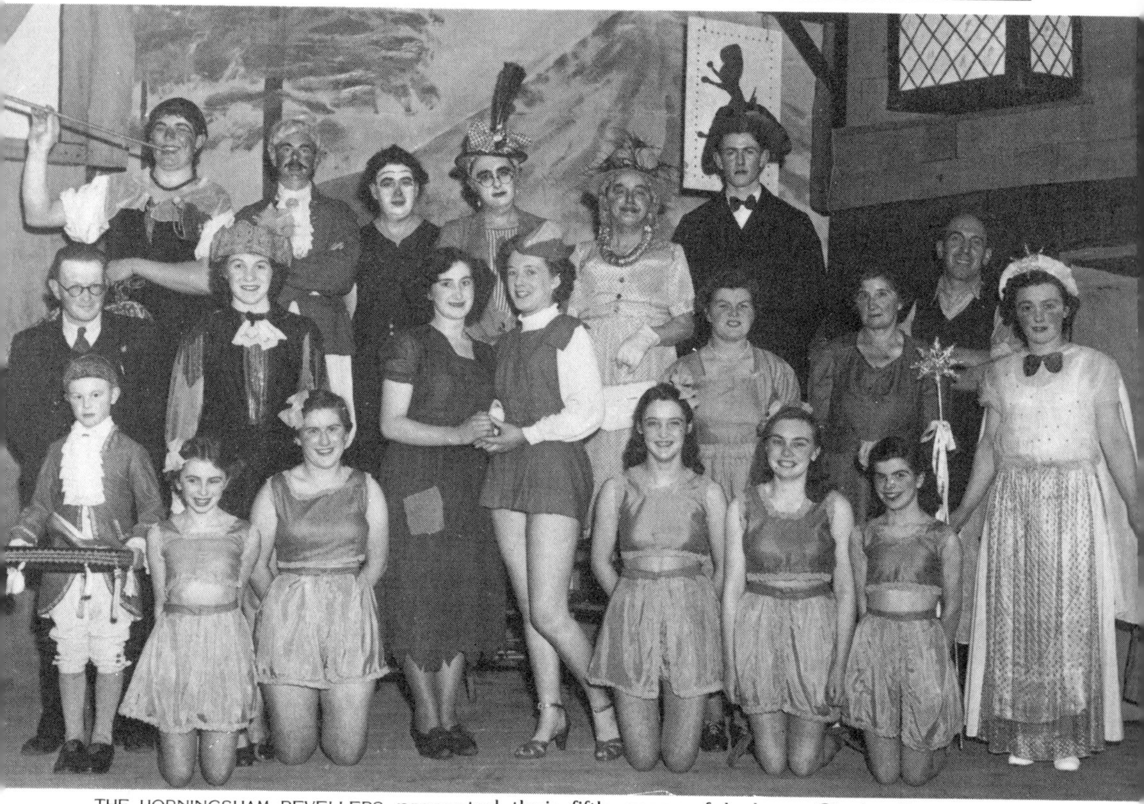

THE HORNINGSHAM REVELLERS presented their fifth successful show, *Cinderella*, a grand pantomime with ten scenes, at the local Village Hall in 1952. Proceeds, as usual, went to local institutions. The cast of *Cinderella* included Joan Edwards, Merigon Dufosee, Sylvia Berry, Susan Barnes, Valerie Taylor, Mary Ford, James Ford (senior), James Ford (junior), Florence Barnes, Ken Doel, William Garrett, Douglas Dicks, Francis Ford, Ann Wheeler, Kathleen Barnes, Vera Trollope, Muriel Doel, Kathleen Alford, Hester Rowe, Margaret Eggleton, Glenys Evans, Janet Dredge, David Taylor, Ben Dufosee and Doris Wheeler. The show was written and produced by Leslie Wheeler. Music was provided by Islay Peet (piano) and Arthur Ford (drums).

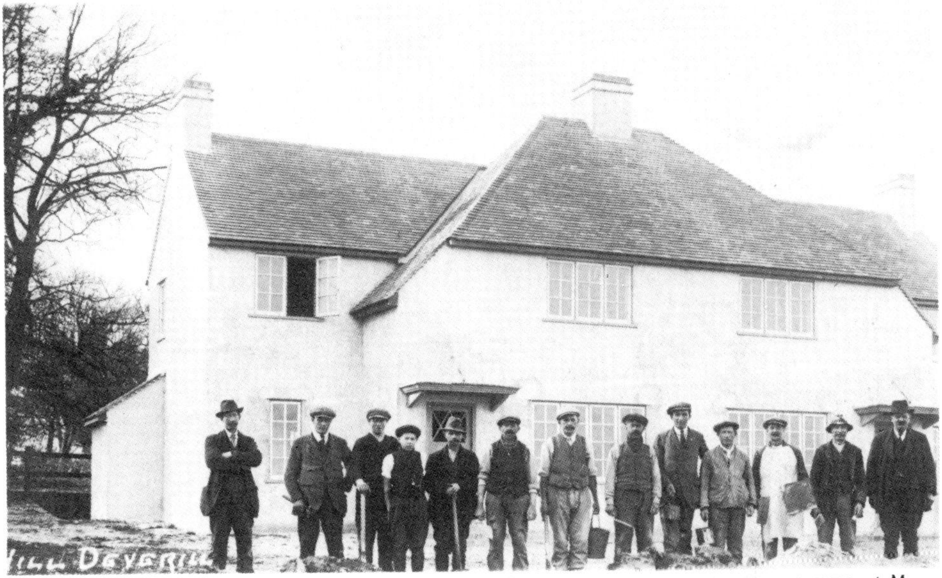

BUILDERS RESPONSIBLE FOR THE CONSTRUCTION OF SIX SEMI-DETACHED COUNCIL HOUSES at Mere Road, Hill Deverill, in 1922. Two more houses at the eastern end of the rank were added by the Warminster & Westbury Rural District Council in 1937.

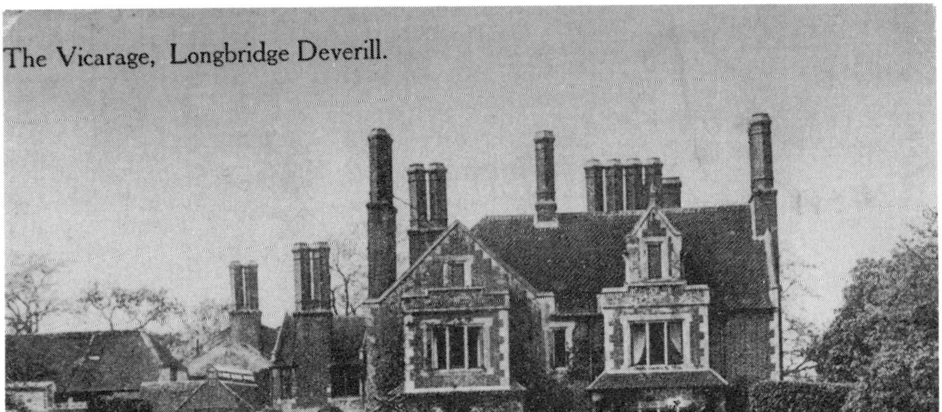

THE VICARAGE AT LONGBRIDGE DEVERILL, in September 1908, when the Revd Penny was vicar.

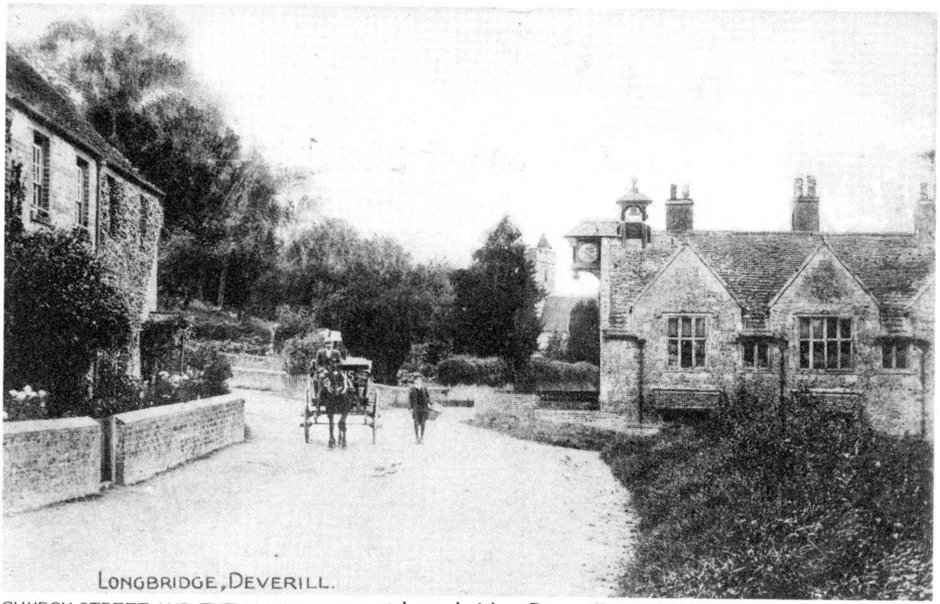

CHURCH STREET AND THE ALMSHOUSES at Longbridge Deverill in 1907. The almshouses were founded in 1665 by Sir James Thynne for six old men and two old women of Longbridge Deverill and Monkton Deverill. The clock, at the west end of the almshouses, is a much later addition. Because of a lack of household clocks, a man ringing a bell used to go round the village to wake up those who were employed at the Silk Mill at nearby Crockerton. Miss Morrice, the daughter of the vicar, Canon Morrice, objected to this and paid for a striking, public clock to be fixed to the almshouses. She also left some money for the upkeep of the clock in the 1880s.

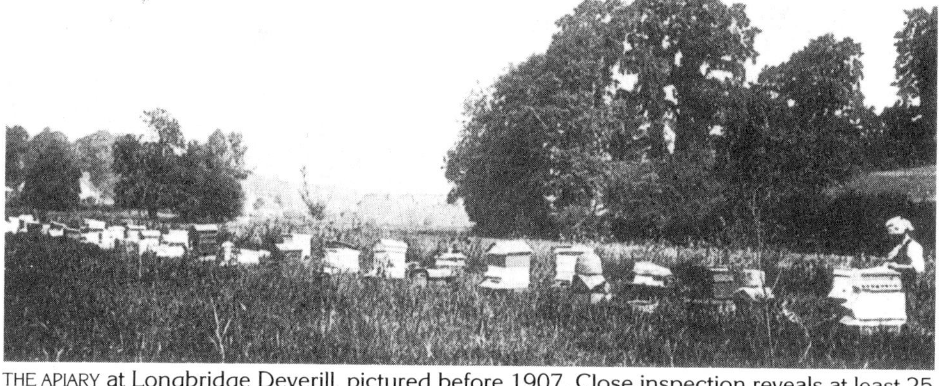

THE APIARY at Longbridge Deverill, pictured before 1907. Close inspection reveals at least 25 hives, both square ones and round ones. The man on the right, attending to a hive, is only protected about the head – he's even got his sleeves rolled up!

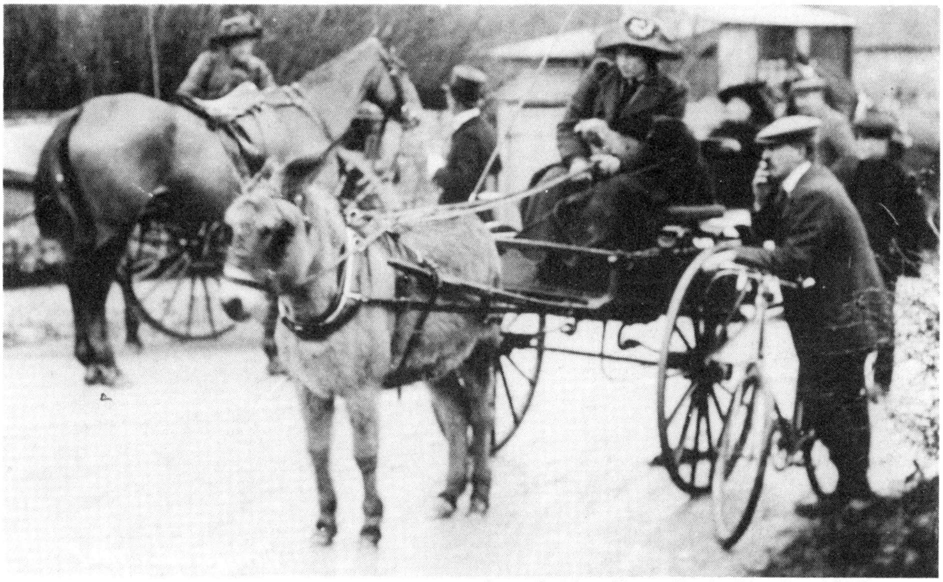

PEOPLE WATCHING A MEET OF THE LOCAL HUNT at Longbridge Deverill, during the 1920s.

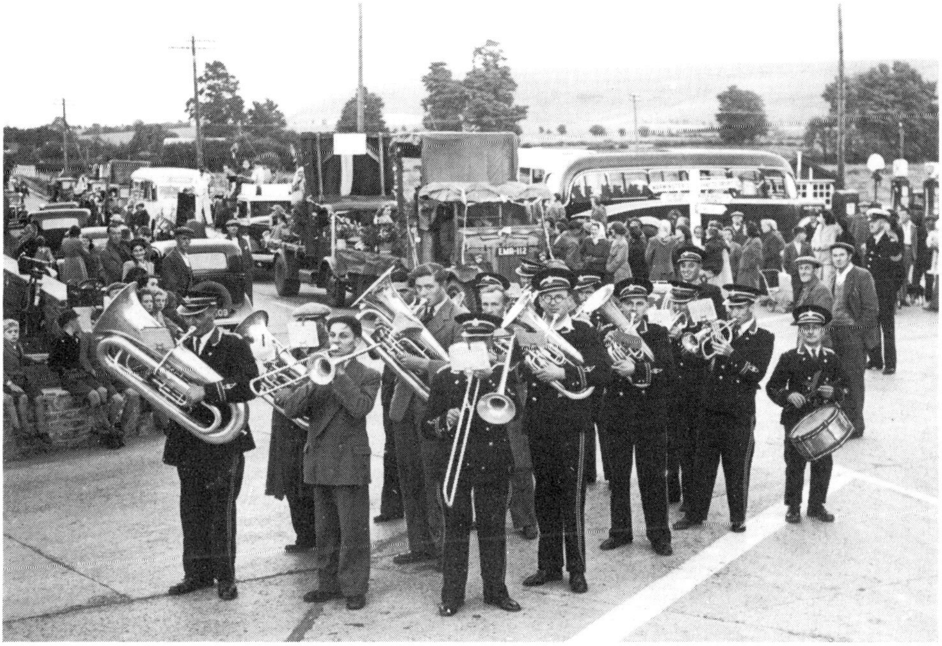

A CARNIVAL PROCESSION after the Second World War at Longbridge Deverill turns out of Sand Street into Church Street. The band appears to be a little disorganised.

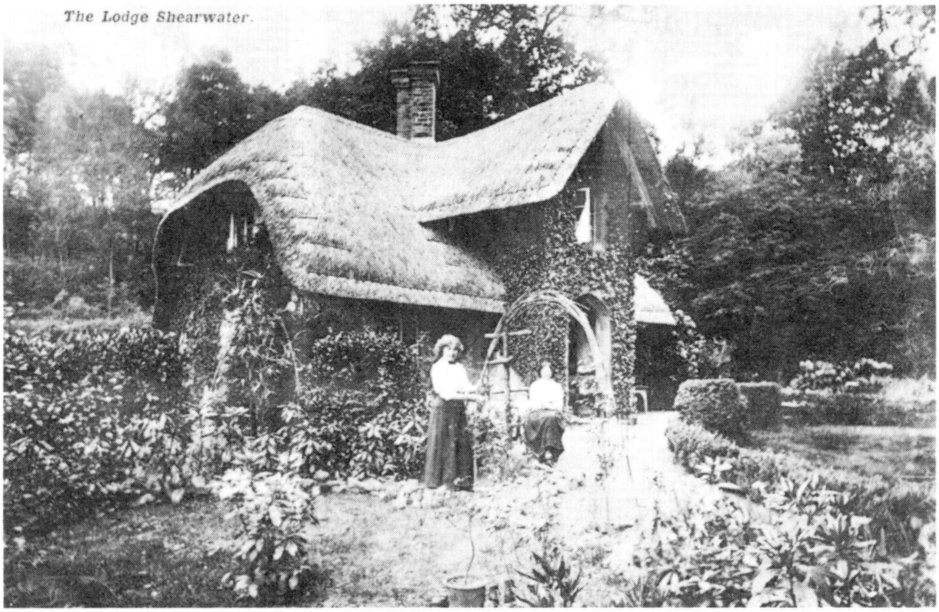

SISTERS BESSIE FELTHAM (LATER MRS STOCKLEY) AND ROSE FELTHAM in the garden of their parents' home at Bargate Cottage (also known as the Lodge), Shearwater *c.* 1900. Bessie, born in 1882, lived to be 101 and she was able to recall the winters during her childhood when ox-roasts were held on the frozen lake, and the 1920s and 30s when Shearwater was the haunt of university oarsmen.

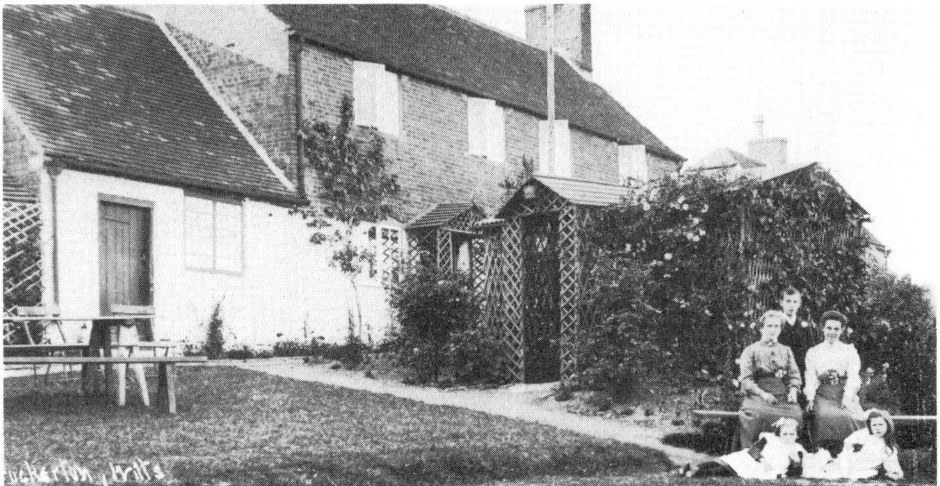

A FAMILY IN THE GARDEN of 69 Jersey Hill, Crockerton, in 1920.

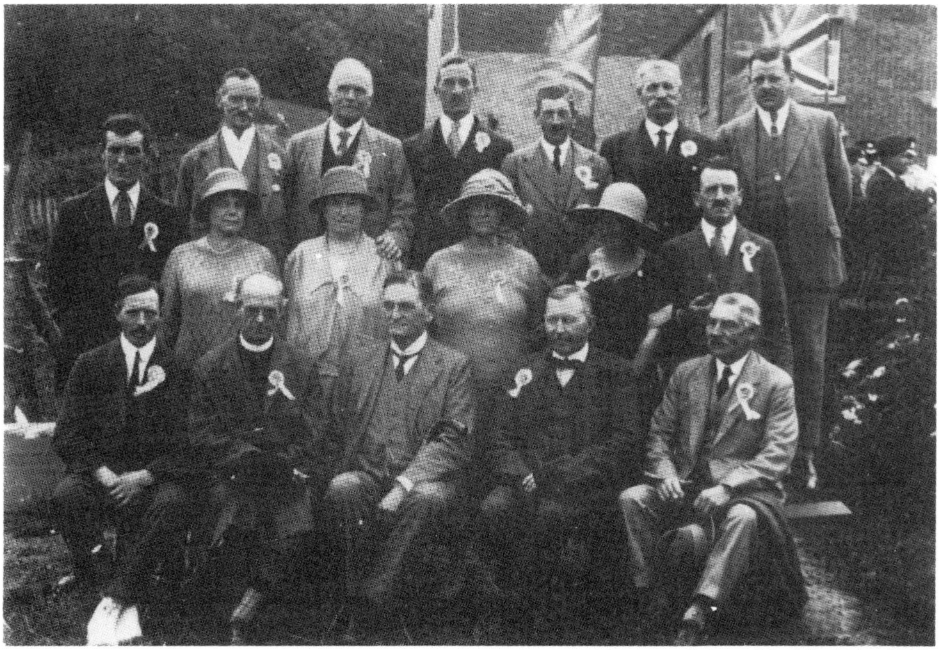

ORGANISERS, OFFICIALS AND JUDGES OF CROCKERTON FLOWER SHOW, pictured behind the Bath Arms in the village, *c*.1920. Lord Bath is sitting in the middle of the front row. Behind them a band is playing.

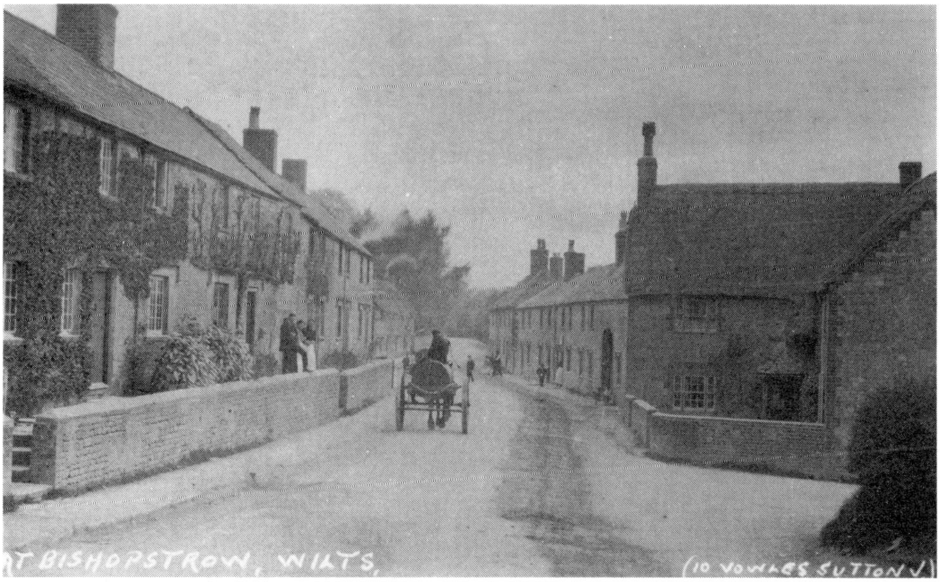

LOOKING NORTH ALONG THE VILLAGE STREET at Bishopstrow, *c*.1916. The horse-drawn vehicle looks like a water cart. These were regularly used for damping down the dust on the roads.

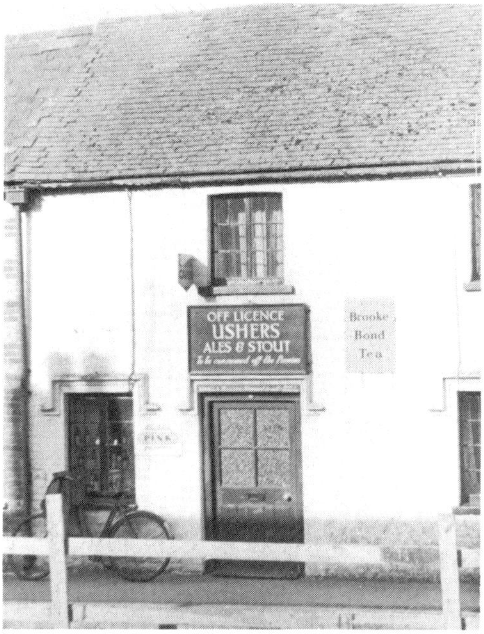

HALLETT'S SHOP at 21 Bishopstrow, pictured during the early 1960s. It is now a private residence.

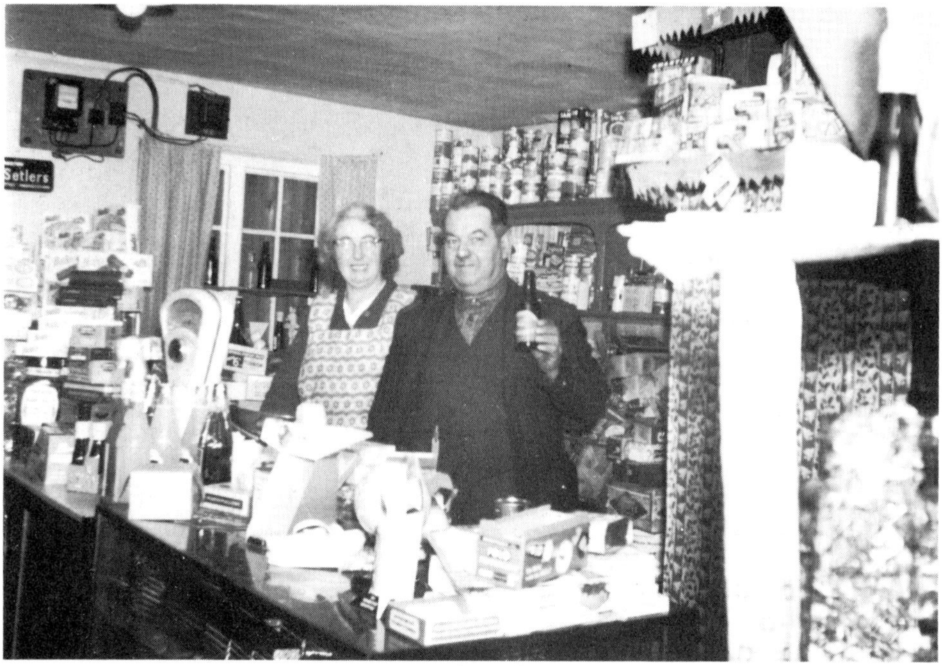

SYDNEY EDWIN HALLETT AND ROSELLA HALLETT (née Fitz) in their shop at Bishopstrow during the early 1960s.

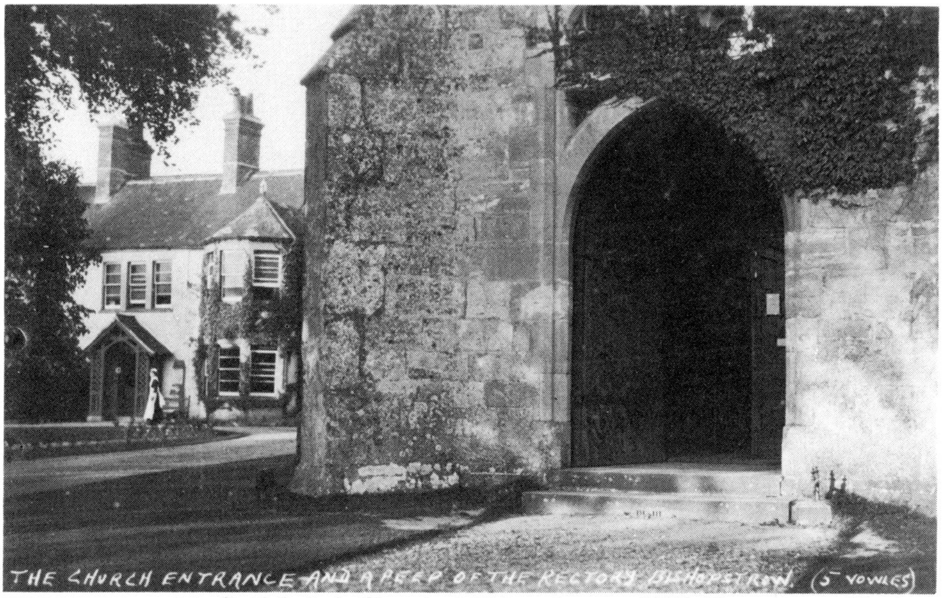

THE RECTORY, next to St Aldhelm's Church at Bishopstrow, *c.* 1915. The rector at this time was Revd George Henry Sanders Atwood (1855–1921) of St Catharine's College, Cambridge. He had come to Bishopstrow in 1883. The Rectory, which dates from 1783, has been a private residence since 1954.

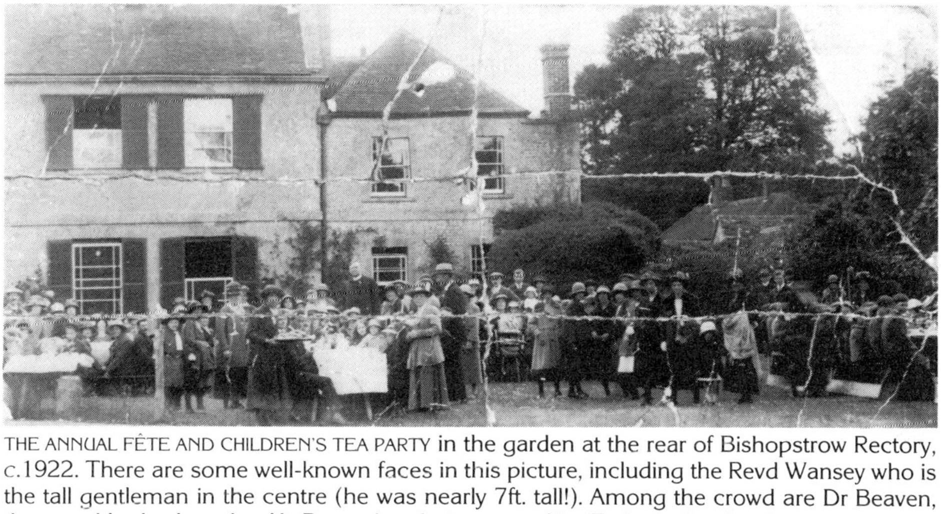

THE ANNUAL FÊTE AND CHILDREN'S TEA PARTY in the garden at the rear of Bishopstrow Rectory, *c.*1922. There are some well-known faces in this picture, including the Revd Wansey who is the tall gentleman in the centre (he was nearly 7ft. tall!). Among the crowd are Dr Beaven, the noted barley breeder, Mr Rutty, the choirmaster, Mrs Erskine, the Girl Guides' mistress, Miss Heath, the school mistress, Mrs Rutty, Mrs Dawkins, Miss Beaven, Miss Fitz, Mrs Payne, Mrs Francis, Mrs Waddington and Miss Emily Stephens. The schoolboys seated on the far right include Bert Dawkins and Gerald Puckett.

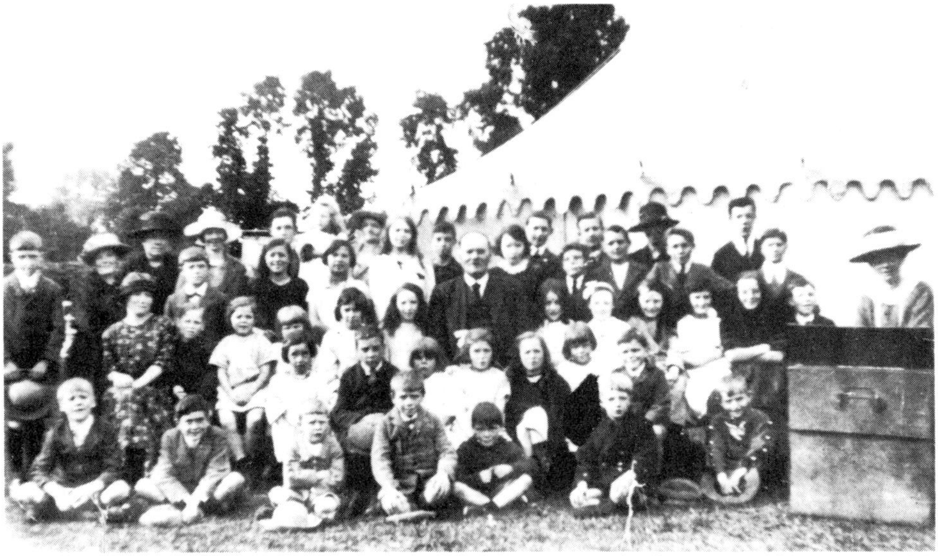

A GATHERING OF BISHOPSTROW RESIDENTS, mostly children, on the Recreation Ground, *c*.1922. The lady on the right is the schoolteacher Miss Heath. She is seated at a portable piano.

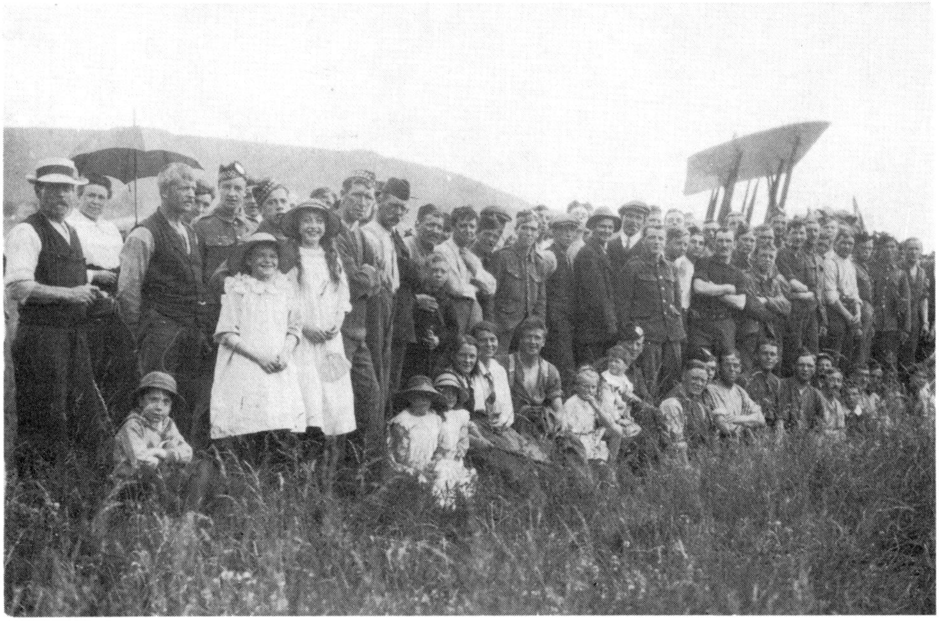

BISHOPSTROW AND NORTON BAVANT RESIDENTS and soldiers, pictured at the scene of a plane crash, in a field between the two villages, during the First World War. The photographer, unfortunately, pictured everyone in front of the plane, but you can see part of it projecting up above the back of the crowd. Scratchbury Hill is in the background.

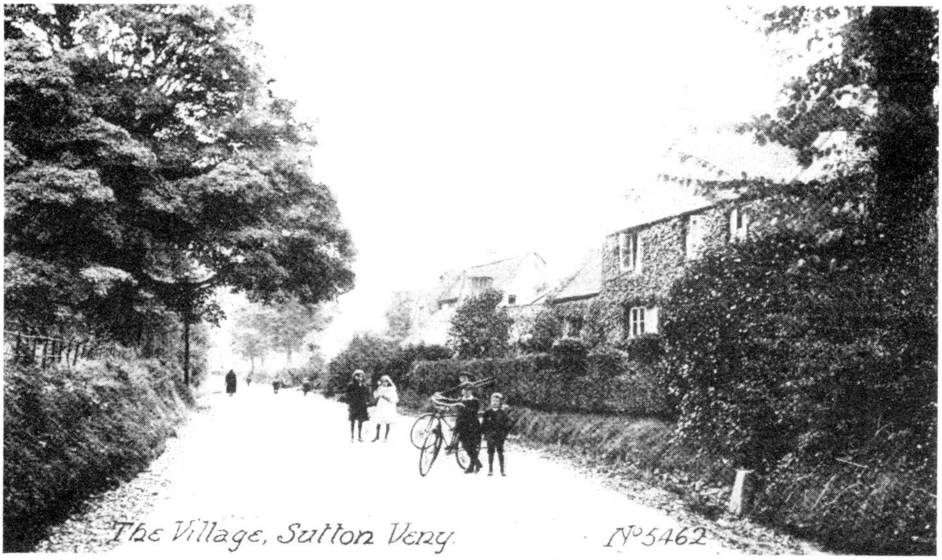

LOOKING SOUTH ALONG THE LOWER PART OF HIGH STREET, Sutton Veny, c.1912. The corner of St John's Churchyard and the park are on the left of the picture. Opposite are Park Cottages. This view appeared on a postcard published by stationer Sidney Pearce Butt, who was also the village postmaster.

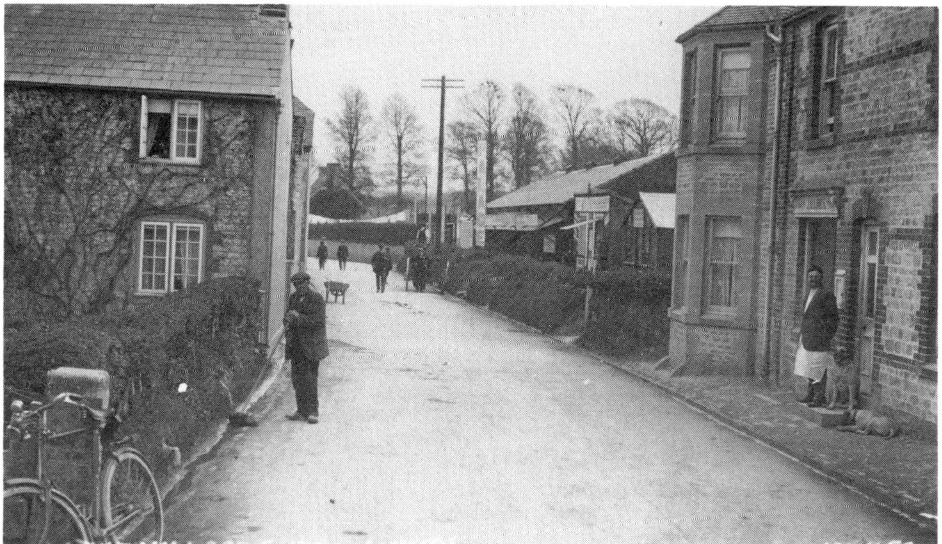

LOOKING SOUTH ALONG SUTTON VENY HIGH STREET during the First World War. J.O. Lines' Bakery is on the right. Further down the street, on the right (next to Dymocks Lane, where the entrance to Walnut Close is today), is the Palace Cinema, a wooden building where the soldiers watched silent films. This was one of three cinemas at Sutton Veny for the troops, the others being at the Quarry and Five Ash Lane.

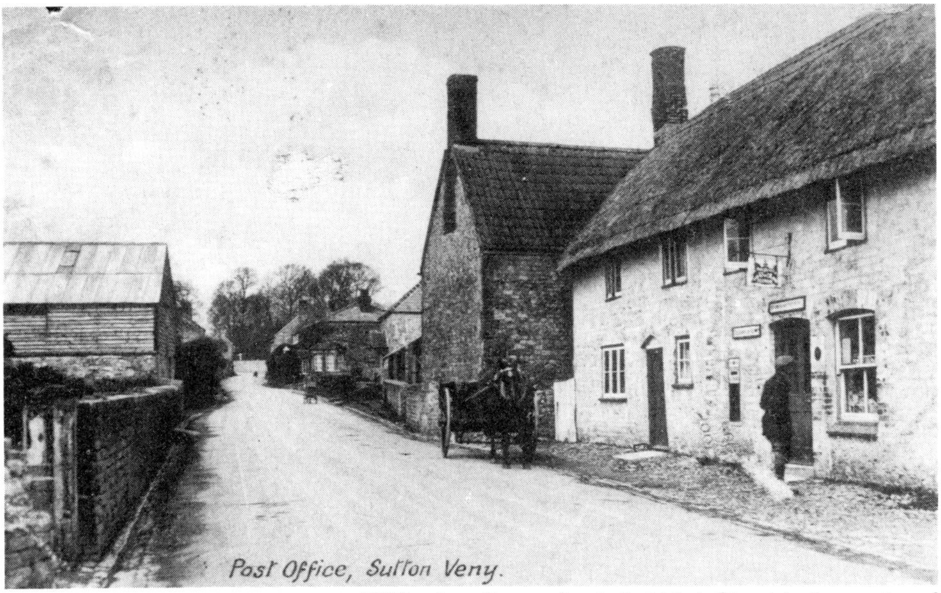

THE POST OFFICE AT SUTTON VENY, c.1900, when it was situated at High Street in the centre of the village. Later the post office was based at Best's Lane, before it returned to the High Street (opposite what was Lines' Bakery) until the property was demolished. It was then installed at Deverill Road in its present premises opposite Sheppard's Garage.

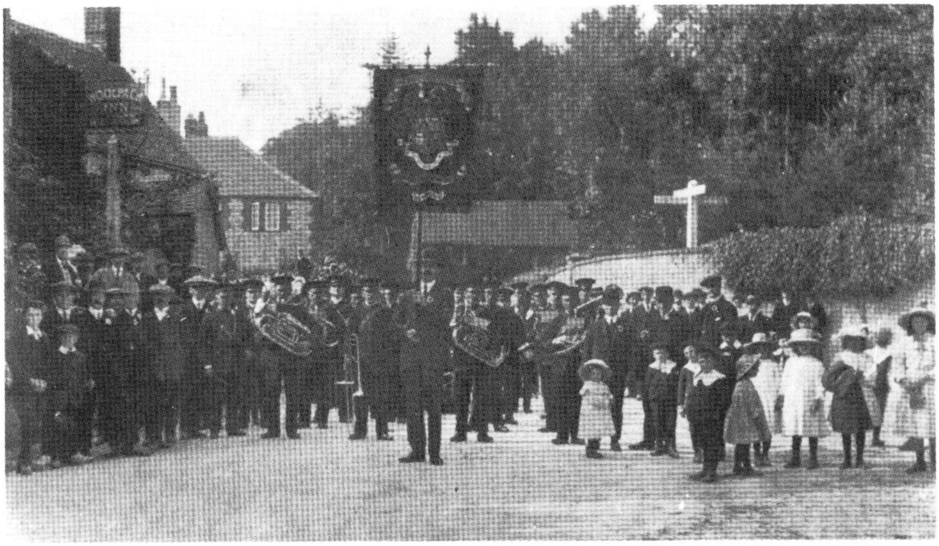

SUTTON VENY RESIDENTS assembled outside the Woolpack, c.1910, when Herbert Ashby was the landlord. It looks like a march, with a band, is about to take place, but the reason for this and the significance of the standard held by the gentleman is unknown.

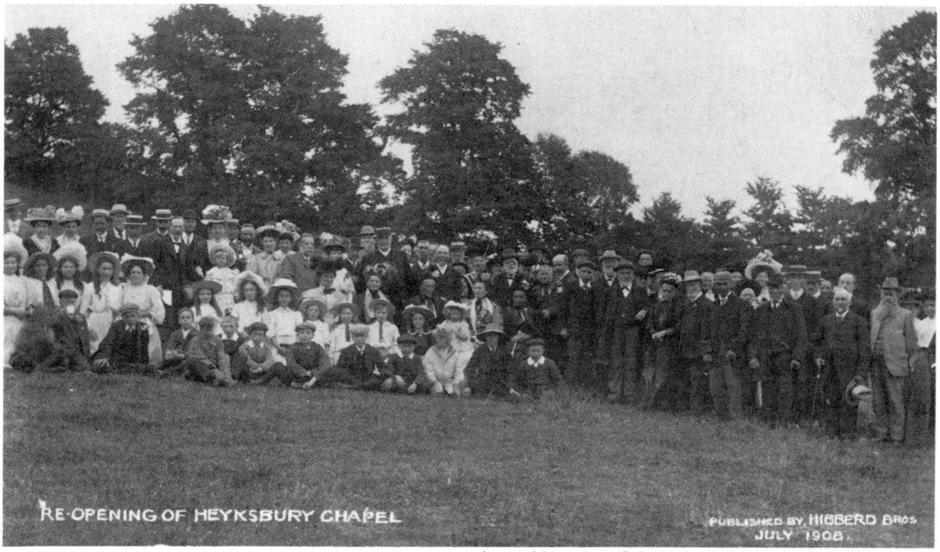

HEYTESBURY CONGREGATIONAL CHAPEL re-opened on Monday 27 July 1908, after a period of renovation. The Revd J.D. Jones of Bournemouth (Chairman-Elect of the Congregational Union of England and Wales) preached the sermon and this was followed afterwards with a public tea and meeting. Mr W.H. Harrison of Bournemouth presided at the meeting and the addresses were spoken by the Revd J.D. Jones, Revd J.D. Perkins (Warminster), Revd P.N. Harrison (Salisbury) and Mr J. Lucas (Warminster).

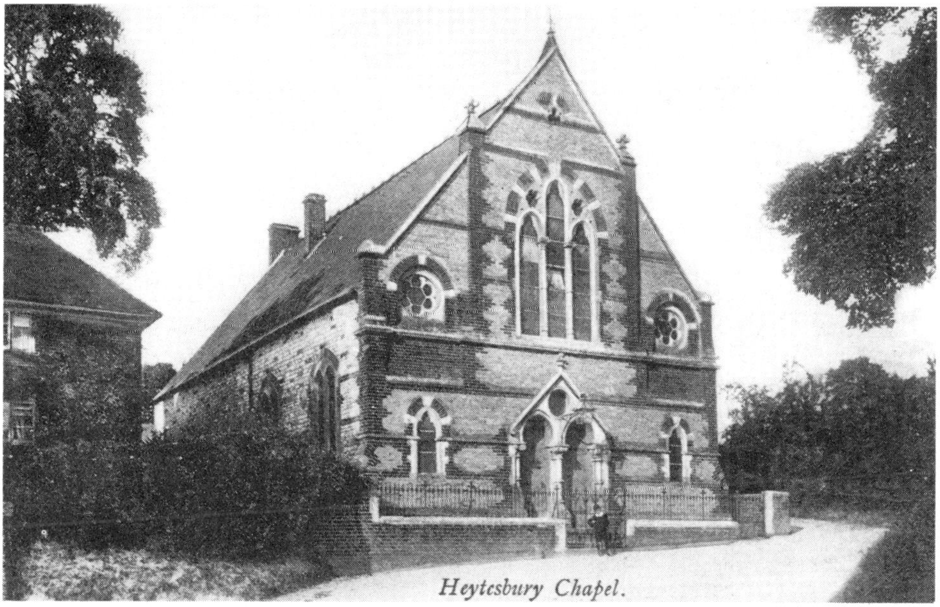

HEYTESBURY CHAPEL, c.1906. It has since been demolished and a house now occupies its site at the northern end of Chapel Road.

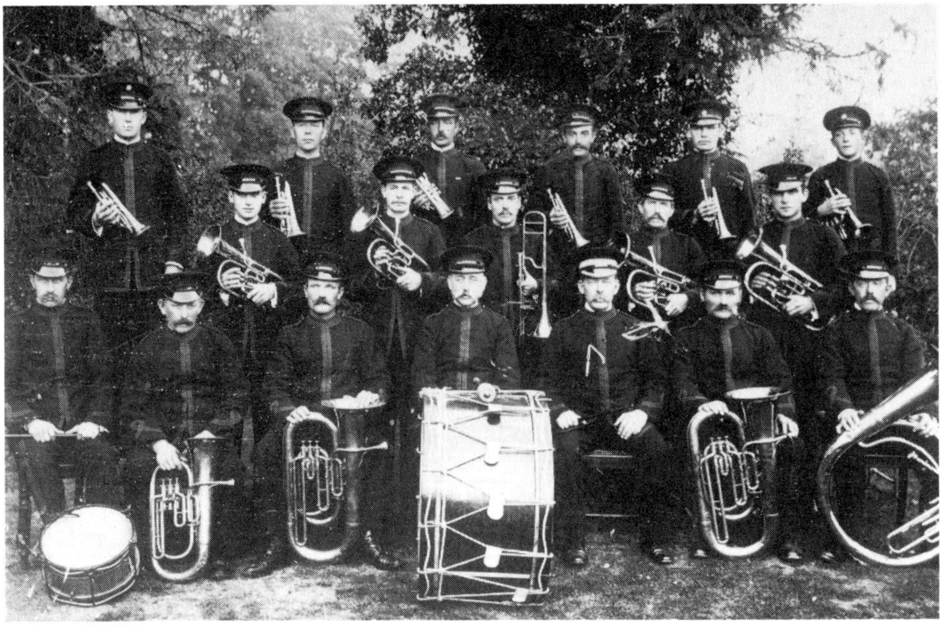

HEYTESBURY VILLAGE BAND in 1905. The musicians from Heytesbury, Norton Bavant, Tytherington, Knook, Codford and Longbridge Deverill are William Morgan, Tommy Stanley, Arthur Reynolds, Reg Gilbert, Bert Sparey, Edgar Ball, William Bailey, Walter Daniels, Bert Blagdon, Elisha Found, Ernest Elling, Barry Bartlett, Albert Dredge, Fred Vincent, Jack Farley, Tom Farley (Bandmaster), Jack Whatley, and Bert Bartlett. Sadly, all the musicians above are no longer alive but the memory of the tuneful pleasure the band supplied at many local events lives on.

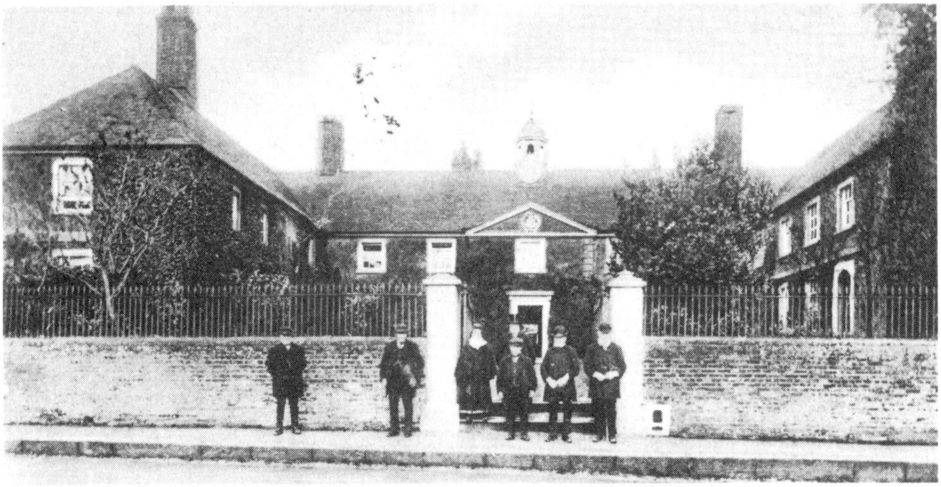

ST JOHN'S HOSPITAL, Heytesbury, was founded as an almshouse by Walter, first Lord Hungerford, in 1472. This picture was taken *c*.1905.

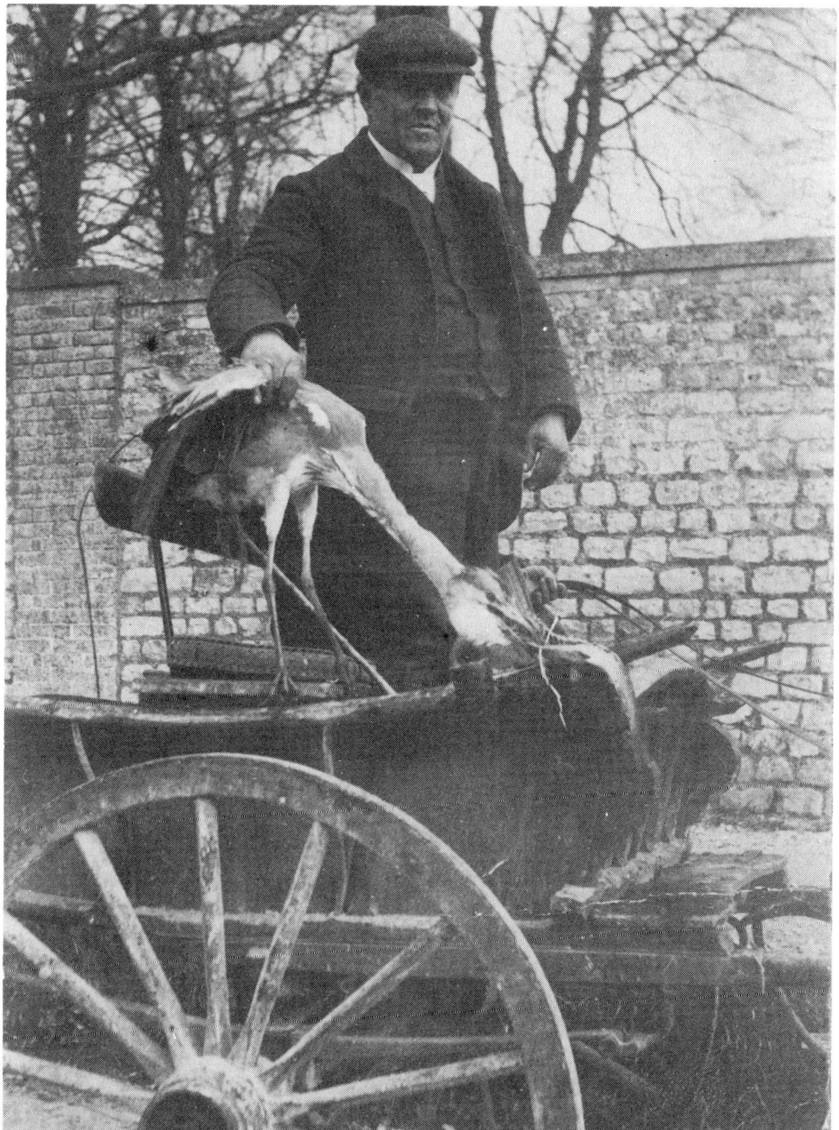

THIS GENTLEMAN IS THOUGHT TO BE TED HURDLE, who was the river-keeper on the Heytesbury Estate. The picture was taken sometime between 1904 and 1912 on the Warminster to Salisbury road at Heytesbury, opposite the turning for Mill Lane. In the background is the wall that surrounds the grounds of Heytesbury House. Close inspection of the picture reveals that the heron, which has obviously been captured by the keeper, has a fish in its mouth. There is a second person on the cart, hidden by Mr Hurdle – the person's left hand is just visible, holding the reins.

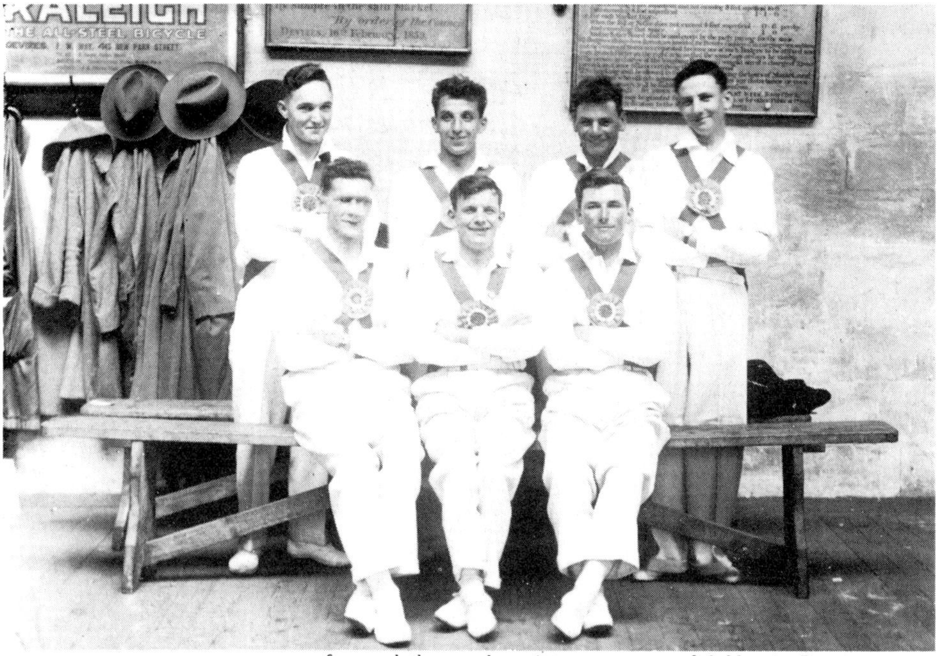

THESE WYLYE VALLEY RESIDENTS formed themselves into a successful Morris Dance team. Among the dancers pictured here, at a Folk Dance Festival at Devizes during the 1930s, are Uriah White from Heytesbury (centre of front row) and Norman Whatley from Langford (back left).

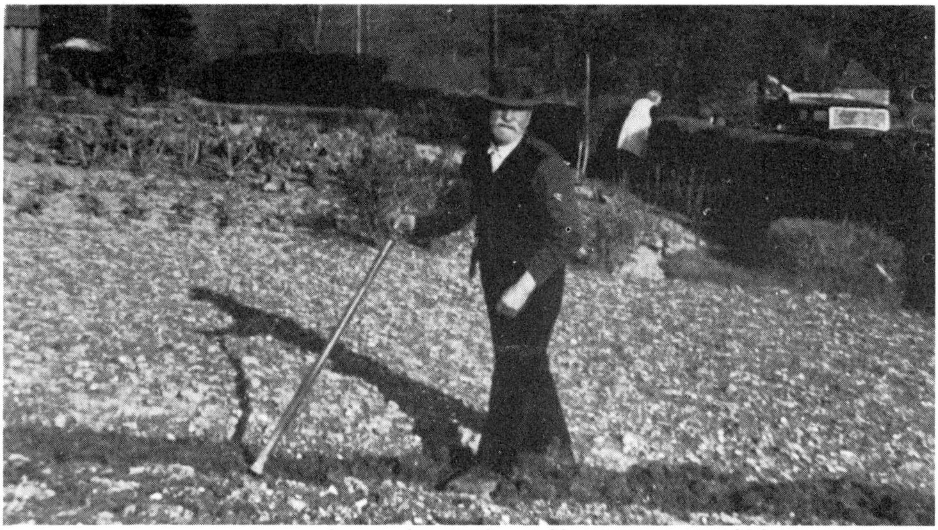

HEYTESBURY RESIDENT TOM DICKS hoeing his garden at Newtown in the 1950s. He worked on the Heytesbury Estate until he was over 80 years of age and he was the last man to drive a horse and cart for them.

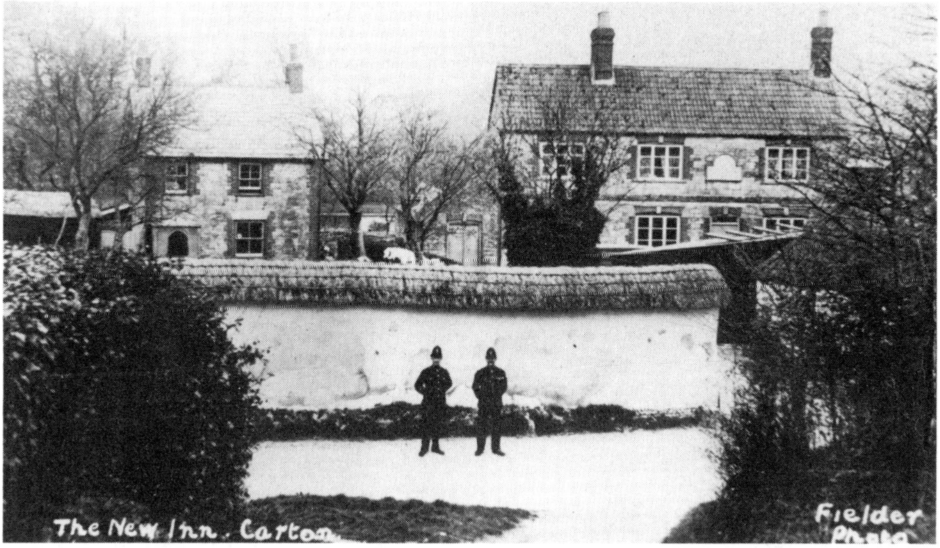

PC 113 WILLIAM PONTING (left) and PC 219 William Henry Hillier pictured outside the New Inn at Corton, *c.*1917. Ponting was born at Malmesbury on 25 October 1894, found employment first as a gardener but joined the police force on 31 August 1914 and was stationed at Trowbridge before moving to Corton on 29 April 1916. He was discharged on 31 August 1917 due to sickness. Hillier was born at Calne on 4 October 1888, worked first as a groom but joined the police on 27 March 1911. He was stationed at Bradford-on-Avon until 15 February 1912, when he moved to the Codford beat. On 5 November 1919 he transferred to North Tidworth.

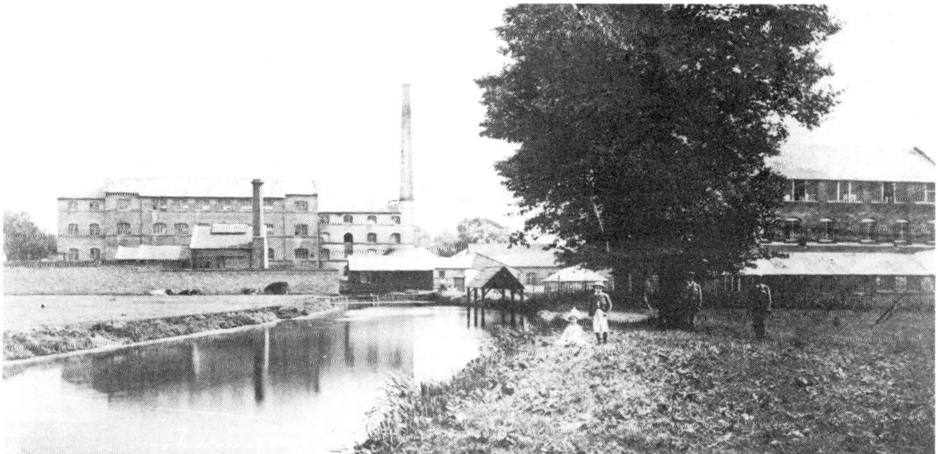

THE CLOTH MILL (Hatch Mill) at Upton Lovell, pictured in the 1890s. It caught fire in 1895 and the owner, William Walker, transferred his business to Samuel Salter's Home Mills at Trowbridge. The fire-damaged ruins and the chimney stood for quite a while afterwards. Today, a house, appropriately named Hatch House, stands on part of the site of the former mill.

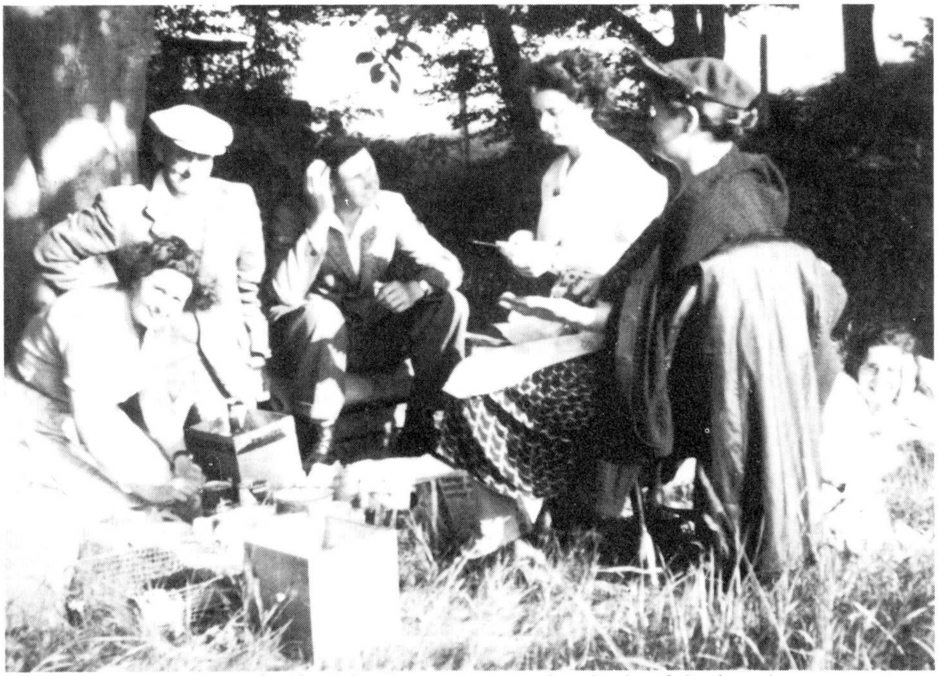

THE PHELPS FAMILY, from Codford, having a picnic in the shade of the beech trees on Ansty Hill, between Knook and Chitterne. They include Kathleen, Bill, David, Alice, Edith and Violet.

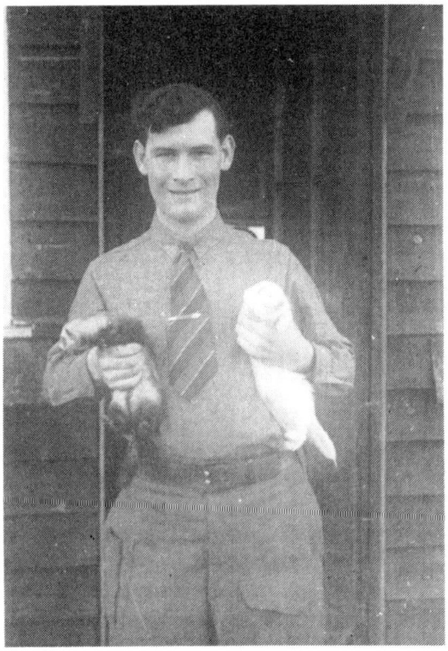

NINETEEN-YEAR-OLD LOUIS PHELPS of Anzac Farm, Codford, pictured with a pair of ferrets in 1946. For some villagers, ferreting was not only a popular pastime, it was also a way of providing a rabbit for the table. If rabbits were plentiful the surplus was sold to local dealers, the money from the sale boosting one's meagre income.

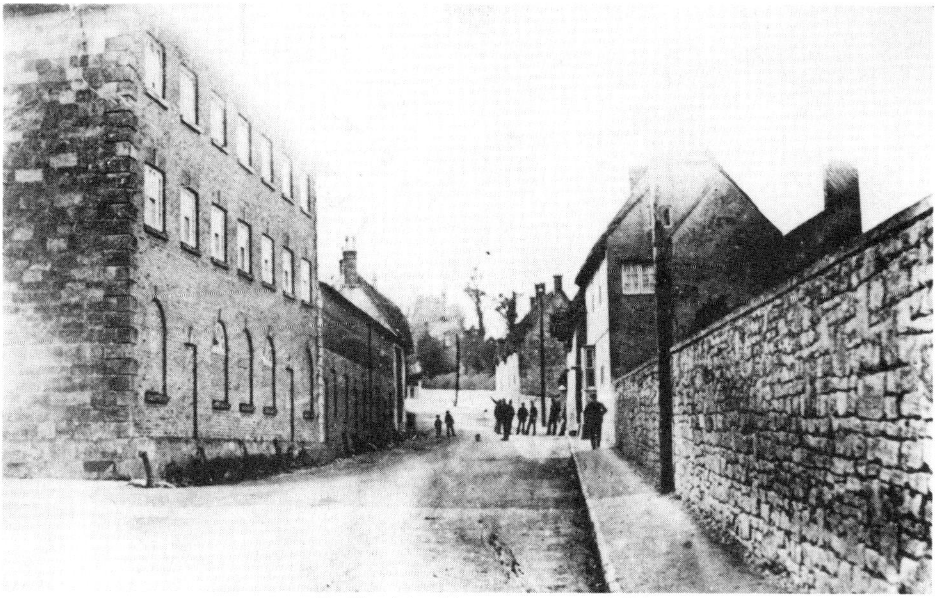

THE UPPER PART OF HIGH STREET, Codford, looking west towards Warminster, before 1900. The Woolstore is on the left. The George Inn, immediately adjacent to the road on the right, was later re-built further back from the highway.

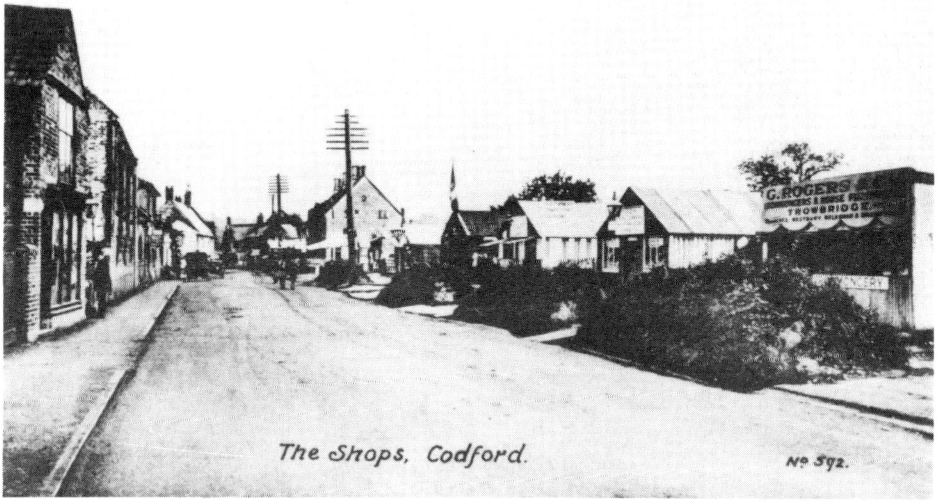

HIGH STREET, Codford, looking east, during the First World War. The temporary buildings on the south side of the road provide shops and other services for the troops in camp around the village. Among the shops are G. Roger & Co. (ironmongers and house-furnishers of Trowbridge), Cook's and S.J. Turner's. The hut with the flag flying is the Young Men's Christian Association.

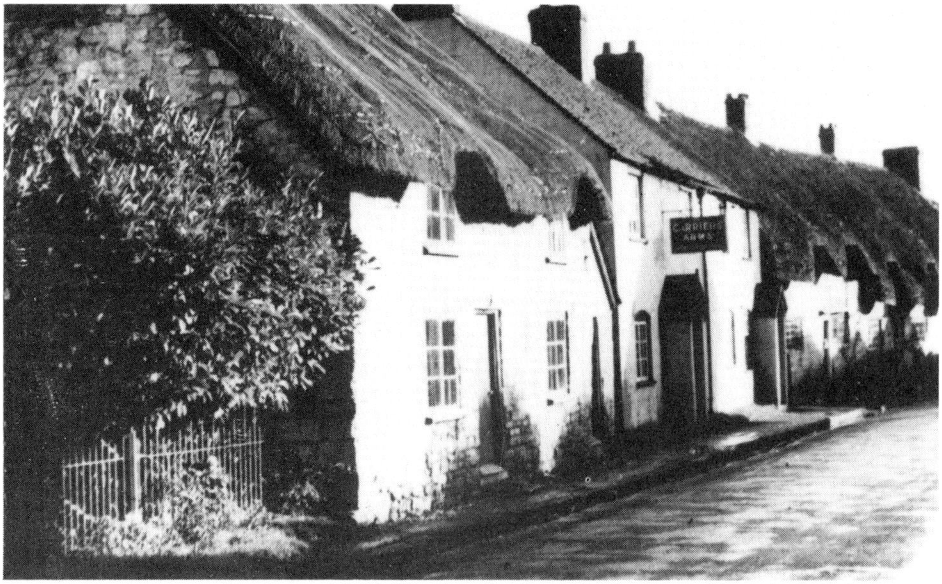

THE CARRIERS ARMS at Stockton, 1947. The landlord at this time was Francis J. Galvin.

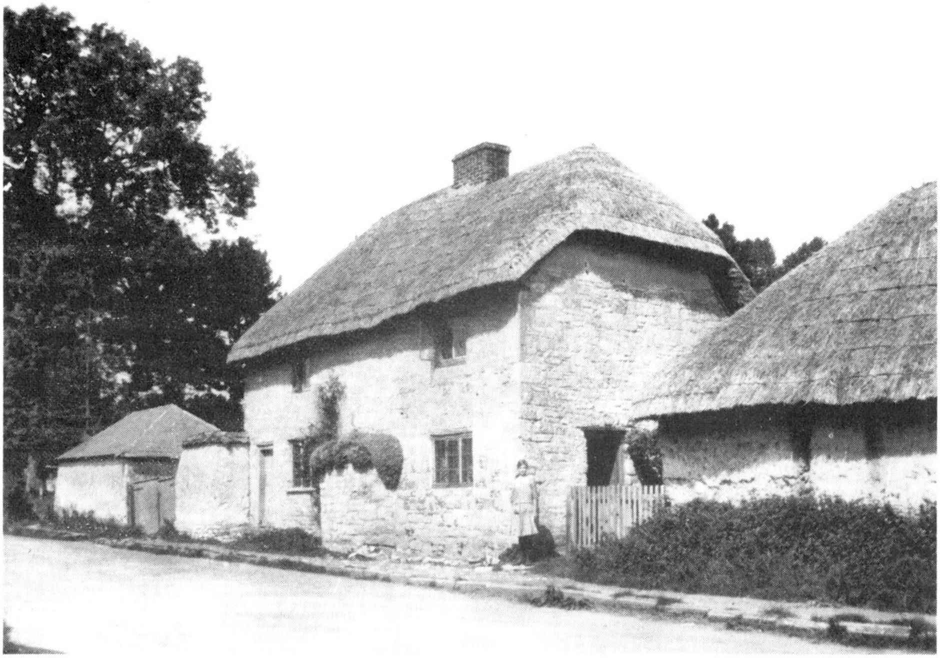

A COTTAGE WITH A BREAD-OVEN IN ITS WALL, on the north side of the street at Stockton *c.*1920. You can still see this charming feature today as you pass by and it is one of several examples to be found in Wiltshire and elsewhere.

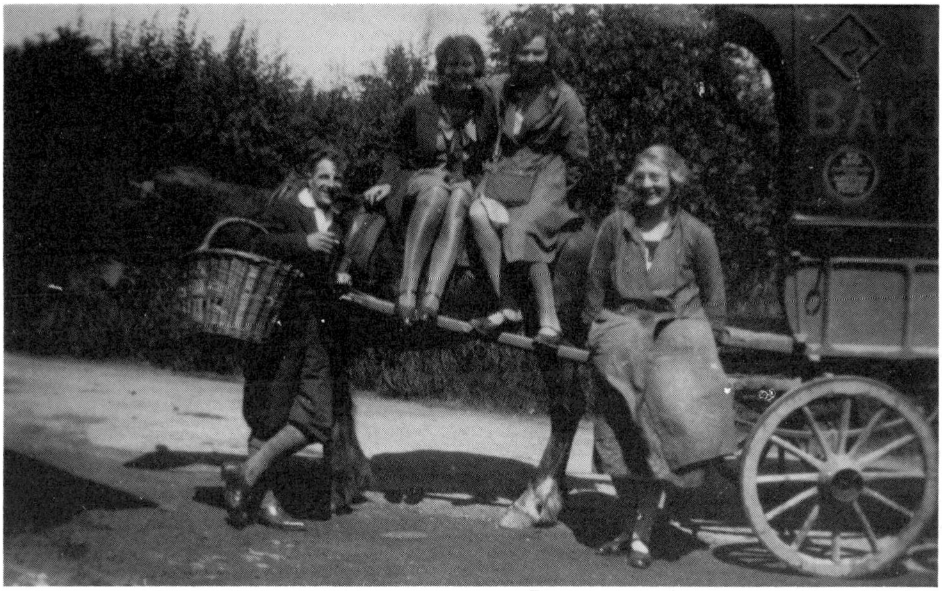

JOHN ROBERT WEARE'S HORSE-DRAWN BAKER'S VAN at Bapton, possibly during the late 1920s. Left to right are an unknown man from the village, Gladys and Phylis Weare (sisters) and their mother Mrs Annie Weare. The business evolved into the village shop ran by Gladys and her husband Roy Bryant. Gladys died in 1985 and the shop continues today in Roy's hands.

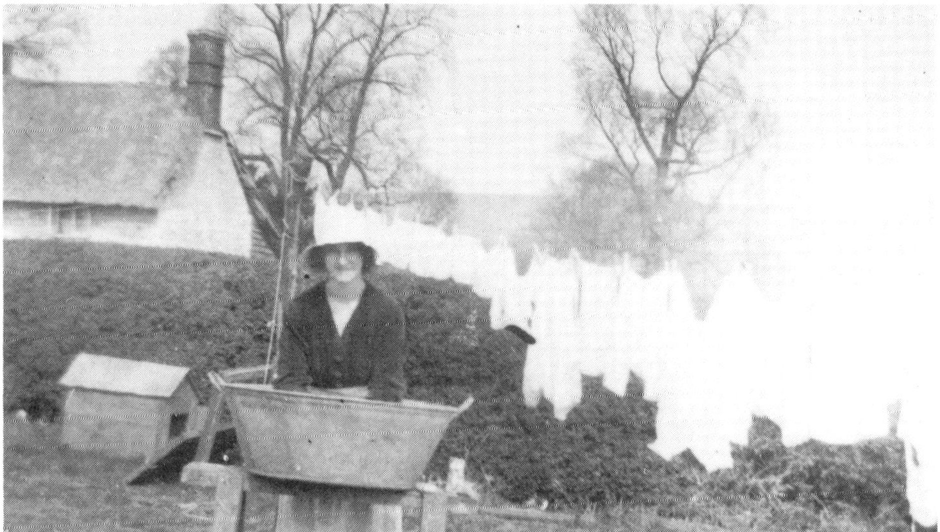

WASHING DAY AT BAPTON, during the 1920s. The lady is unknown. A galvanised wash-tub of water at waist height on a bench in the garden, a clothes line and the unpredictability of the English weather – a far cry from today's automatic washing machines, tumble driers, spinners and rotary clothes' lines.

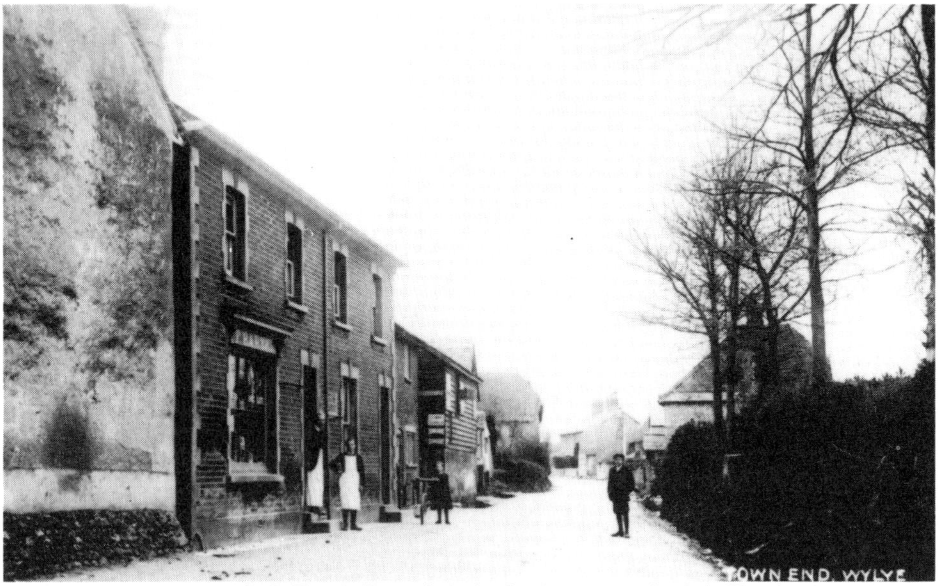

TOWN END AT WYLYE in 1915. Frank Barter's baker's shop is on the left. Frank is standing in the doorway. The two boys in the picture are Frank's sons, Howard and Victor. The girl with the bicycle is Frank's daughter, Freda.

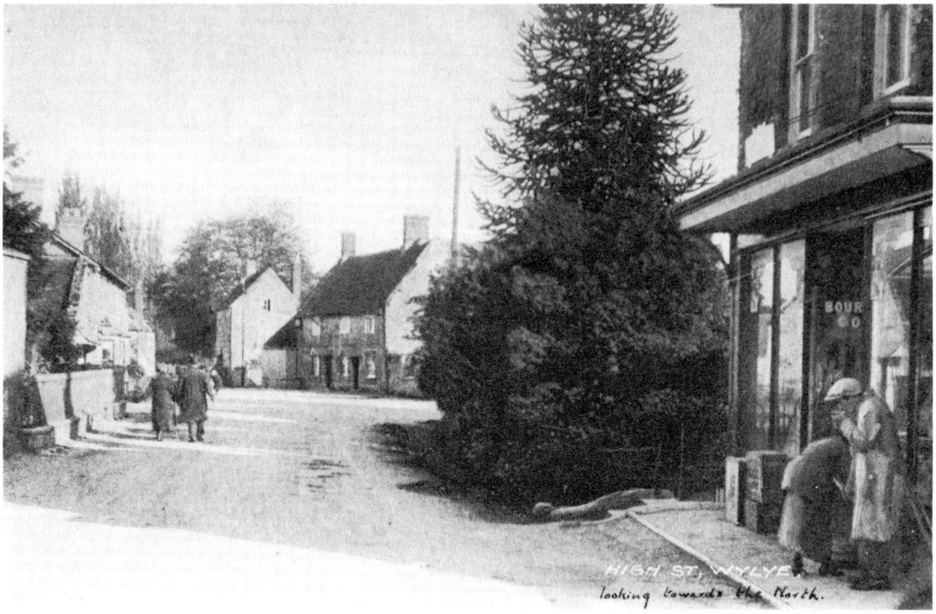

HIGH STREET, Wylye, looking north towards the Bell Inn (centre). It's hard to imagine that this is the main road connecting London with Exeter! The shop, on the right, is still the village shop and post office today.

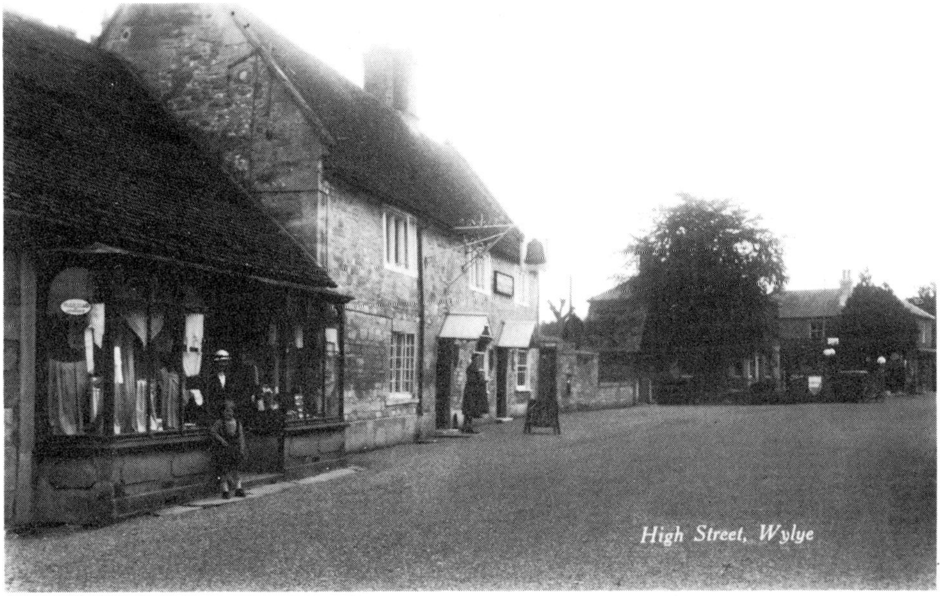

HIGH STREET, Wylye, *c.*1937, looking south past the Bell Inn towards the garage. The Bell Inn has a board outside advertising 'TEAS'.

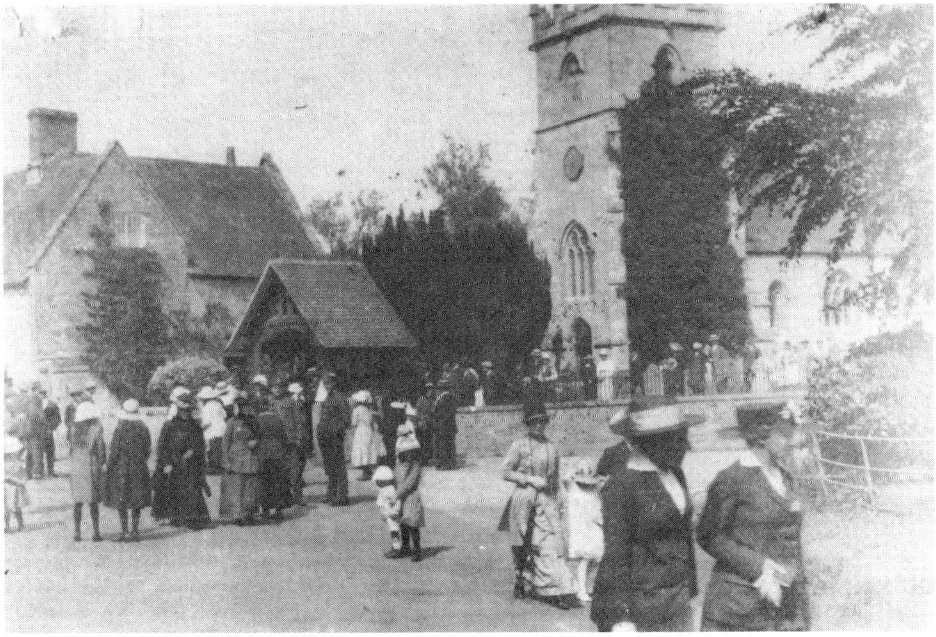

CONGREGATION LEAVING ST MARY'S CHURCH, Wylye, one Sunday morning in 1919.

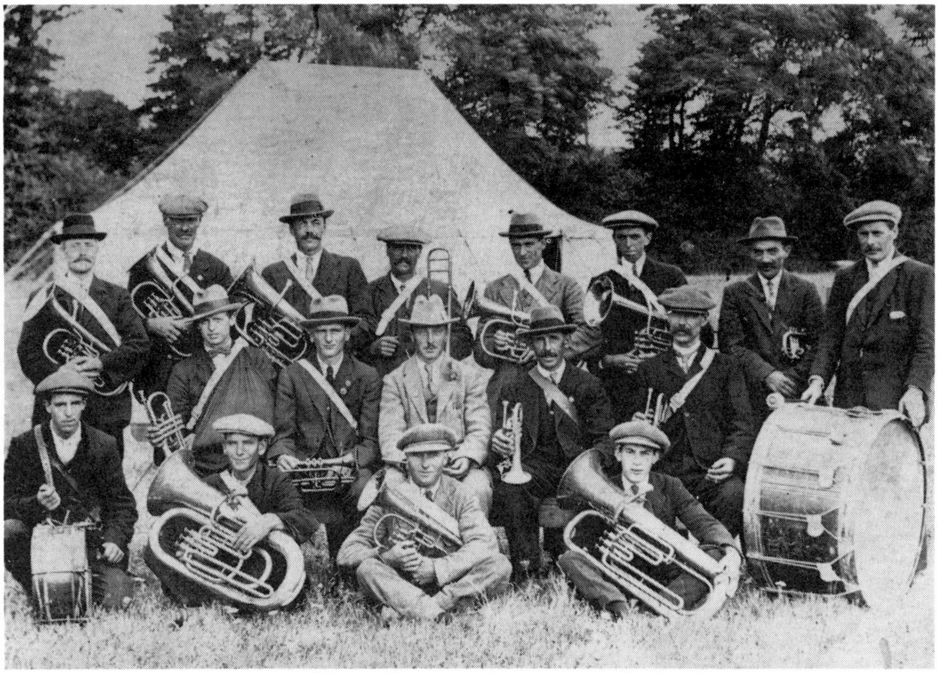

WYLYE BAND during the early 1920s. The musicians include S. Small and Arthur Cox.

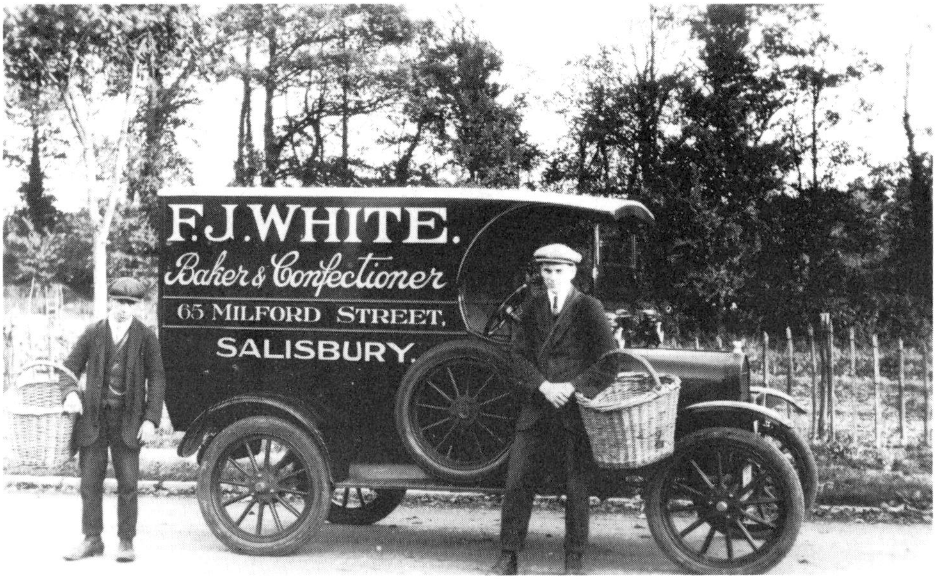

BREAD AND CAKES being delivered in Hanging Langford in 1925. The van, as can be plainly seen by the sign-writing, is that of F.J. White, Baker & Confectioner, of 65 Milford Street, Salisbury.

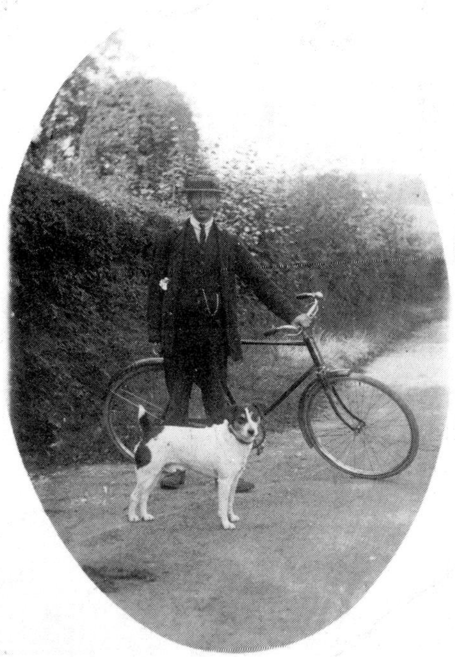

FARMER TOM SMITH, pictured with dog and bicycle at Hanging Langford, *c.*1920.

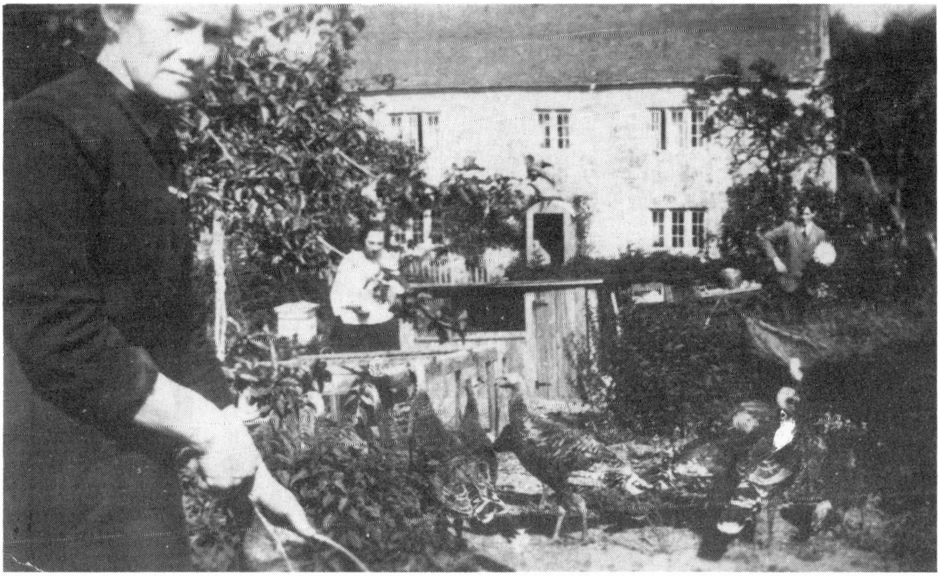

THIS LADY IS FEEDING TURKEYS on ground opposite Pear Tree Cottage, Hanging Langford, during the 1920s. To the left of the lady in the centre is a beehive and an apple tree, and it looks like the man on the right has just cut a cauliflower. Turkey meat, honey, fruit and fresh vegetables were obviously available for the cottager's table.

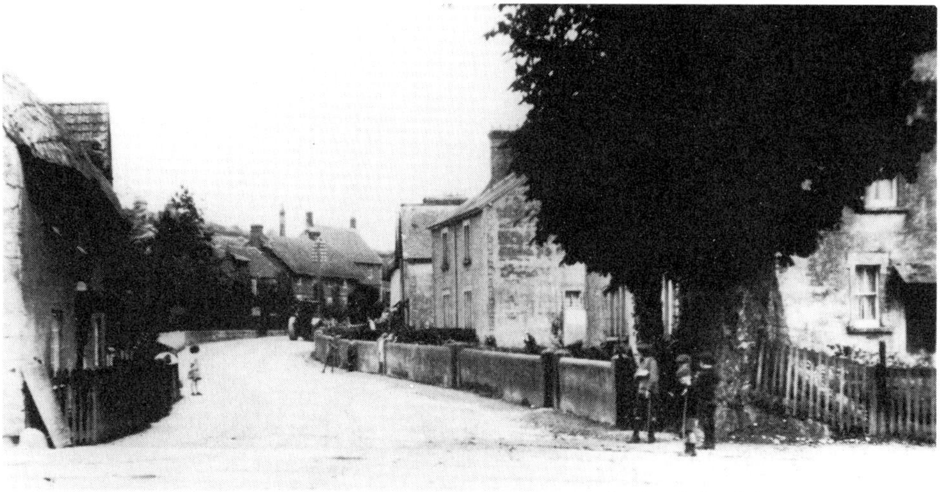

THE MAIN STREET AT STEEPLE LANGFORD, looking east towards Stapleford from the junction with Duck Street (to Hanging Langford) c.1920. The little boys, on the right by the tree, have just watched the traction engine pass by. There have been several changes since this picture was taken: the chestnut tree is gone; the thatched house on the right is now tiled and its porch and doorway removed, being replaced by a window; the house on the right now has a brick porch built around its door.

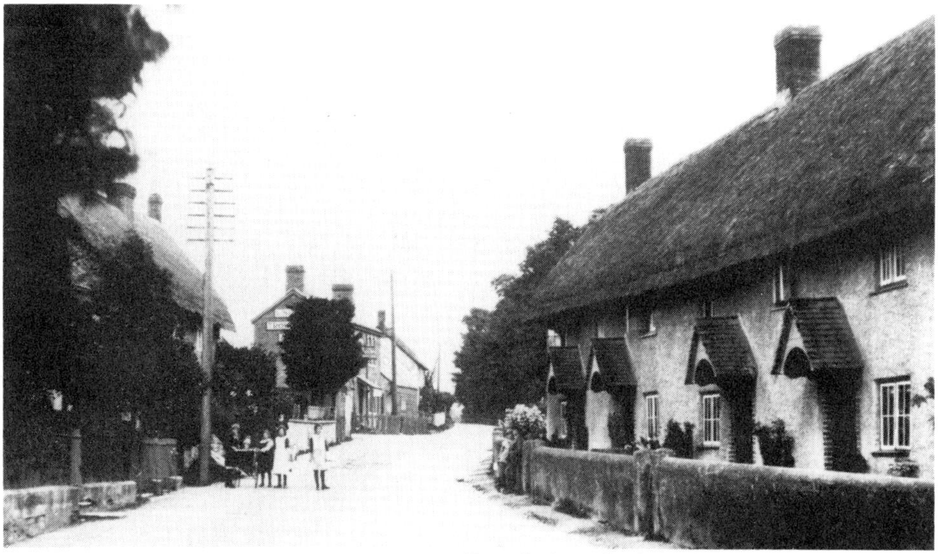

THE MAIN A36 BRISTOL–SOUTHAMPTON ROAD, at Steeple Langford, looking east again, before 1920. The four thatched cottages on the right have since been changed to two tiled dwellings, now called Lantern Cottage and Streetly Cottage. The yew tree, to the left of the picture centre hiding the Bell Inn beyond, still exists. The Bell is still an Ushers House today. The thatched cottages at the end of the road, past the Bell, no longer exist. Their site is partly occupied today by a bus shelter and a small layby.

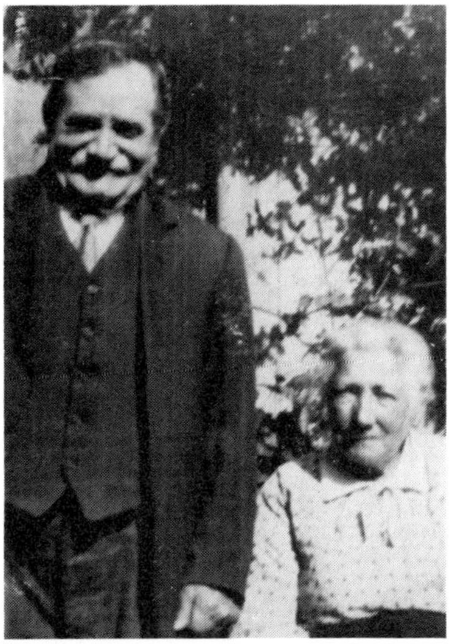

MR JOHN WHATLEY and his second wife, Ginny, during the 1920s. John Whatley was church caretaker at All Saints, Steeple Langford, for nearly 50 years.

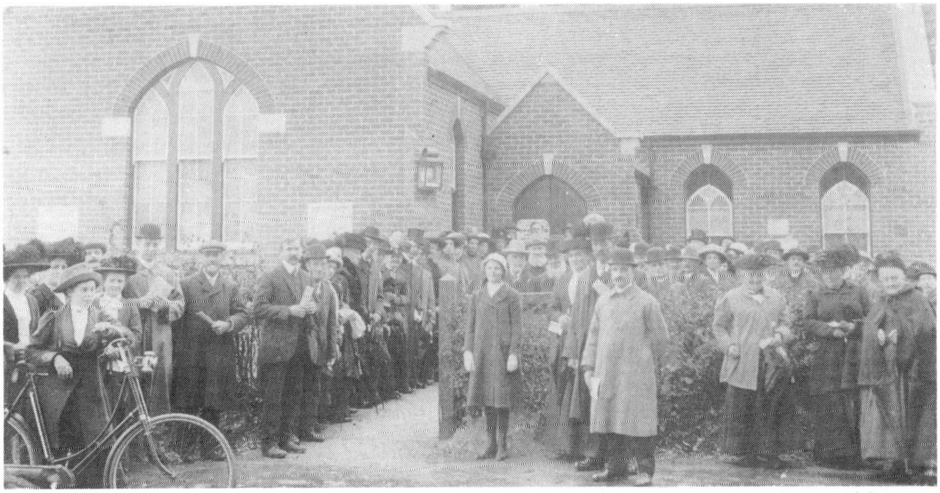

THE OPENING OF THE UNITED METHODIST CHAPEL AND SCHOOLROOM at Stoford, on the afternoon of Wednesday 16 October 1912. The chapel and schoolroom had seating for around 100 persons. It was built by Messrs Wort & Way of Salisbury, in red brick with stone dressings, at a total cost of £571 3*s*. 6*d*. The site, north of the A36 road, was given by Mr F.R. White of Porton. The crowd includes Revd R.W. and Mrs Gair (Milford St Chapel, Salisbury), Revd E.C. Bartlett (District Chairman, Sandown, Isle of Wight), Revd E.O. Dinsley (London), Revd J.H. Green (Salisbury), Mr and Mrs F.R. White, Mr and Mrs E.G. Warren, Mr and Miss J. Hinxman, Mr G. Williams (Shrewton), Mr J.E. Pinder, Mr and Mrs F. England, Mr T. Godwin (Downton), Mr and Mrs Axton, Mr H. Rivers, Mr J.F. Penn, Mr S.R. Naish, Mr W. Shepherd, Mr E.H. Cooke, Miss Evelyn White (organist), Mrs Young, Mr E. Chipp, Mrs Gregory, Master Edgar Tryhorn, Mr J. Forest, Mrs Sturgess and Mr Bernard White. It rained just after this photograph was taken. A tea was held afterwards at the Clubroom at the Swan Inn, and this was organised by the Womens Missionary Auxiliary and secretary Mrs Penn.

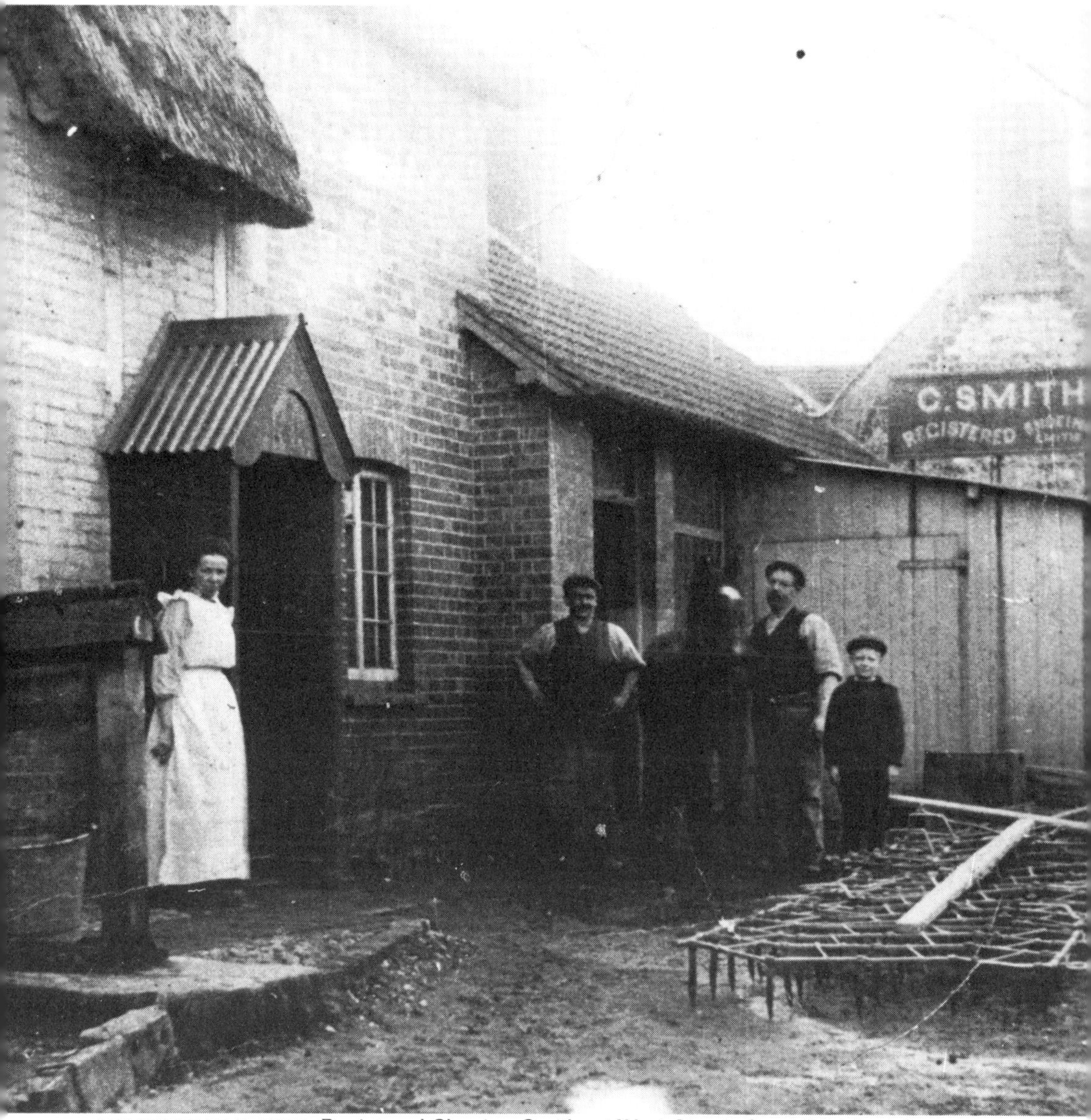

THE FORGE OF C. SMITH, Registered Shoeing Smith, at West Street, Great Wishford, between 1900 and 1905. A pony awaits attention, while a set of drag harrows, on the right, are in for repairs. The shed in the background has been replaced by a wooden garage, and the single-storey building in the corner (behind the men) has since been made into a two-storey residence, now called Garden Cottage. The house, where the lady is standing, has a tiled roof instead of thatch today, and has had the porch removed. This is now called Forge Cottage. The well-hood, on the left, has also been removed.

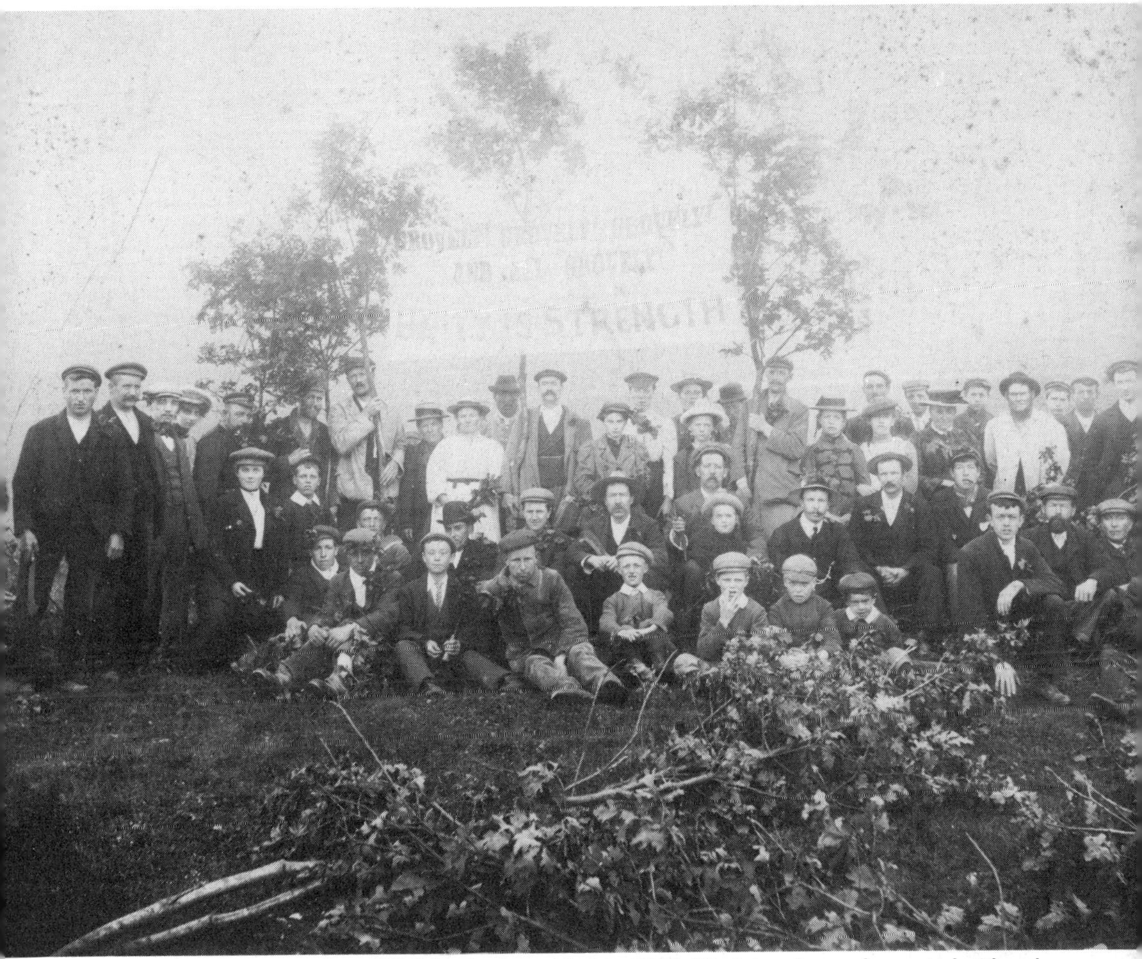

THE OAK APPLE CLUB, Great Wishford, assembled in 1904. Their lapels are decorated with oak apples and leaves, according to the custom, and some of the men are holding the bill-hooks they used to cut the oak boughs from Grovely Wood.

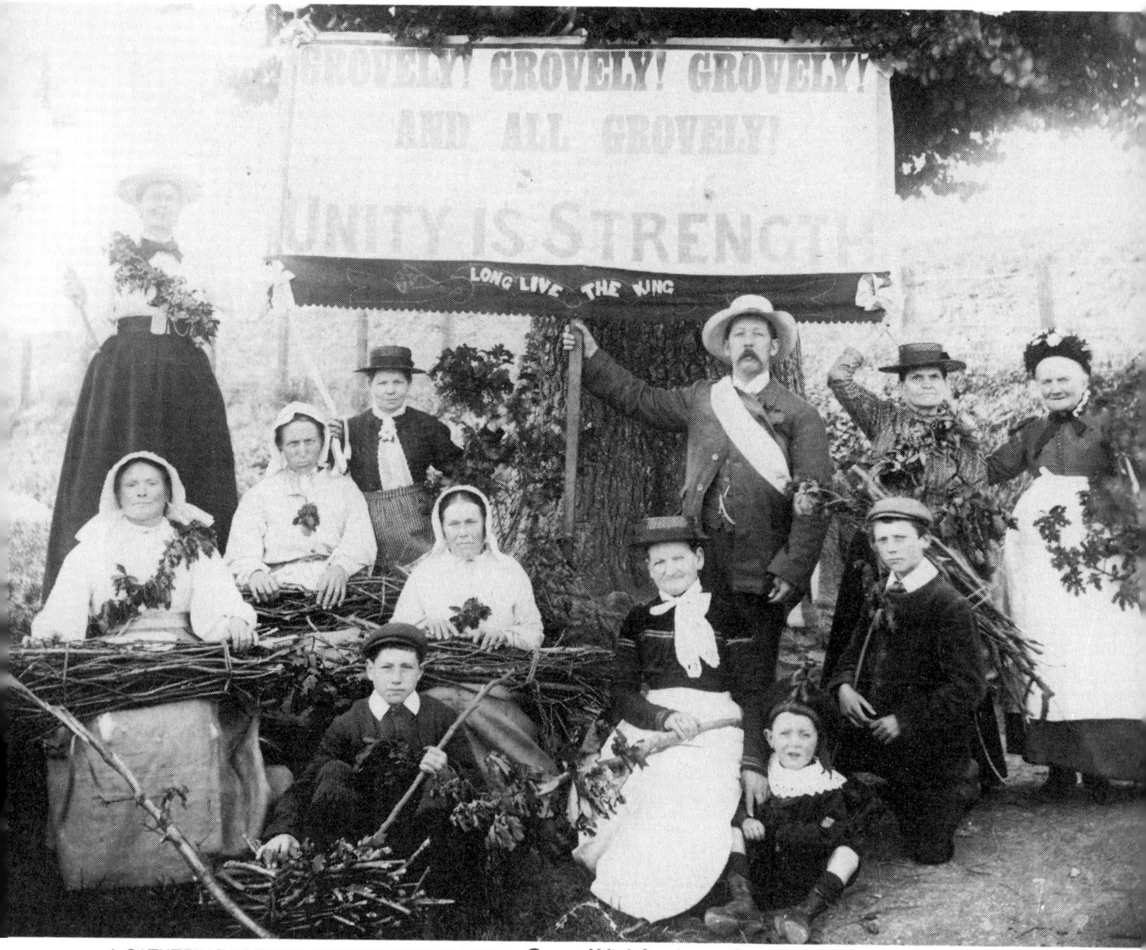

A GATHERING AROUND THE TOWN END TREE, Great Wishford, on Oak Apple Day, 1906. Among those here are Mrs Pile, Mrs Down, Mr Scott, Mrs Newton, Mrs Everett, Mrs King, Mrs Burton, Mrs Head, Johnny Shergold, Jim Head and Cecil Sweet.

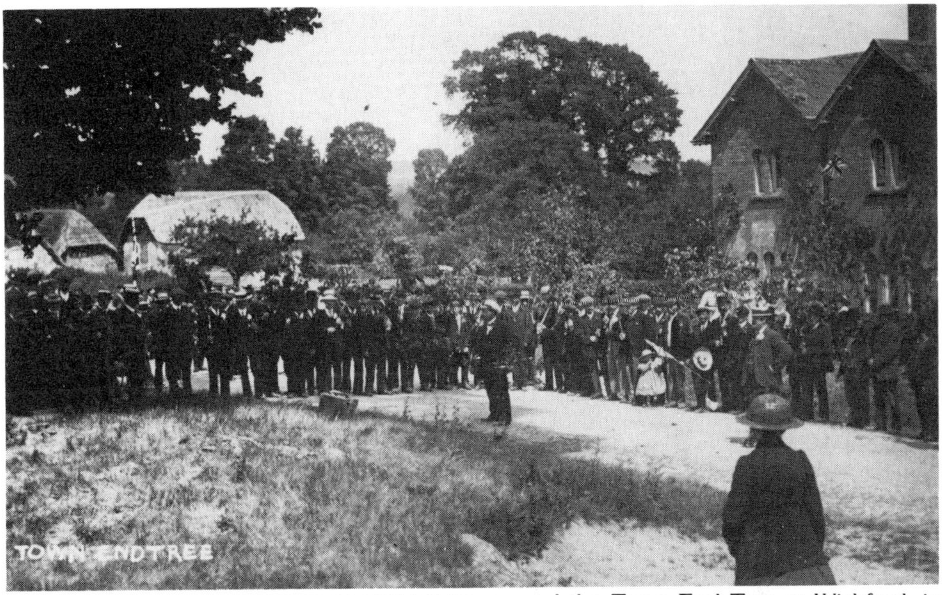

THE GENERAL MEETING OF THE OAK APPLE CLUB, around the Town End Tree at Wishford, in 1910. The Club Chairman, Mr A.E. Scott, is standing at the edge of the road, centre of picture.

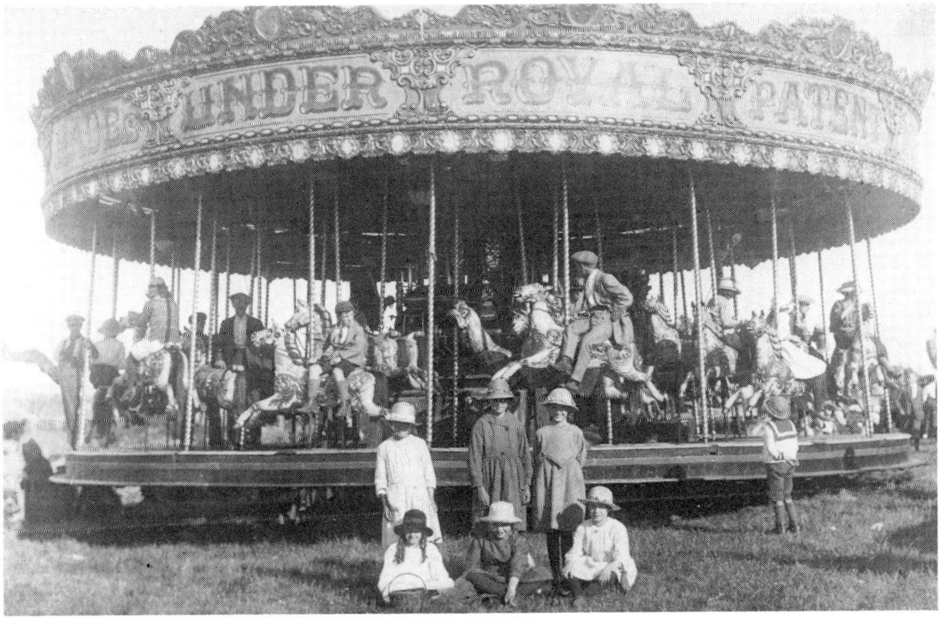

CHILDREN AND ADULTS enjoying a ride on a steam roundabout at Wishford Oak Apple celebrations, between 1918 and 1920.

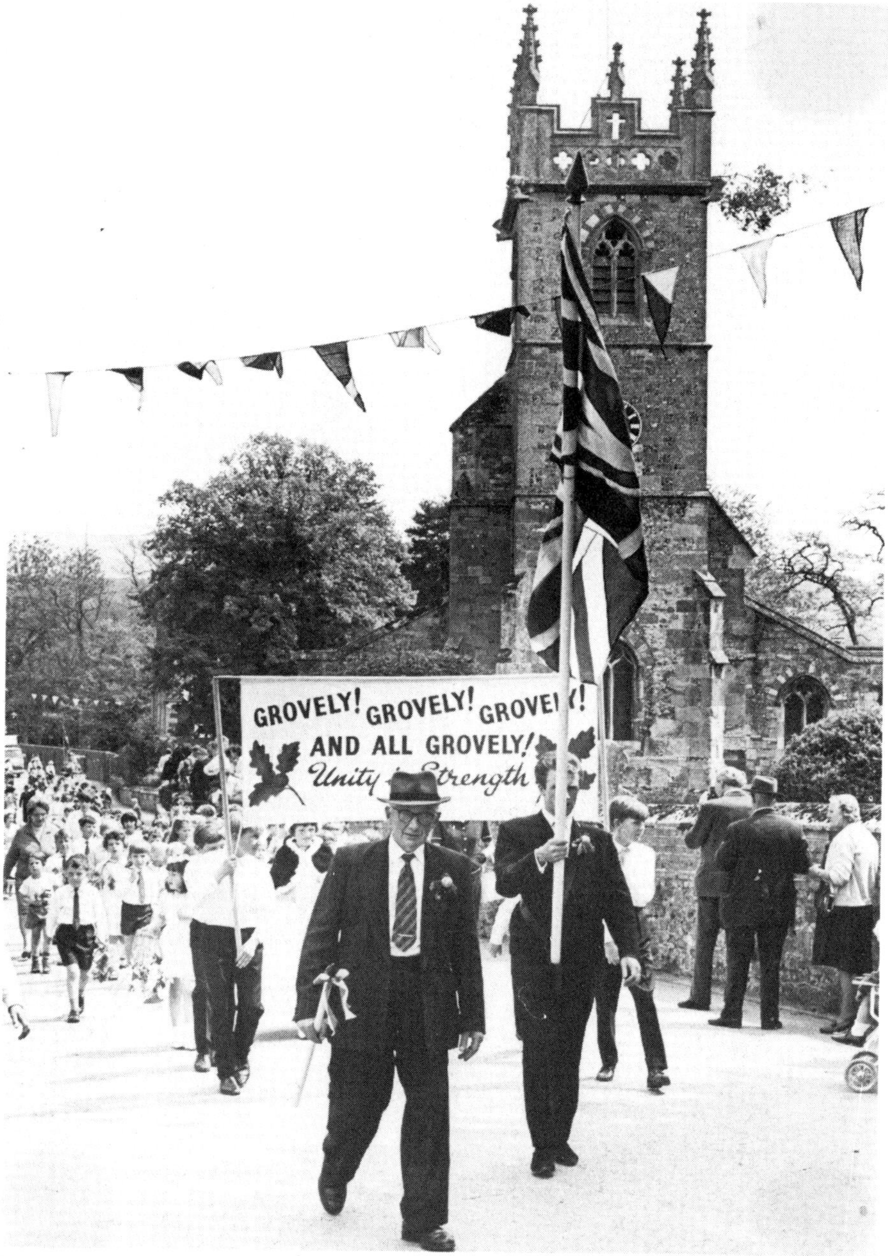

THE OAK APPLE PROCESSION makes its way up West Street, Great Wishford, during the 1950s/60s. The banner proclaiming 'Grovely, Grovely, Grovely, and all Grovely – Unity is Strength' is followed by the schoolchildren clutching their sprigs and branches of oak boughs.

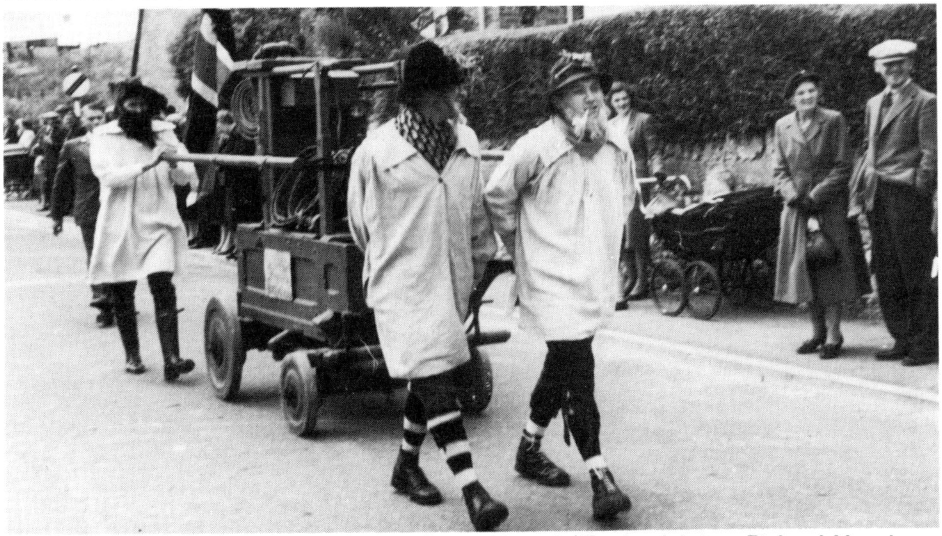

GREAT WISHFORD has one of the earliest fire engines in England. It is a Richard Newsham, four-wheel model, for use by 10 or 12 men, and it was patented in 1725. Since 1972 it has been kept in the north aisle of St Giles Church. Here we see the fire engine being trundled around the village during one of the Oak Apple processions. The photograph was probably taken during the 1950s.

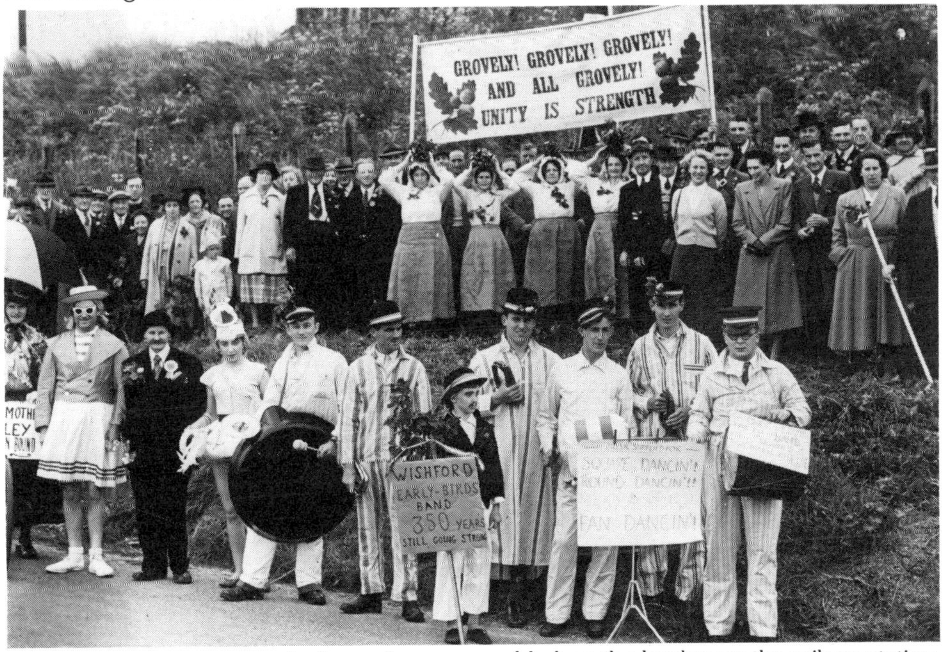

WISHFORD RESIDENTS, some in fancy dress, assembled on the bank near the railway station, for the Oak Apple celebrations in 1953.

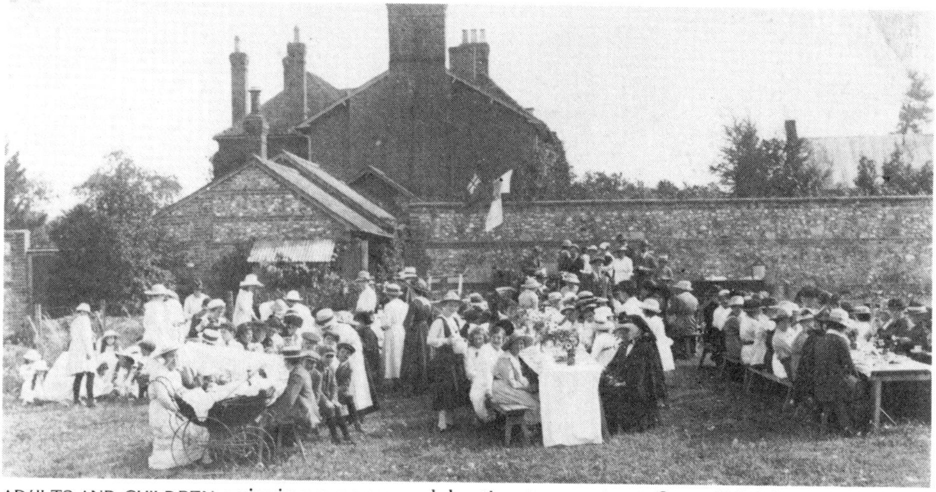

ADULTS AND CHILDREN enjoying a peace celebration tea-party at Great Wishford, in 1919.

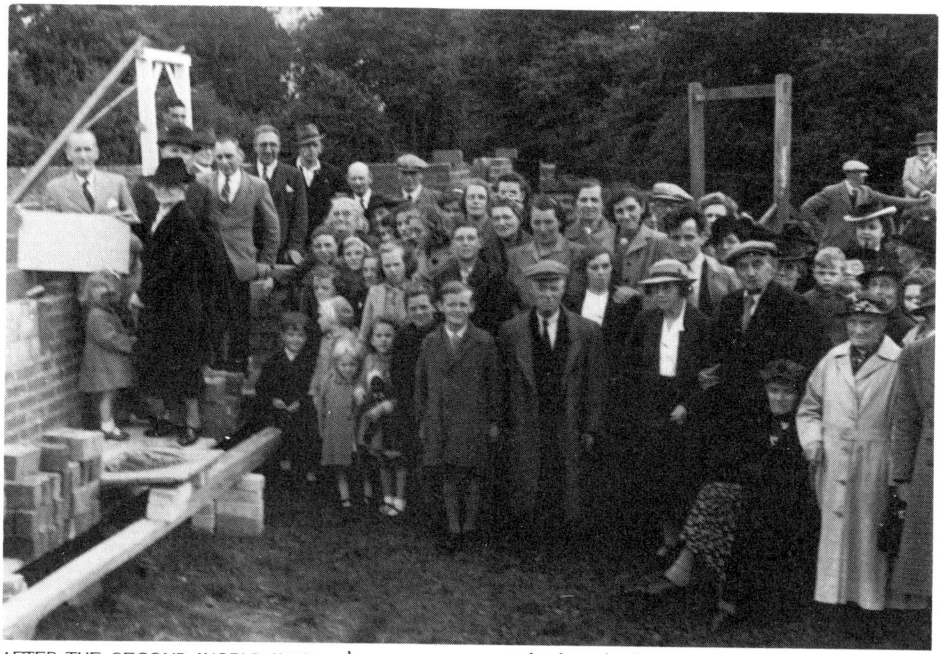

AFTER THE SECOND WORLD WAR, when peace was declared, the people of South Newton wanted to commemorate the peace in a tangible form that would be useful to villagers. From one of the oldest inhabitants came the suggestion of a bungalow for elderly people. The idea was approved and building went ahead. This photograph shows Mr and Mrs Chalke laying the foundation stone, which is held by Mr Harry Winzar, Chairman of the Parish Council. Today, South Newton residents are the proud owners of two Peace Memorial Bungalows for elderly people, now run by the Charity Commissioners.

SECTION THREE

Down on the Farm

This section attempts to portray life on the land between 1900 and 1960, when mechanisation came in and the old traditional methods went out. The Norfolk four-course rotation, once a part of a farmer's tenancy agreement, is hardly seen today – replaced by continual wheat growing on some farms. Water-drowning is another forgotten art. Throughout the year, farmers in the Wylye Valley were allowed to flood the meadows, anytime between 6 p.m. and 6 a.m., when the mills were not working, using a system of dykes, ditches and hatches to divert water from the River Wylye. The practice ensured a rich growth of grass, up to one foot in height, providing ample grazing for dairy cattle (usually shorthorns) throughout the summer months. Water-drowning, which required good management and constant labour to keep the ditches and dykes free-flowing, is now a dead craft.

Until the Second World War, farming had changed little in a hundred years. At the turn of the century there were about 120 farms in the area covered by this book, and together they employed over a thousand men. Each farm had a big staff, from a bailiff down to the women and children who were employed with stone-picking and birdscaring, and there were dairymen, carters, shepherds and day-labourers. Just about everybody who lived in a village was employed on a farm or in some sundry trade.

Looking back, most people have a romantic view of farming. They talk of when the cornfields were red with poppies and how, during haymaking time, the farmer always had a barrel of cider for the men. They remember the horses and the binder, and the stooks of corn; and all the senior citizens I know say that the summers when they were young, unlike now, were long and hot. That's all probably true but it has to be said that it was hard work for the farm labourer and few of today's farmworkers would wish for the return of the pre-mechanised days.

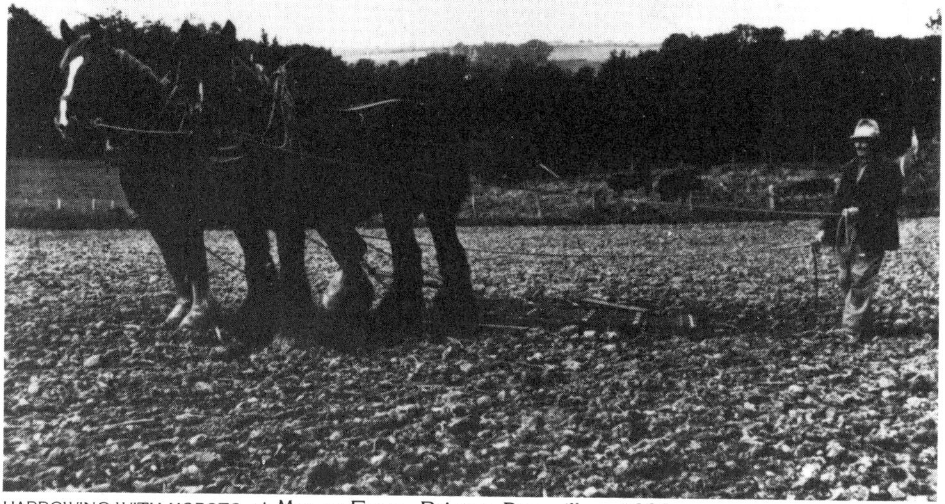

HARROWING WITH HORSES at Manor Farm, Brixton Deverill, *c.* 1920.

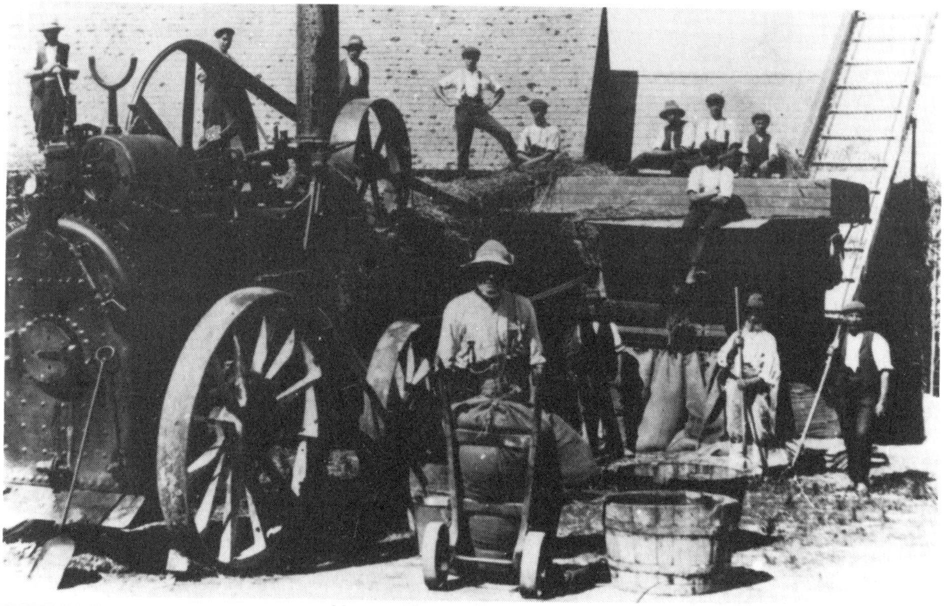

THRESHING WITH STEAM POWER at Manor Farm, Brixton Deverill, *c.*1920. The farm labourers include Thomas Ridout and Tom Massey. Note the huge 2½cwt. sack of grain on the sack truck.

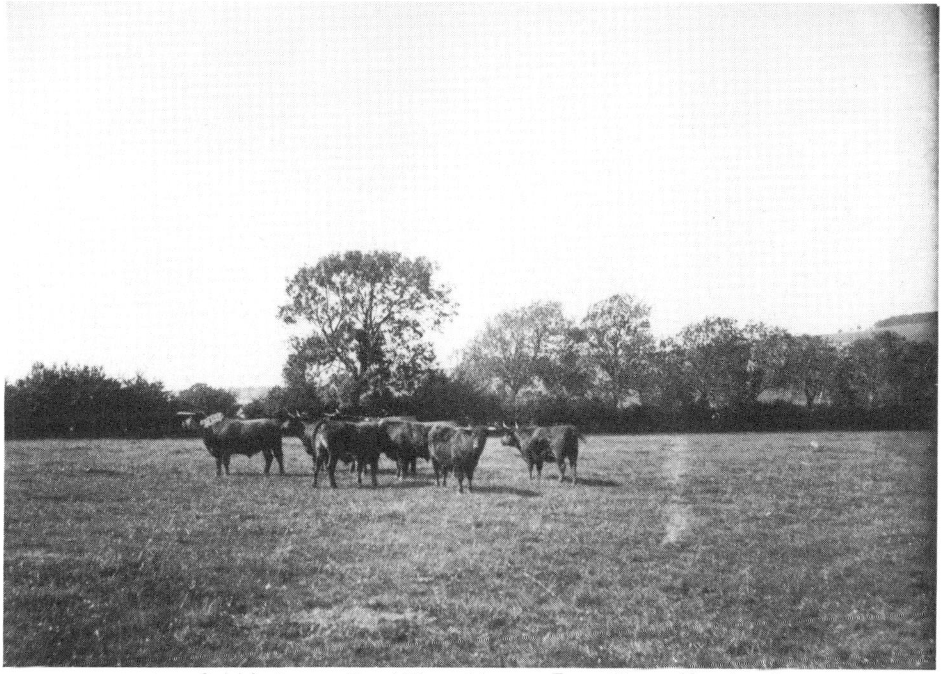

DEVON STEERS in a field between Ryc Hill and Lower Barn Farm, Horningsham, exact date unknown. Bidcombe Hill is in the distance, on the far right of picture.

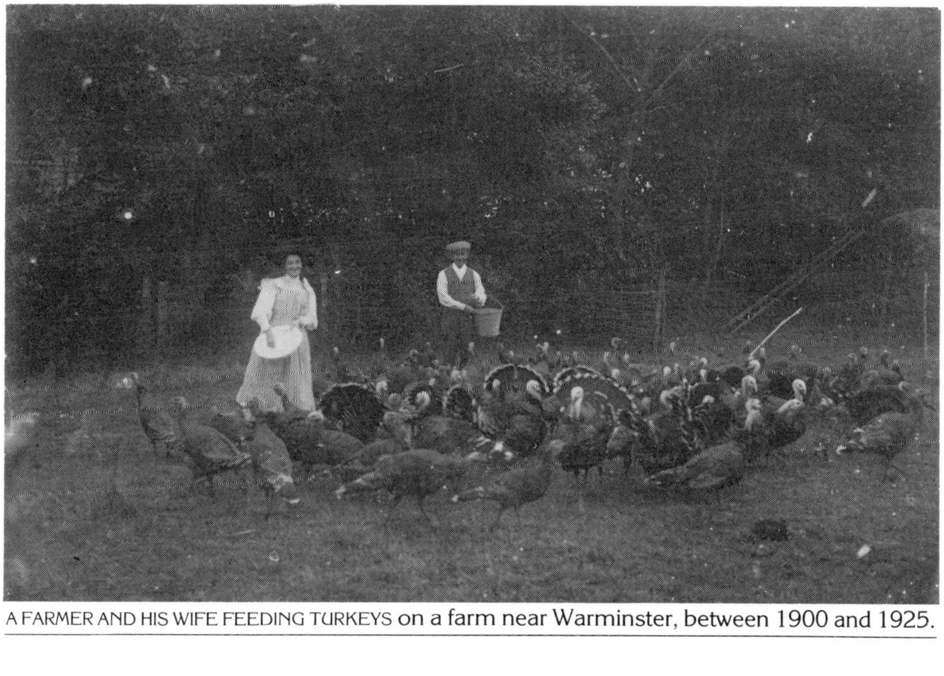

A FARMER AND HIS WIFE FEEDING TURKEYS on a farm near Warminster, between 1900 and 1925.

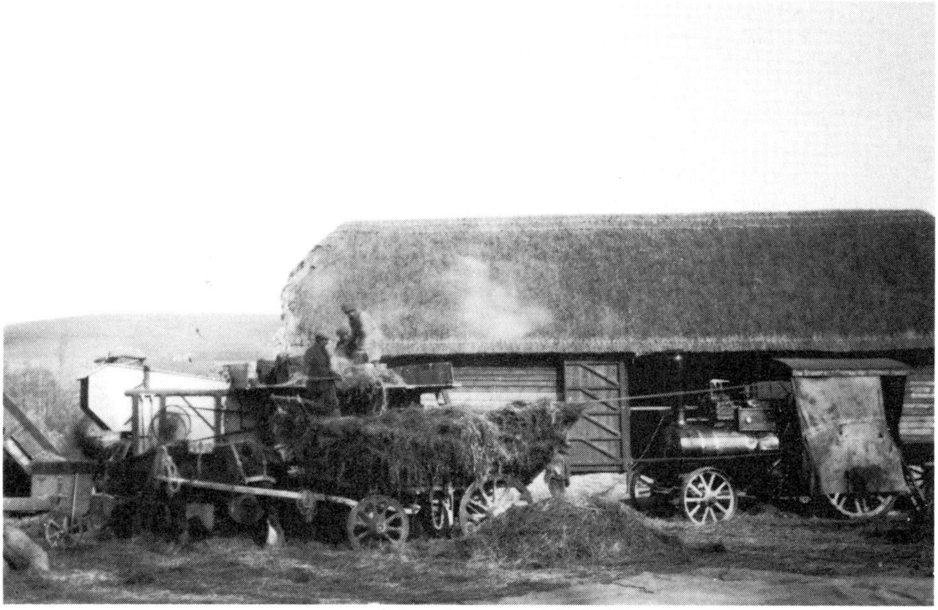

THRESHING WITH STEAM POWER near Warminster, *c.*1940. The exact location remains a mystery, but it could be in the Deverills. The traction engine is signpainted 'Tom Standfield, Contractor, Verwood, Dorset'. He, obviously, travelled many miles undertaking work.

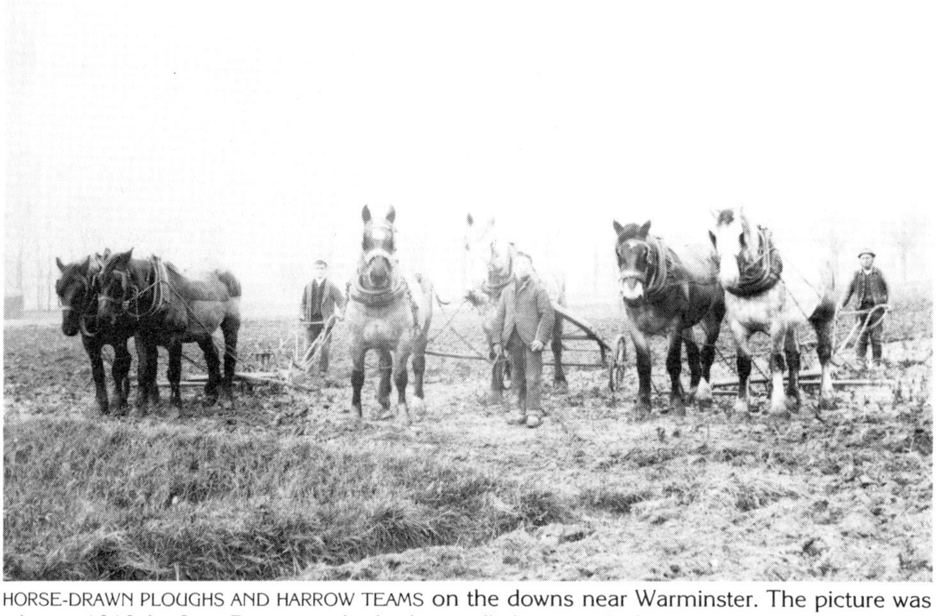

HORSE-DRAWN PLOUGHS AND HARROW TEAMS on the downs near Warminster. The picture was taken, *c.*1910, by Sam Burgess, who had a small photography business and grocery shop at Brook Street, Warminster.

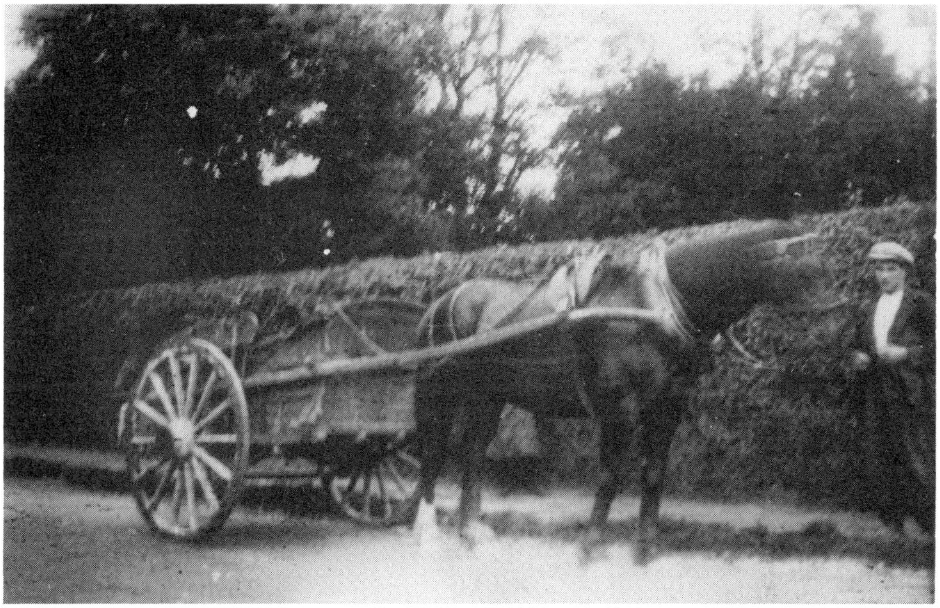

HORSE AND MILK FLOAT belonging to Mr Paddock of Knapp Farm, Bishopstrow, c.1930. The picture was taken near Temple Corner at Bishopstrow. The man on the right is dairyman, William Hallett.

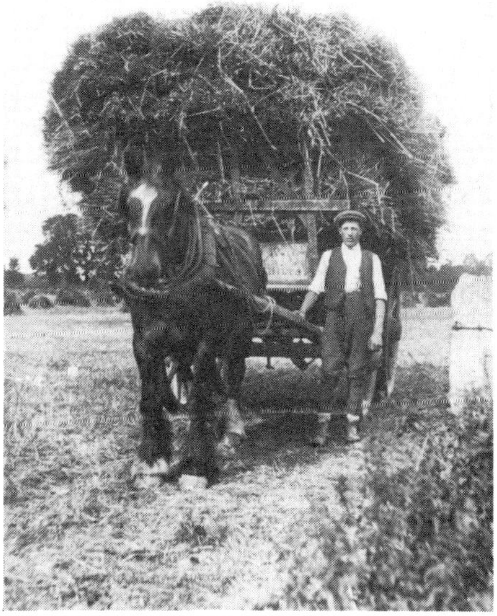

HORSE AND CART, loaded with hay, leaving a field at Knapp Farm, Bishopstrow, c.1935. Knapp Farm was farmed by Jimmy Paddock. The gentleman leading the horse here is believed to be Vic Forsey, who worked for Paddock.

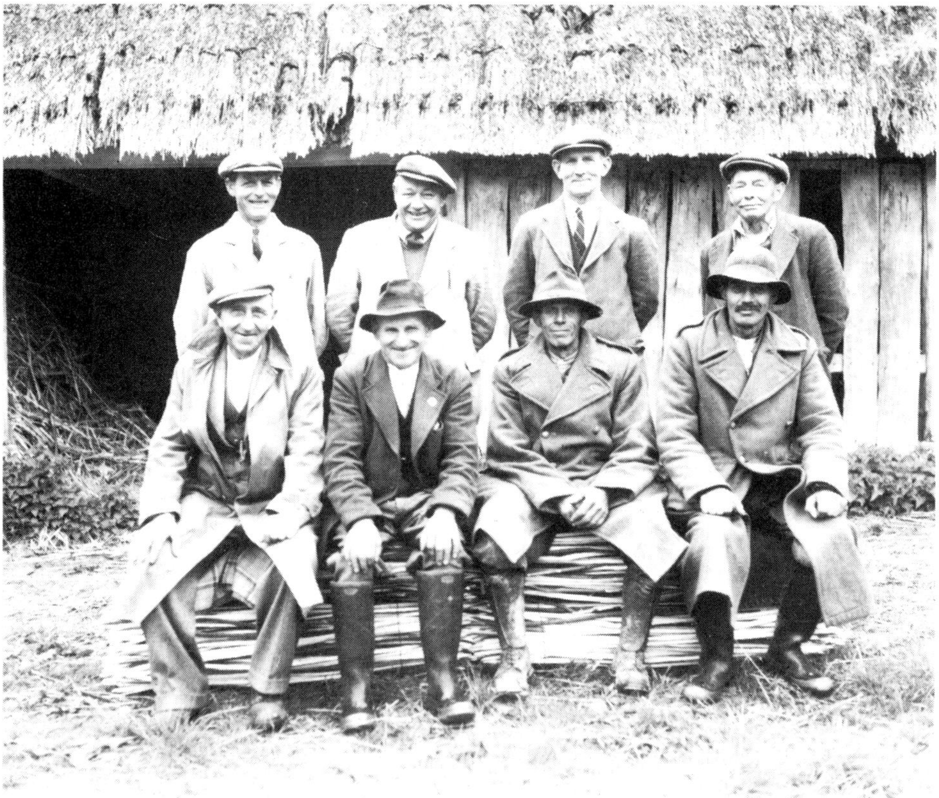

STAFF AT BISHOPSTROW FARM, pictured just after the Second World War. Back row, left to right: Jack Brooks, dairyman; farmer Mark Gauntlett; Harry Northeast, dairyman; and George Everley. Front row, left to right: Herbie Mitchell, carter; Percy Parham, shepherd; Fred Burroughs,carter/foreman; Fred's brother, Harry Burroughs, carter, who was always affectionately known as 'Uncle' or 'Har'. Fred and Harry had another brother, Jesse, who is omited for some reason from this photograph. He lived with his mother at North Farm Cottages. Mark Gauntlett retired from the farm in 1964, moving to Ilfracombe, where he died soon afterwards after tripping out of his bath. The Rice family from Devon took over the tenancy after Gauntlett and Laurence Rice farms Bishopstrow Farm today.

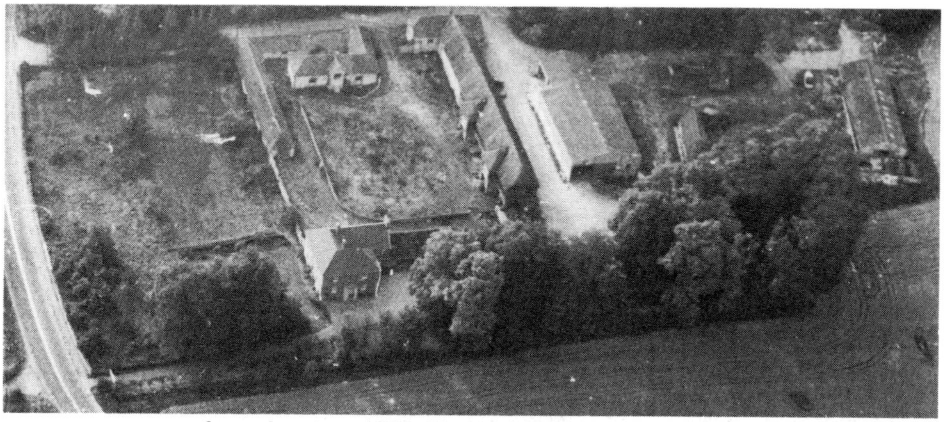

BISHOPSTROW FARM, from the air, *c*.1970. The A36 Warminster–Salisbury road is visible on the left. The traditional, thatched barns (property of the Ministry of Defence), in the centre of the picture, were destroyed by an arsonist during the early hours of Saturday 21 August 1976. The contents of the barns included 50 tons of hay and straw, two tons of cattle cake, one ton of cattle feed and half a ton of cattle minerals, plus tyres and machinery parts, which belonged to the farm's tenant, Mr L. Rice. Total damage was put at nearly £50,000.

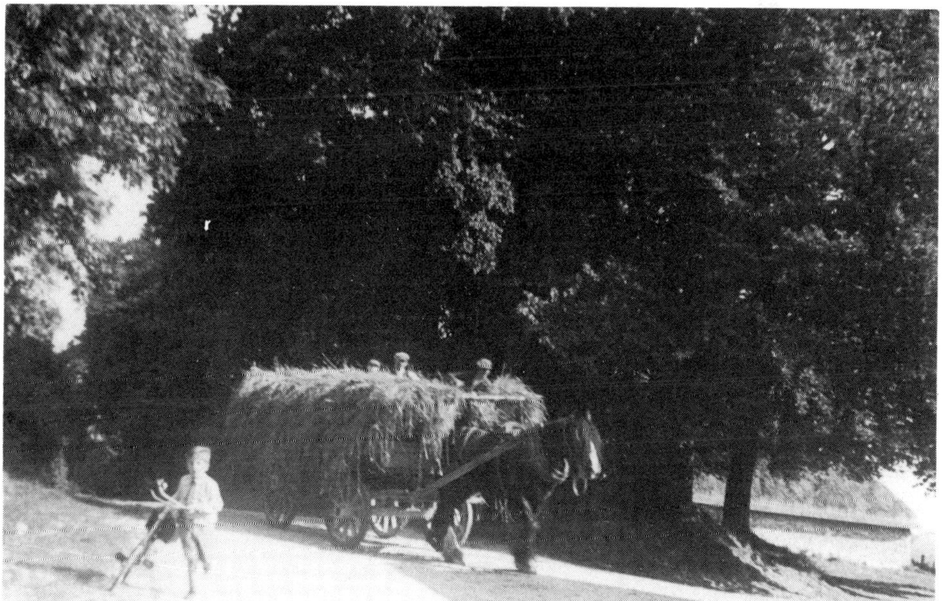

A CART LOAD OF HAY turns off Cox's Drove into Bishopstrow Farm during the late 1920s/early 30s. Farmer Gauntlett's carts and wagons featured the name 'S.W. Farmer' painted on them – this was the name of a previous tenant at Bishopstrow Farm. Farmer was a partner in the firm of Frank Stratton & Co.

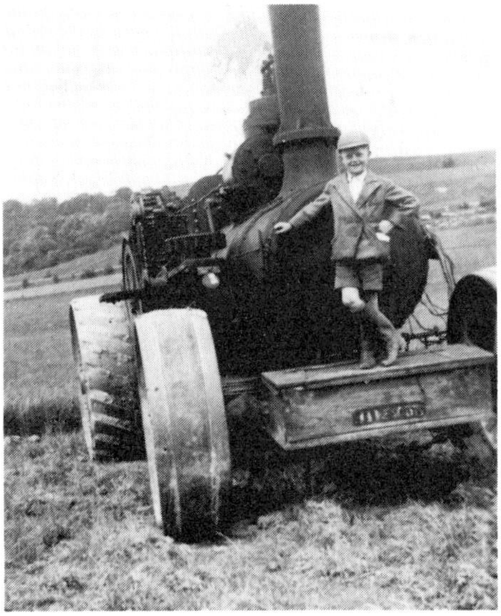

BOREHAM SCHOOLBOY, Bill Symes, standing on a Fowler Compound traction engine, in a field east of Morgan's Drove, Bishopstrow Farm in 1935. You can see Battlesbury Hill in the distance. The farmer, Mark Gauntlett, owned two of these engines. Using a cable, the engines towed ploughs and cultivators, etc. backwards and forwards across the fields. The track from Bishopstrow Farm to the fields north of the railway was unsurfaced and the huge traction engines, making their way to and from work, made deep ruts during the winter time. In really bad weather the track became impassable. The drivers were Bill Dixon and Topper Hiscock. The engines, which weighed about 22 tons each, were scrapped during the 1950s.

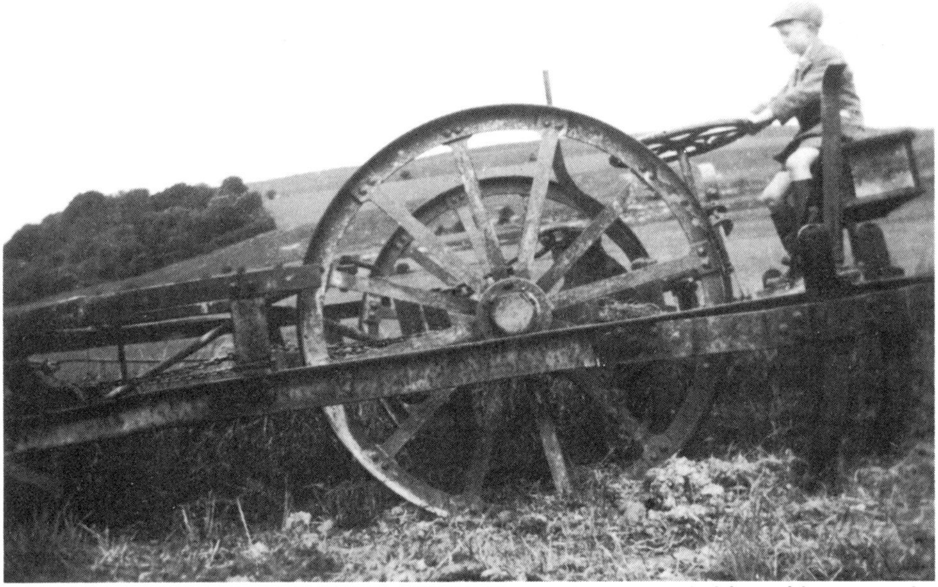

BILL SYMES, again *c*.1935, on the scarifier which the engines hauled by cable across the arable land, after ploughing, at Bishopstrow Farm. The picture was taken in the same field, just east of Morgan's Drove. Battlesbury Hill is visible in the background. Tom Haines, whose job on the farm was looking after the dry cattle, was usually the operator of the scarifier. He also steered the plough as it was hauled across the field, to and from the engines. The field here was too wide for the machinery to be towed across in one go, and one engine was positioned in the centre of the field, the other at the edge.

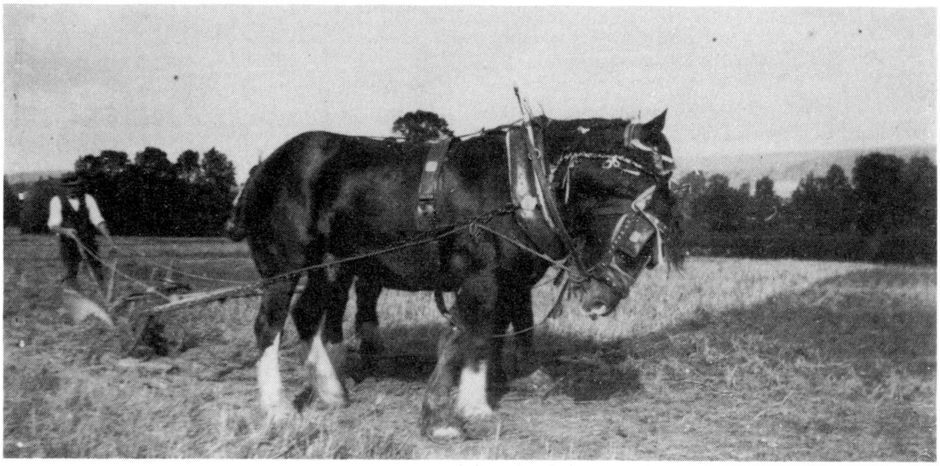

A SCENE FROM A PLOUGHING MATCH organised by the Warminster and Mere branch of the Farmers' Union, at Greenhill Farm, Sutton Veny, on Saturday 13 October 1923. Despite the heavy marl soil of the chosen fields and 1½in. of rain the day before, there was good support for the event, which was later reported as successful. Ploughing commenced at 9.30 a.m., each team being given half an acre. There were 51 horse teams and four tractors in competition. At 11 a.m. bread, cheese and ale were served before work continued until 2.30 p.m. The judges were A. Compton (Nunney), C. Isaac (Sevington), A.E. Mitchell (Downton), W. Pullen (Swindon), E. Parrott (Warminster) and Mr Jeans (Sutton Veny).

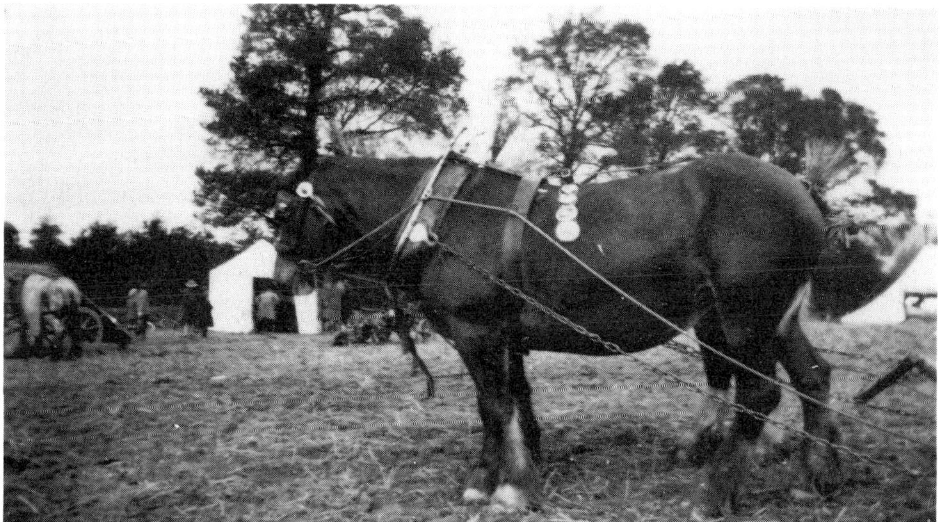

HORSES ENTERED BY A. LONG (an employee of Mr G.F. Benham at North End Farm, Sutton Veny) for the ploughing match held at Greenhill Farm, Sutton Veny, on 13 October 1923. Mr Long entered two classes: Class 2, for carters aged 25 and over with single plough; and Class 8, for best turn-out. He was not among the prizewinners for Class 2 but came third for best turn-out.

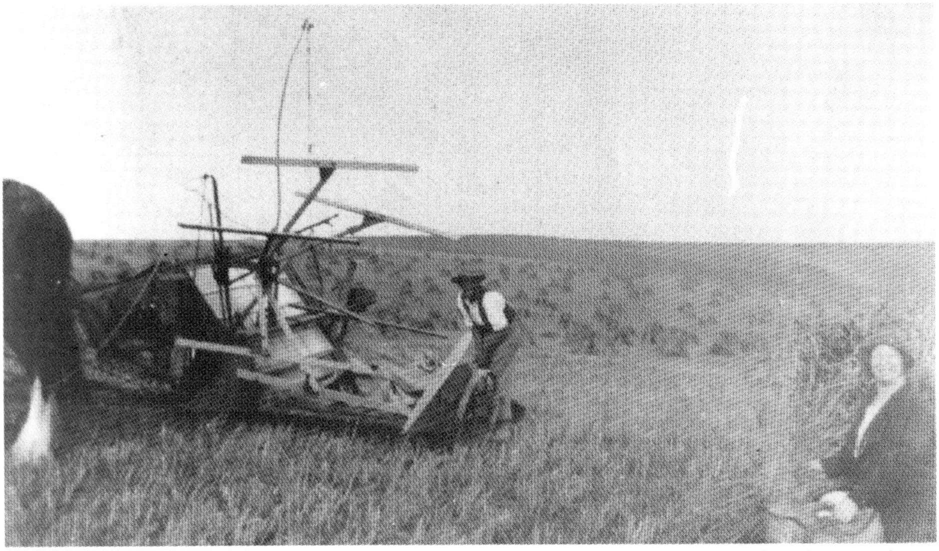

FRANK PEARCE adjusts the horse-drawn binder during harvest time on the downs above Knook. The photograph was taken sometime between the two world wars. The lady in the bottom right corner is Margaret 'Tiny' Dredge, who lived at Knook.

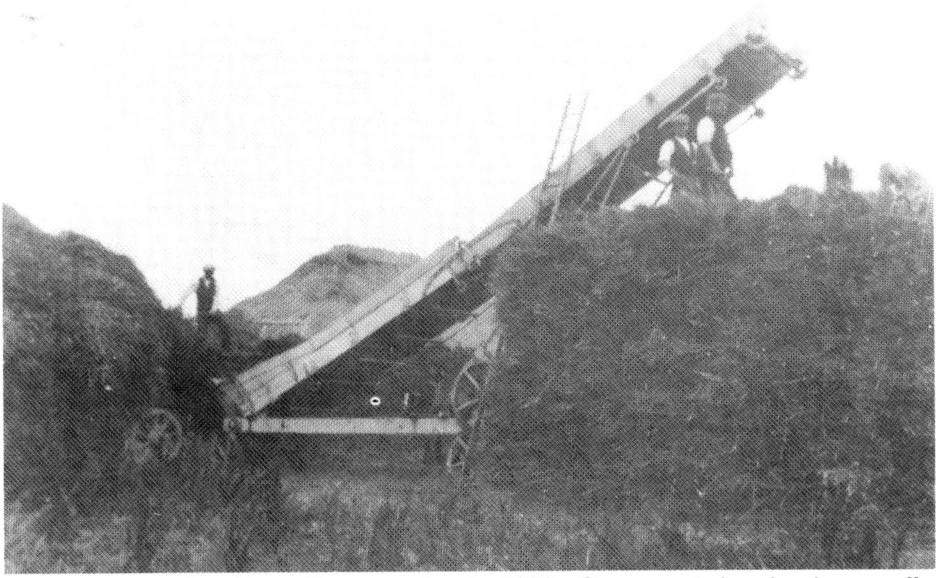

BUILDING A RICK at East Farm, Knook, during the 1930s. One man pitches the sheaves off a horse-drawn cart, on to the elevator which takes the sheaves up to at least four men who are building the rick. The elevator was folded up and lowered after use for easy transport and storage.

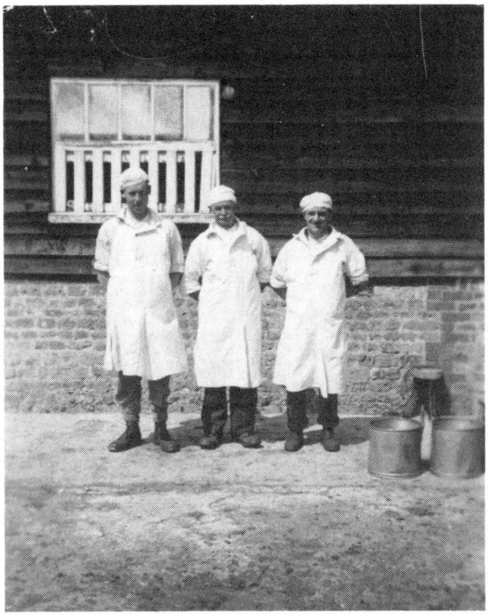

DAIRYMEN AT NORTH FARM, Norton Bavant, c.1945. Roy 'Ginger' Richards is on the left, the man in the middle is unknown, and William Hallett from Bishopstrow is on the right.

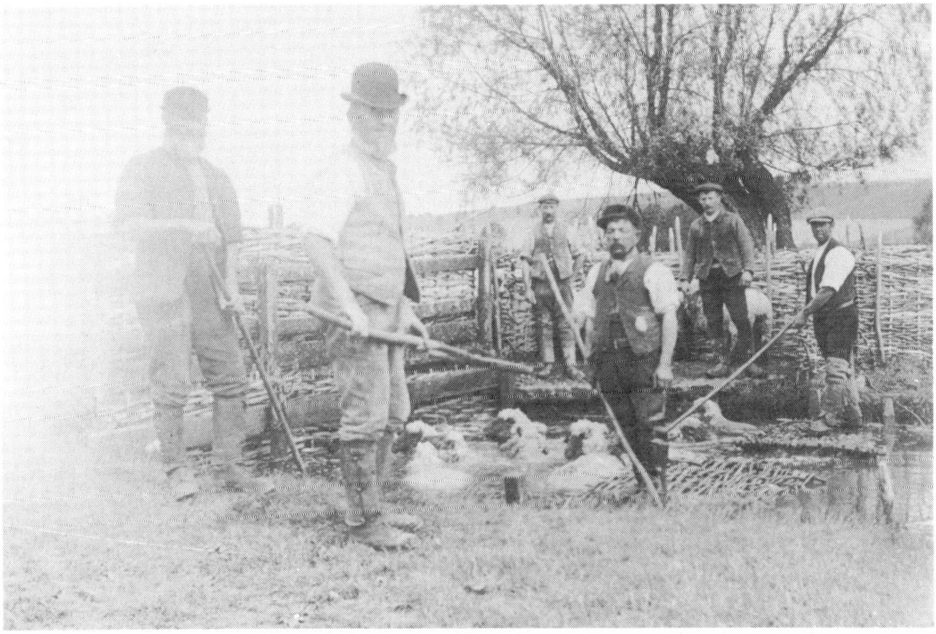

MR THOMAS HOUSE, second from left, dipping black-faced sheep at Stockton, in the years just after the First World War. One of the men helping is Mr Robbins, who is third from the right. Note the hurdles which form not only the surrounding fences, but also provide something for the dippers to stand on.

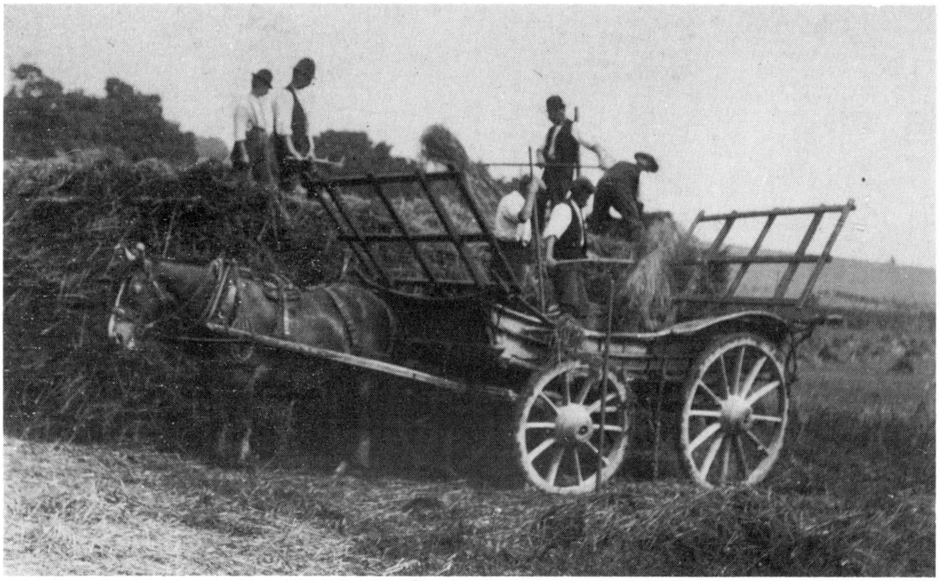

SIX FARM LABOURERS making a rick near Codford, during the summer of 1923. When all the straw was in a rick, the men 'tucked the sides' and 'thatched the top', making it waterproof. The wagon is a prime example of the 'Wiltshire' type. Malmpit Hill is in the background.

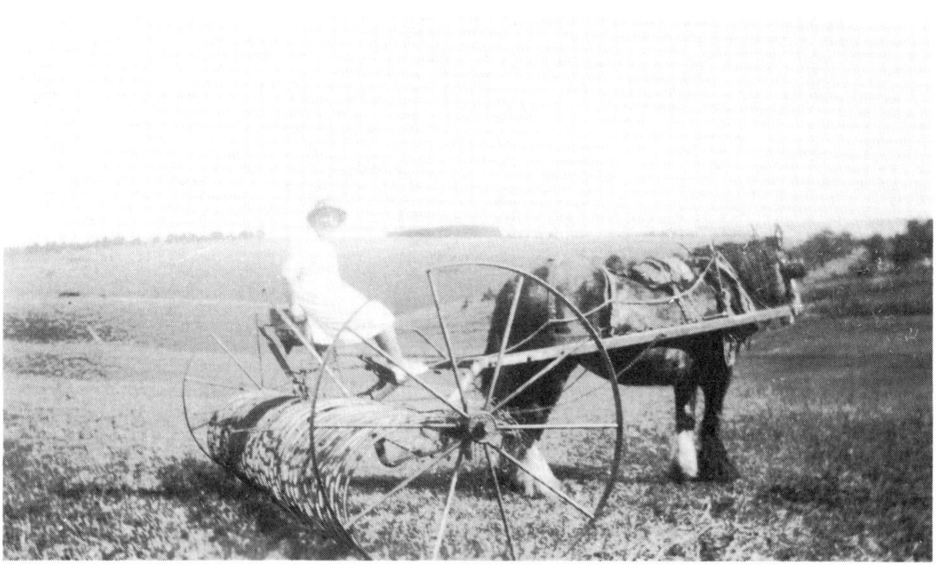

NELLIE ROBBINS, with a horse-drawn hayrake, on land farmed by the Stratton family at Codford, c.1934.

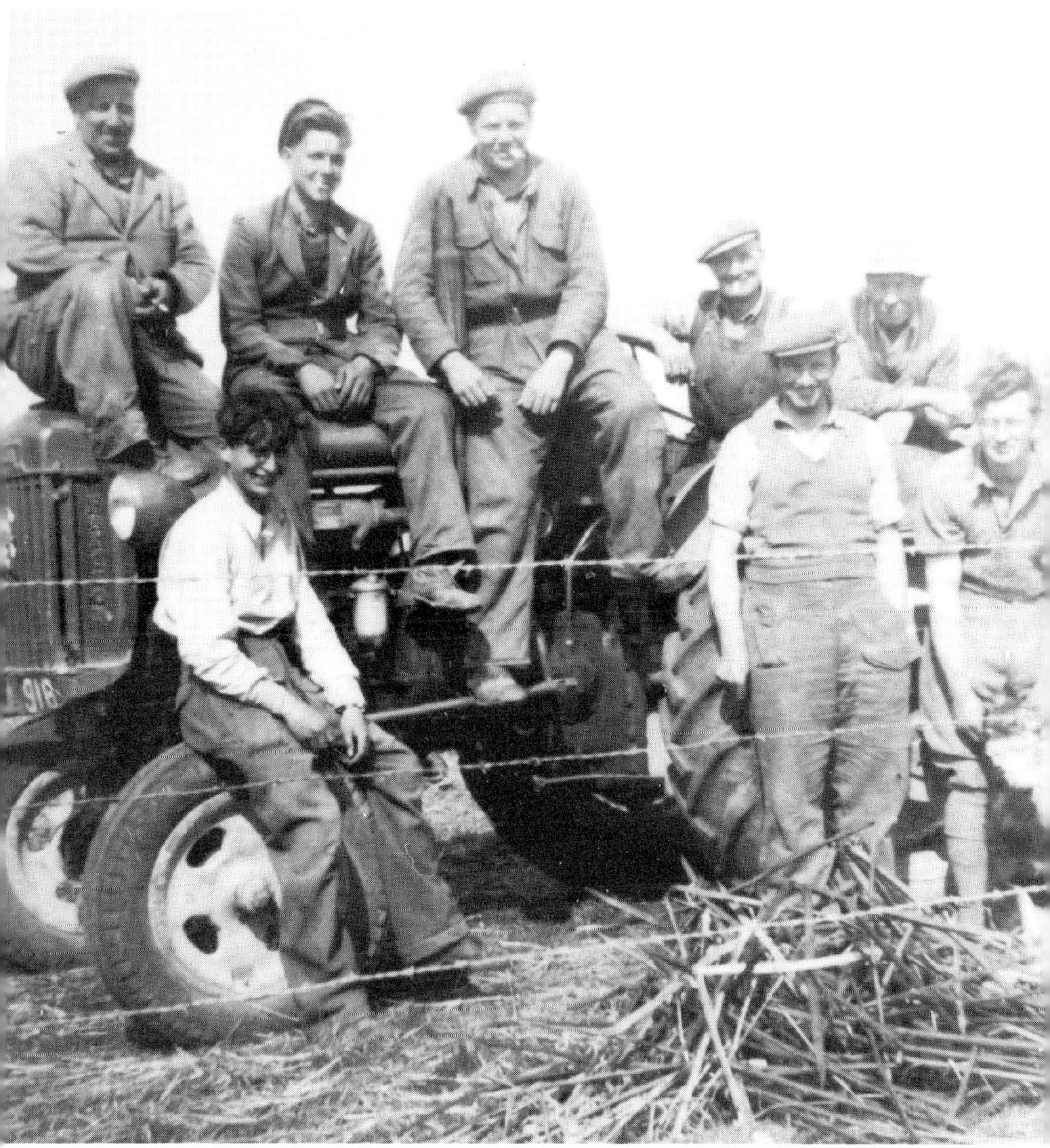

THIS PHOTOGRAPH, TAKEN BY LOUIS PHELPS on 24 April 1953, shows the threshing gang around a Fordson tractor at Collins' Farm, Codford. The men include Ron Sutton, Peter Patterson, Frank Satchell, Herb Diaper, Peter Carter and Harry Wright. The sticks in the bottom right corner are spars thrown out of a rick when the thatch was taken off.

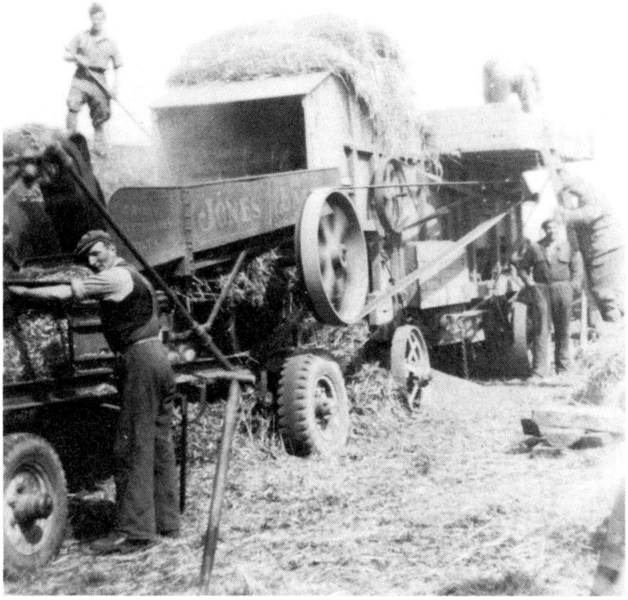

THRESHING AT COLLINS' MANOR FARM, Codford, on 24 April 1953. Frank Satchell is standing next to the Jones' baler. Harry Wright, top left, is pitching the sheaves off a cart on to the top of the thresher, where a third man cuts the twine and feeds the sheaves into the threshing drum – a tiring and dangerous job.

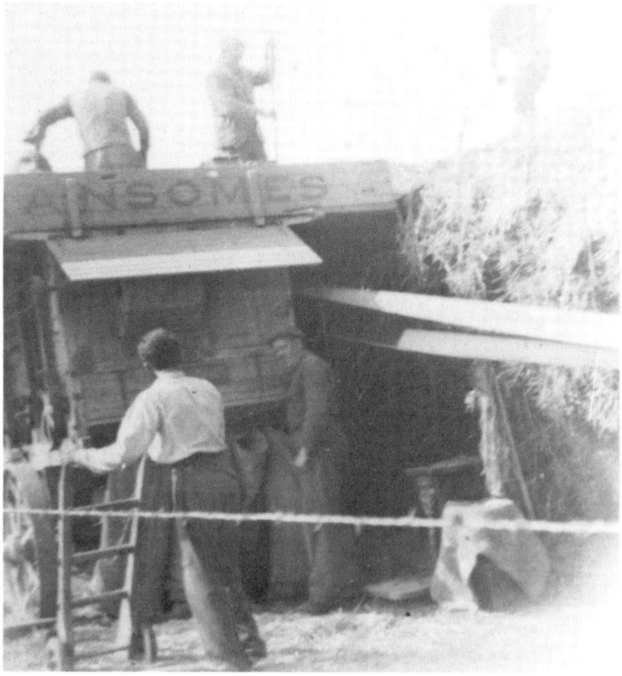

ANOTHER THRESHING SCENE at Collins' Manor Farm, Codford, on 24 April 1953. The thresher bears the maker's name, Ransomes of Ipswich. Threshing was not only hard work, it was also very dusty, and few farmworkers lamented the coming of combine harvesters.

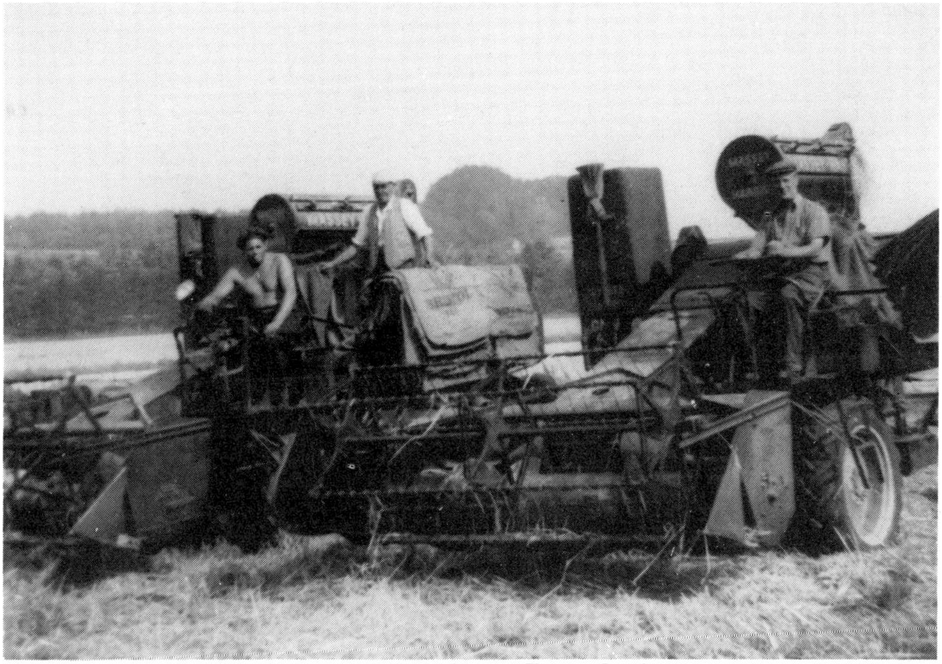

TWO MASSEY HARRIS COMBINE HARVESTERS, at Manor Farm, Codford, on 1 August 1952. The drivers are Peter Patterson and John Beaumont. Herb Diaper is the man in the middle, standing on the grain-bagging platform.

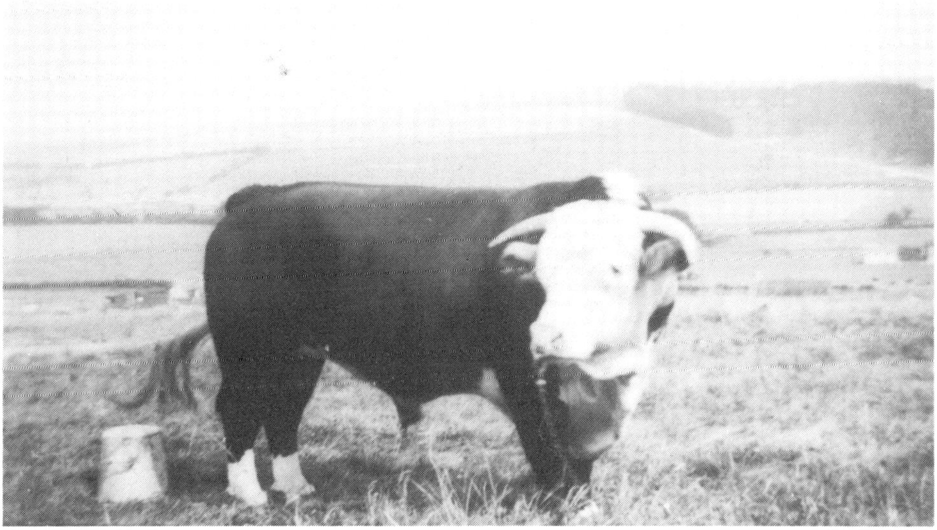

PEDIGREE HEREFORD BULL belonging to William George Phelps at Anzac Farm, Codford, in 1955. Farmer Phelps always bought his stock bulls from pedigree sales at Hereford or Salisbury. Codford Punchbowl can be seen in the background, top right of the picture.

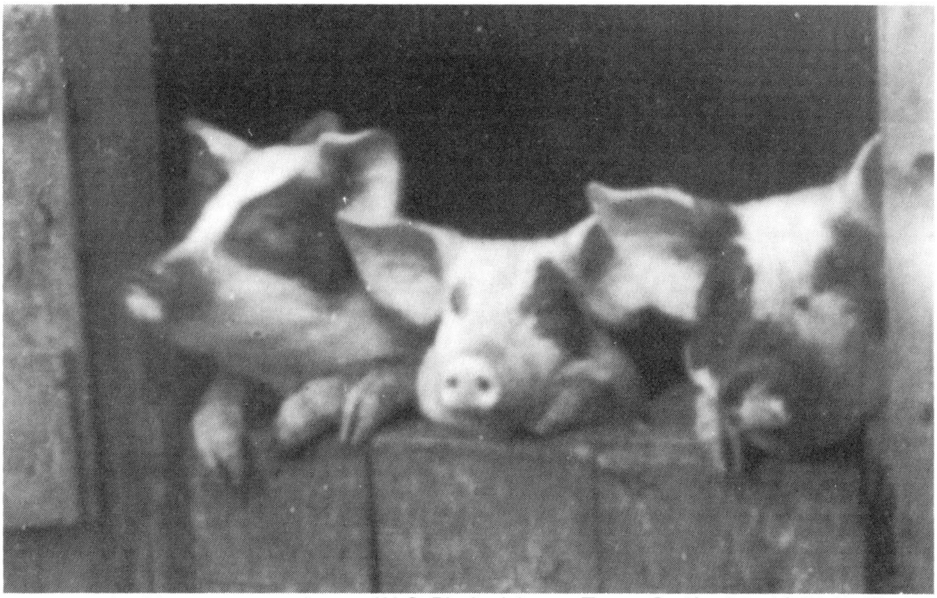

THREE PIGS looking over a sty door at W.G. Phelps' Anzac Farm, Codford, in 1955. Mr Phelps reared up to 50 pigs at a time, both porkers and baconers, buying young stores for fattening at local markets.

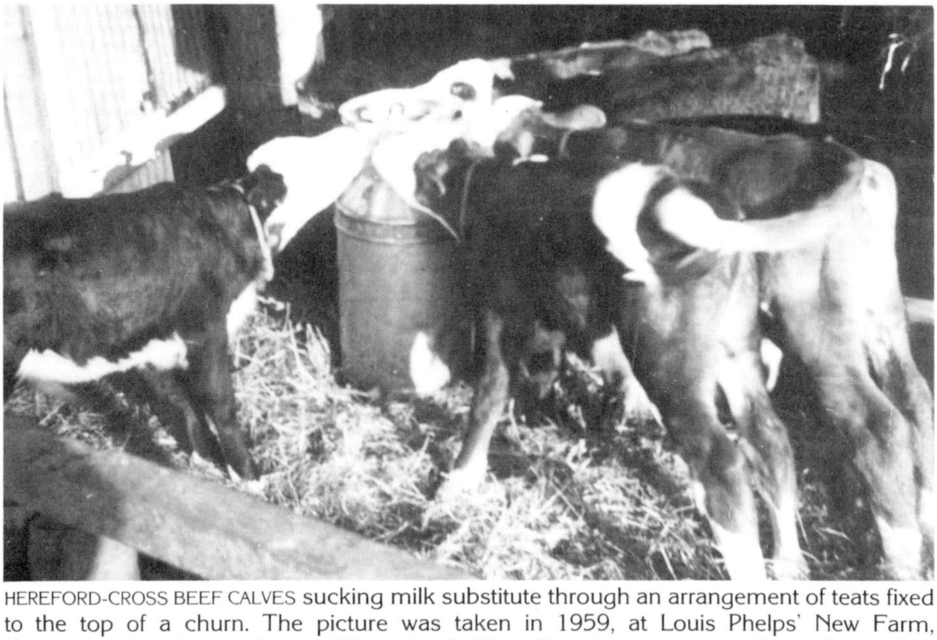

HEREFORD-CROSS BEEF CALVES sucking milk substitute through an arrangement of teats fixed to the top of a churn. The picture was taken in 1959, at Louis Phelps' New Farm, Heytesbury, just below Corton Wheatsheaf. (New Farm's address was later changed to Tytherington).

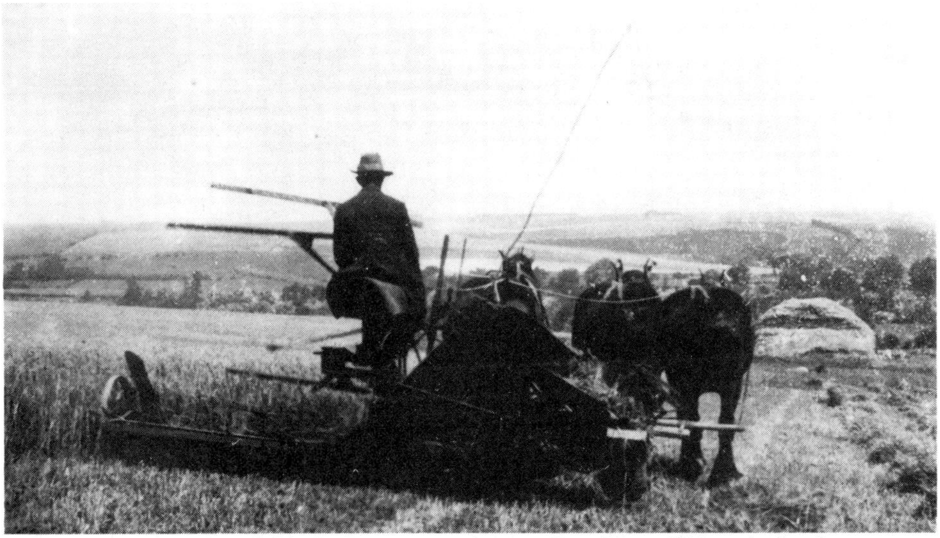

THE BINDER AT WORK in a field of winter-sown wheat at East Farm, Wylye, during the summer of 1933. The crop was sown at the rate of three bushels per acre, costing 4s. per bushel. A wheat crop usually followed rape, turnips or other roots which had been folded by sheep. The land was prepared by ploughing, cross-ploughing and then harrowing. The wheat was sown by broadcasting before the end of November, and when the germinated wheat reached a height of around two or three inches the field was rolled to make the soil firm around the roots.

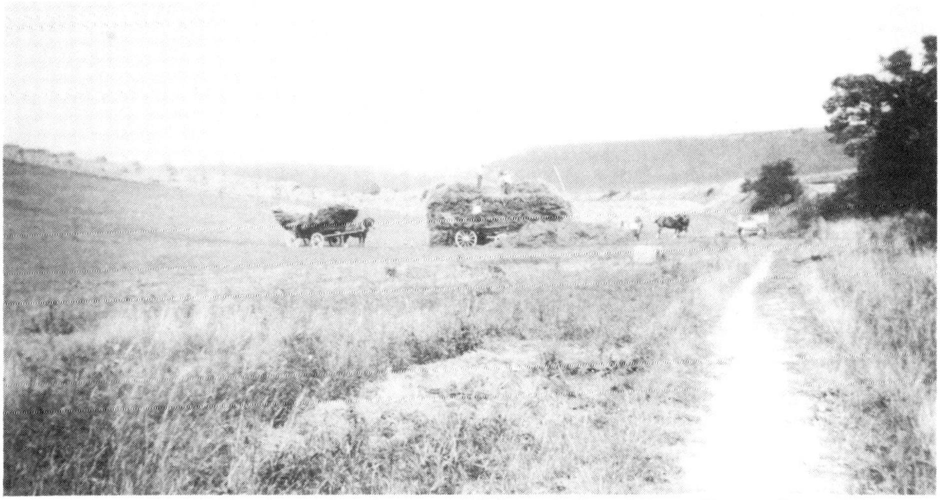

A HARVEST SCENE at Yarnbury Castle, near Wylye, during August/September 1933. The average yield for wheat that year was 28 bushels to the acre. At Salisbury Market, during the previous year, the price obtained for wheat was £1 for eight bushels. After harvesting, poultry were folded across the stubble to 'glean' the fields. The straw was sold to thatchers for 9*d*. per bundle.

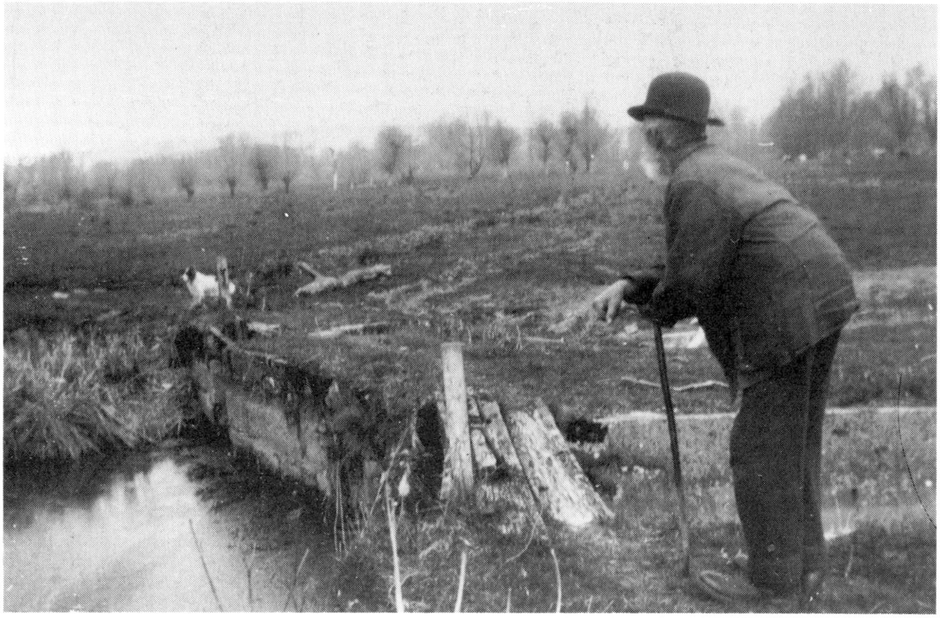

WATER-DROWNER, MR A.E. NOBLE, pictured in the meadows near Wylye in 1933. He was the most efficient drowner in the district, working at his craft from boyhood until he was nearly 80 years of age.

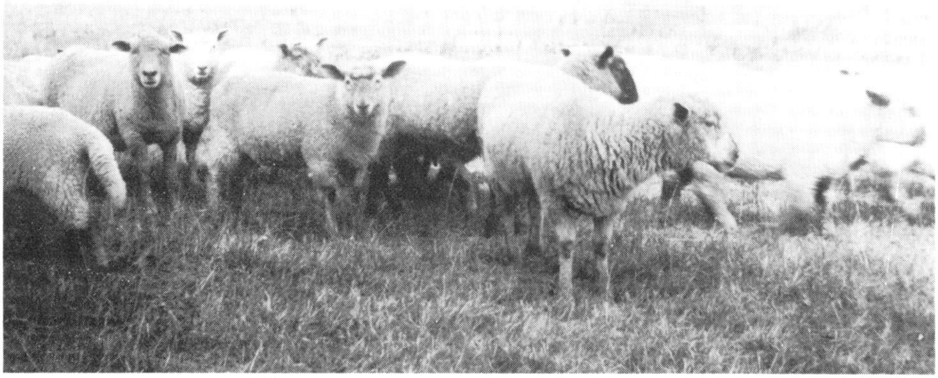

SHEEP FROM EAST FARM, Wylye, on the downland slopes near Bilbury Rings during the summer of 1933. The East Farm flock of mixed breeds numbered 300 before 1920 but had increased to 700 by 1931. East Farm sent 350 adult sheep and 200 lambs to market in 1933.

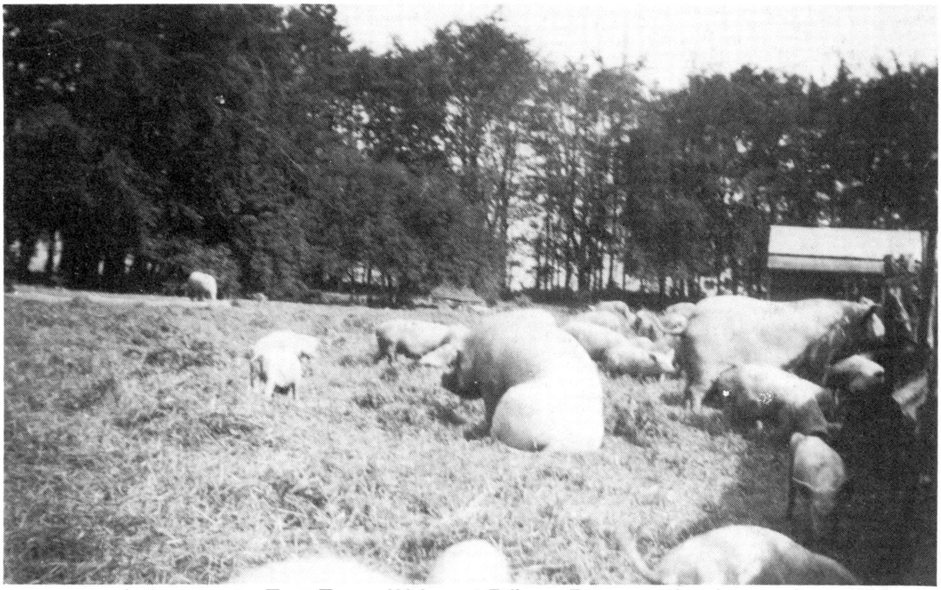

BACON PIGS, belonging to East Farm, Wylye, at Bilbury Rings on the downs above Wylye in 1933. Around 100 large white and saddleback pigs were reared on the poor land at Bilbury that year. When fattened to a weight between 12 and 15 score pounds the pigs were sent by road transport to a bacon factory in Trowbridge, about 20 miles away.

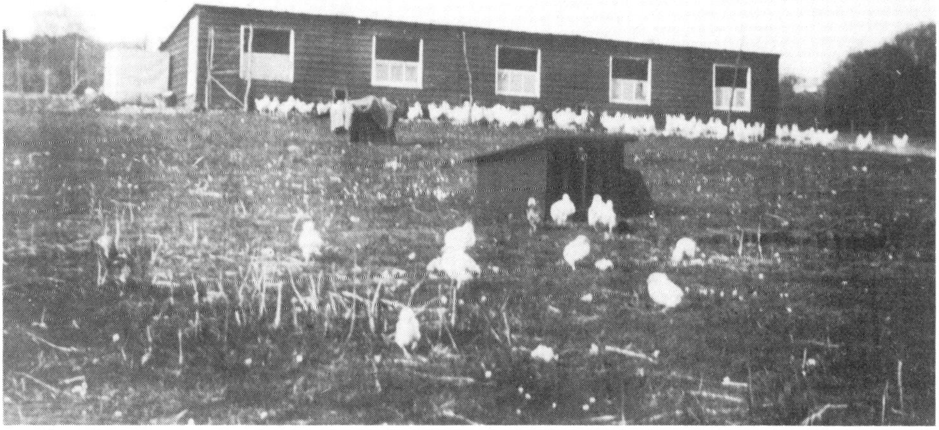

POULTRY AT WYLYE in 1933. In April 1934 eggs became very cheap, as far as the consumers were concerned, selling between 9*d*. and 1*s*. per dozen. One week at Salisbury Market, where the majority of poultry keepers in the Wylye Valley sent their eggs, the highest price realised was only 7½*d*. per dozen.

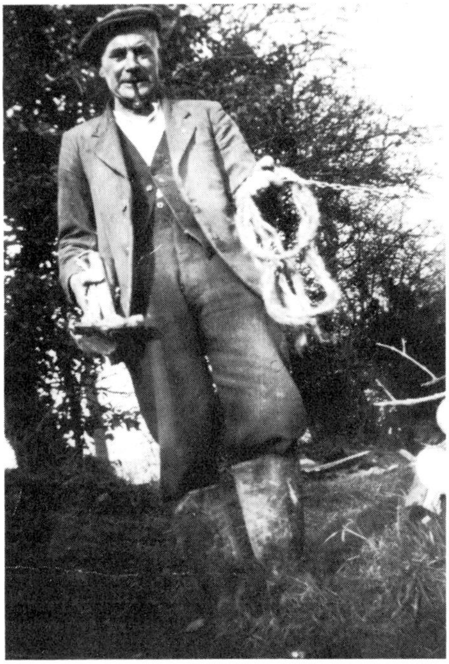

ARTHUR COX, who was for many years in the employ of the Hooper family at Deptford Farm in the 1950s.

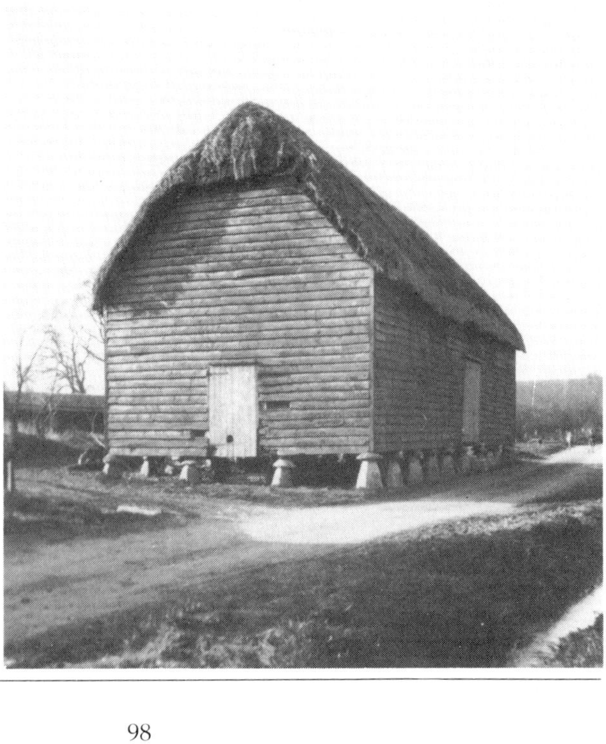

A 'STAFFLE' OR 'STADDLE' BARN at Hanging Langford, pictured during the 1920s. Barns like this were used for storing grain after threshing. The staddle stones made it difficult for rats, mice and other vermin to get at the precious grain.

SECTION FOUR

Road and Rail

Two roads, running almost parallel, one either side of the River Wylye, connect Warminster with Wilton. The 'back road', south of the river, is the more scenic and serves mainly agricultural traffic, village commuters and sightseers. It has recently been added to the Wiltshire Cycleway routes. The A36 Bristol–Southampton trunk road, to the north of the river, is a very busy road. The increase in motor traffic over the years has brought its toll of accidents. Local residents, who campaigned in the 1970s, seeking improvements to the A36, used the slogan 'The Death Valley' on their posters and publicity material. Thankfully, there have been some road improvements in recent years. The holiday traffic jams at Wylye and Deptford are now a thing of the past, thanks to the construction of a bridge and a dual carriageway to carry the A36 over the A303 Exeter–Andover road. Heytesbury is now bypassed; a further bypass is under construction at Steeple Langford; and there are also plans for one at Codford. The long-awaited Warminster Bypass (due for completion Autumn 1988) will also ease congestion and make the town more pleasant to live, work and shop in.

These developments are a far cry from the roads of yesteryear. For example, in 1908, Heytesbury had the unique distinction of being the only village in the district with a main street coated with tar. This was a great boon for the villagers because the houses and shops had only a narrow pavement between them and the road, and in the summer months the dust swept up by passing vehicles was a nuisance. The only way of dealing with the dust was to periodically dampen it down by sprinkling the roads with water from a barrel on a horse-drawn cart. The dust, the mud and the holes in the road which were filled with stones also presented problems for travellers.

The railway through the valley, between Warminster and Salisbury, was constructed in 1857, and it was originally a single line with a passing loop at Wylye. Other loops were added later: at Wilton (1867), Heytesbury (1888), and Codford and Wishford (1898). These arrangements proved insufficient for the amount of traffic and the line was doubled: between Wilton and Salisbury in 1896, Codford–Wylye in 1900, and Wylye–Wishford in 1901. There were stations at Heytesbury, Codford, Wylye, Langford (closed 1857), Wishford and Wilton. These closed for passenger traffic in September 1955, as part of the cuts implemented nationwide by Dr Beeching. Freight traffic was also denied soon afterwards. Today, the trains make no official stops between Warminster and Salisbury, and complete the 19½ mile journey in around 20 minutes. Diesel now, of course!

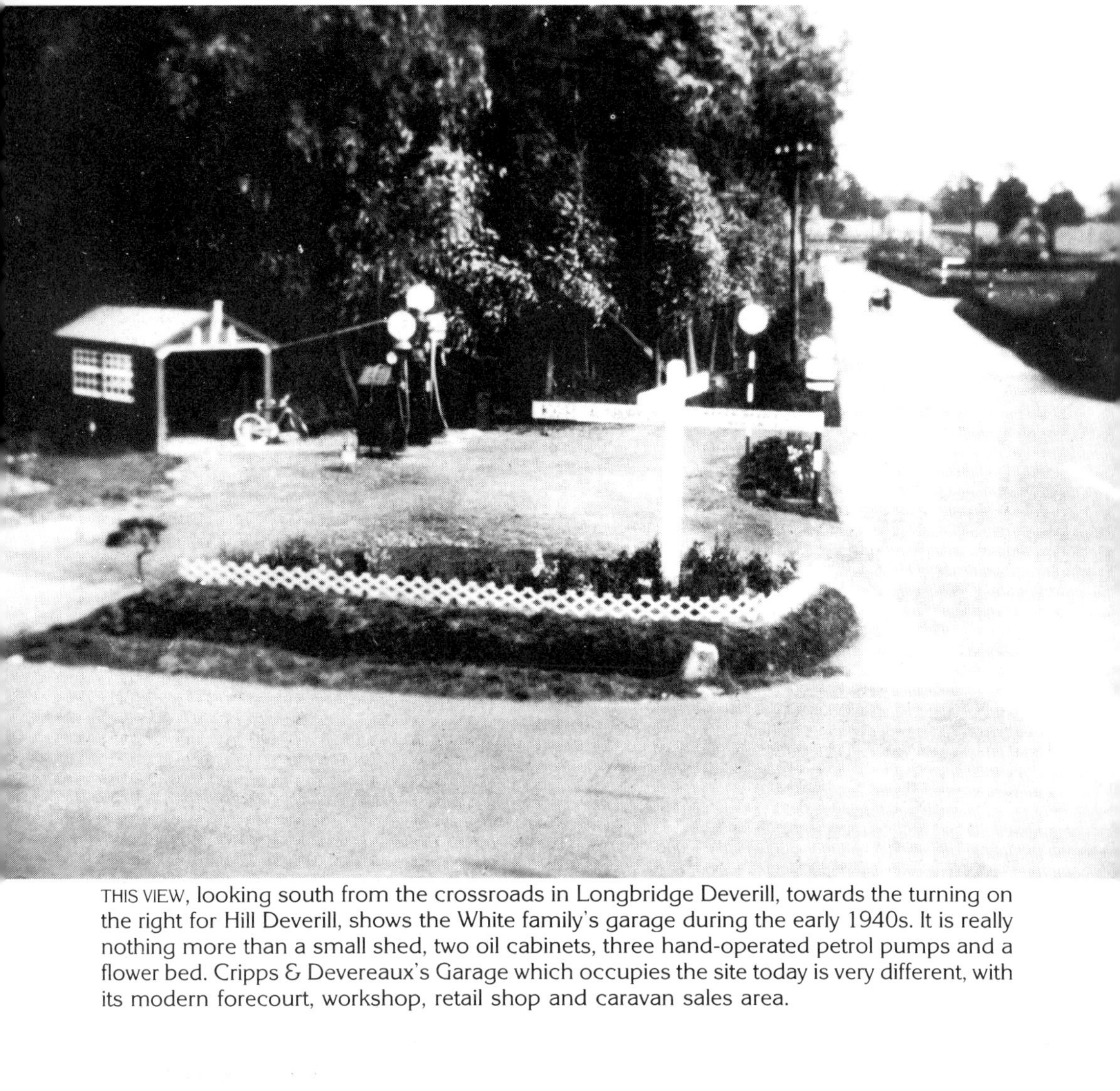

THIS VIEW, looking south from the crossroads in Longbridge Deverill, towards the turning on the right for Hill Deverill, shows the White family's garage during the early 1940s. It is really nothing more than a small shed, two oil cabinets, three hand-operated petrol pumps and a flower bed. Cripps & Devereaux's Garage which occupies the site today is very different, with its modern forecourt, workshop, retail shop and caravan sales area.

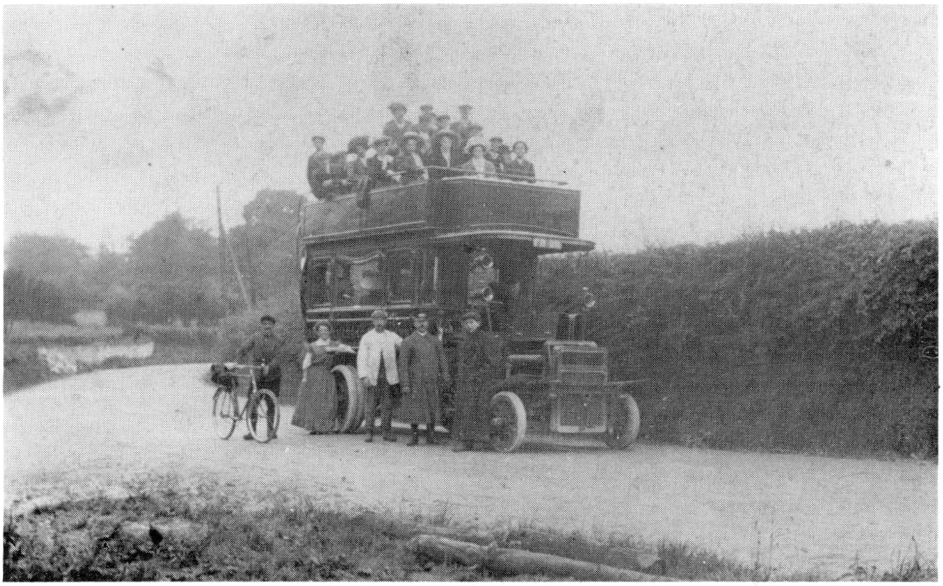

BATH ELECTRIC TRAMWAYS BUS, pictured near Warminster (exact location unknown), c.1925.

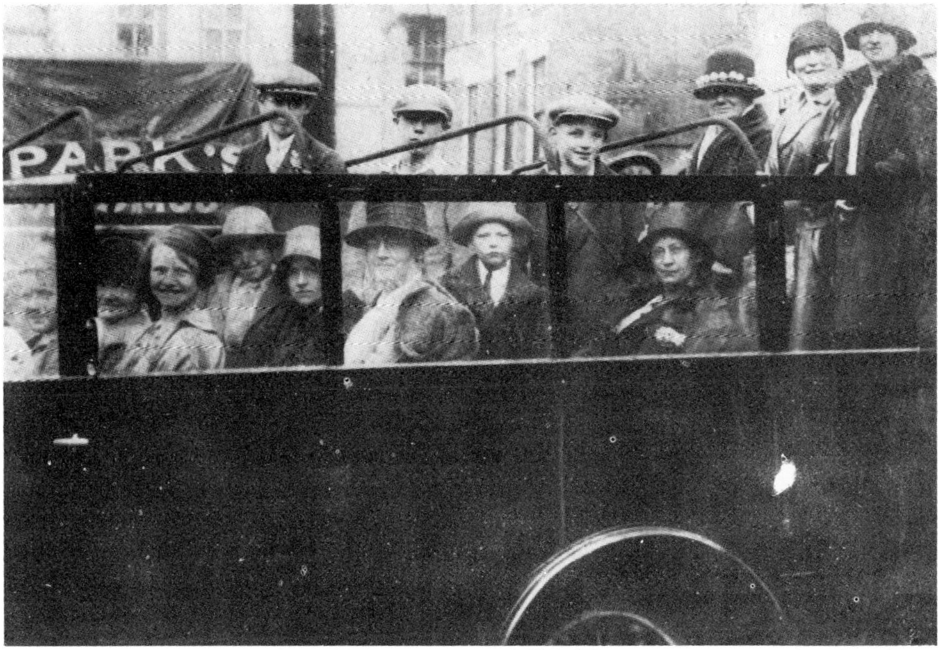

A SUNDAY SCHOOL OUTING from Bishopstrow in 1926. The passengers in the charabanc include George Long, Bill Maslen, Cecil Puckett, George Field, Mrs Field, Mrs Long, Mrs Fitz, Rosella Fitz, Kathy Butcher and Mrs Butcher.

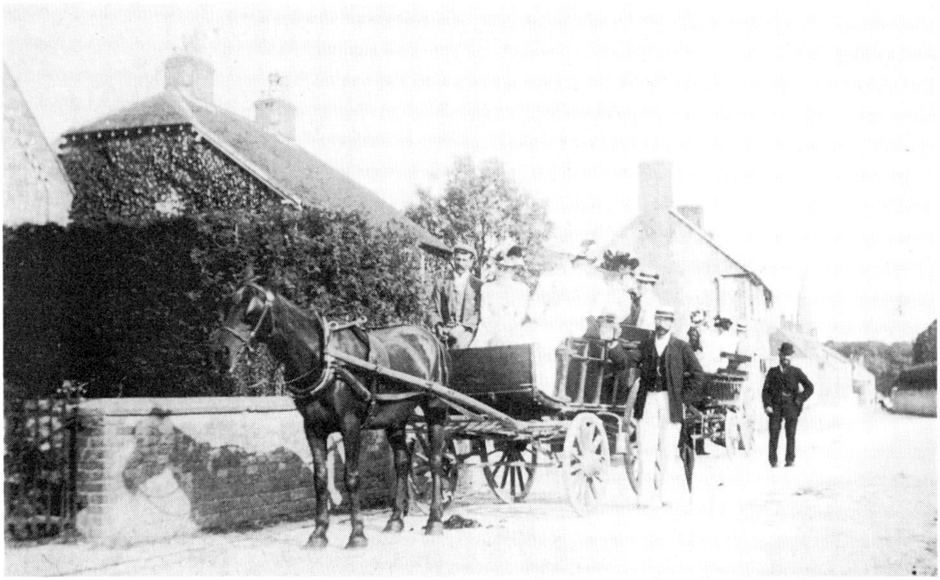

TRAVELLERS ON THE ROAD near the Manse at Sutton Veny, just after the turn of the century.

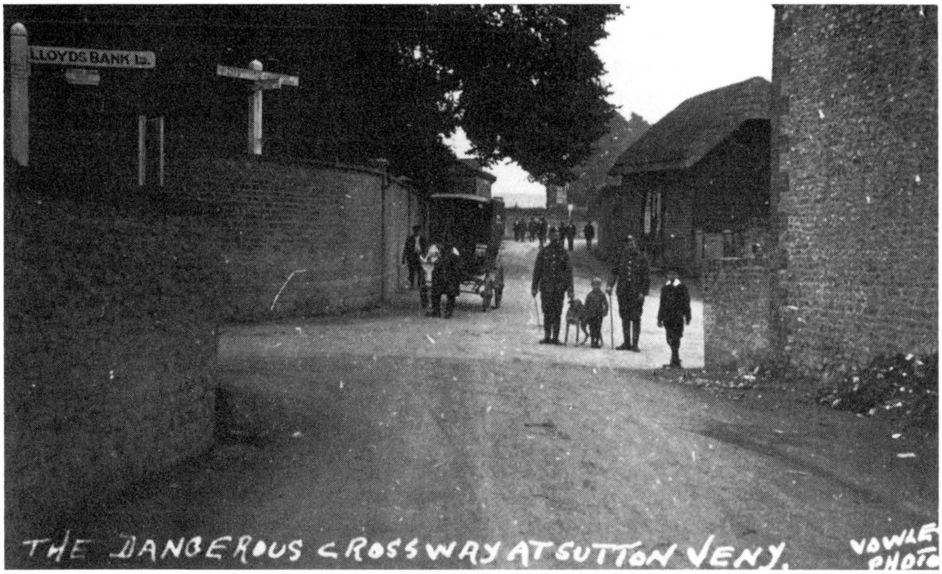

THE PHOTOGRAPHER MR A. VOWLES titled this picture 'The dangerous crossroads at Sutton Veny'. The picture was taken c.1916, and looks from Deverill Road towards Norton Road, at the top of the village. Those in the road include soldiers with a dog, children and a man leading a horse and cart. The walls and the three-fingered signpost, on the far side, are still the same today. The signpost on the left points to Lloyds Bank, which was situated in a house nearly opposite the Woolpack in the village.

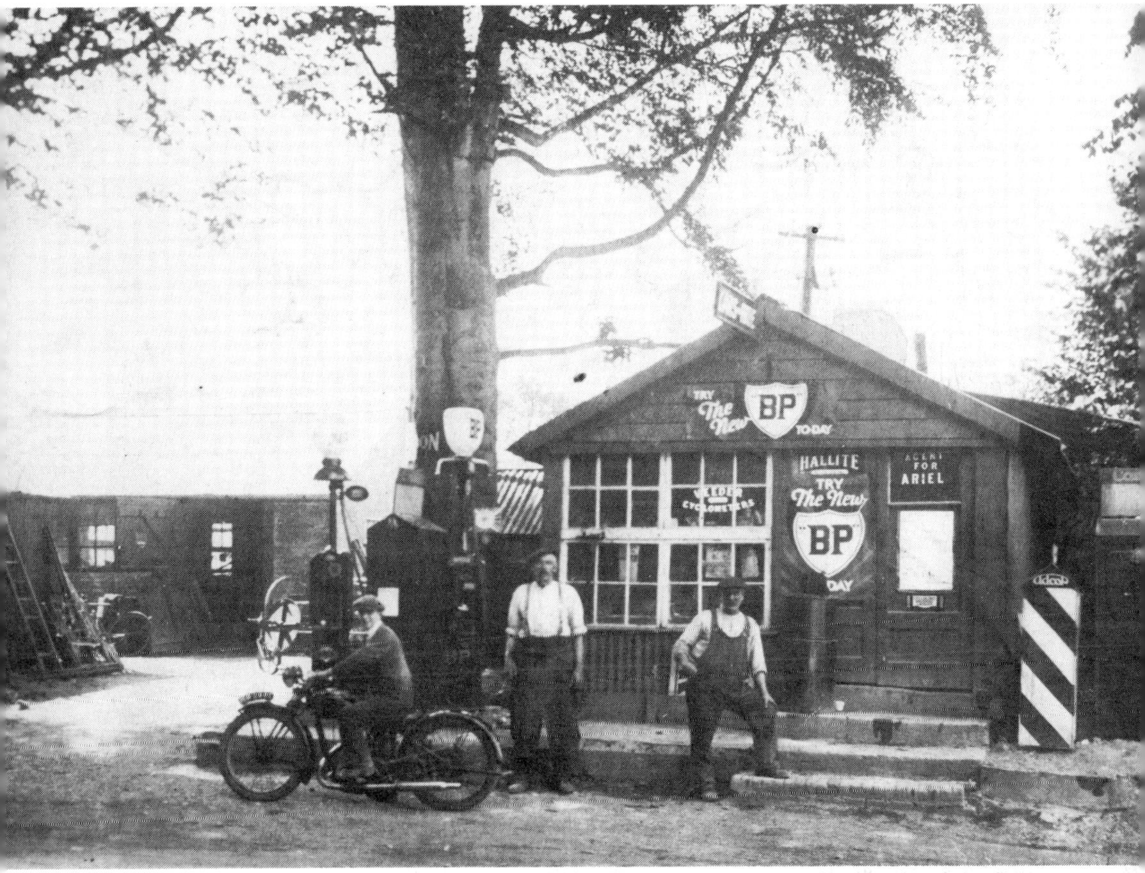

THE GARAGE AT HEYTESBURY, during the 1920s. The garage was in the hands of the White family from before 1899 until 1948. The men are Uriah White on the left, on what looks like a New Imperial motorbike, Dick Skinner in the middle, and William Uriah White (Uriah's father) on the right. The signs advertise 'Cars For Hire', BP petrol, Veeders cyclometers and Castrol oil. In the yard, to the rear, a hay tedder awaits welding repairs. Heytesbury still has a garage on this site today – Griffins – and although it doesn't sell petrol, it has been modernised and presents a very different scene to the one we see here.

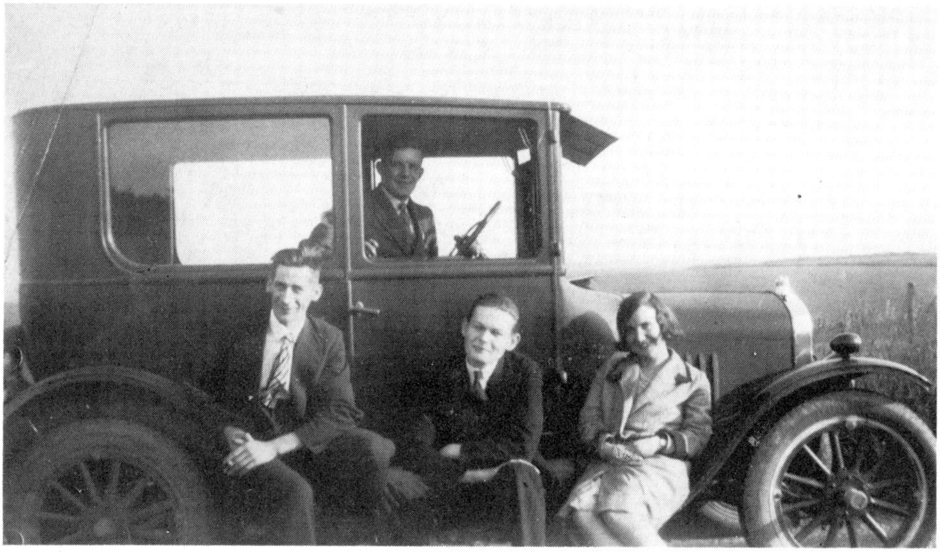

A FINE CAR, POSSIBLY A FORD, in the late 1920s. At the wheel is Heytesbury resident, Uriah White. Seated on the running board, left to right, are Joe Monnington (Uriah's brother-in-law), the gentleman in the middle is unknown and Uriah's sister, Phoebe. Notice the sun visor above the windscreen and the spoked wheels.

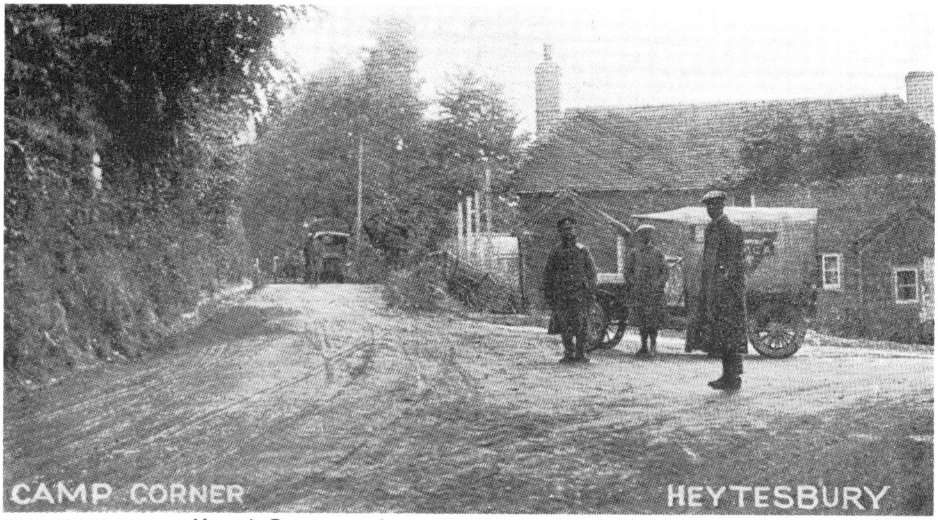

CAMP CORNER, near Knook Camp, on the eastern side of Heytesbury, where the road forks left for Chitterne and right for Knook and Upton Lovell. The picture was taken during the 1914–18 War. The house in the background is the old Turnpike, long since demolished to make way for road improvements. The van is carrying supplies for the use of Australian troops at the YMCA, Knook Camp. The photograph has been reproduced from a postcard sent to Melbourne, Australia, over 70 years ago. This card has made the return journey – it is now in the possession of Heytesbury resident, Elizabeth Hibbs.

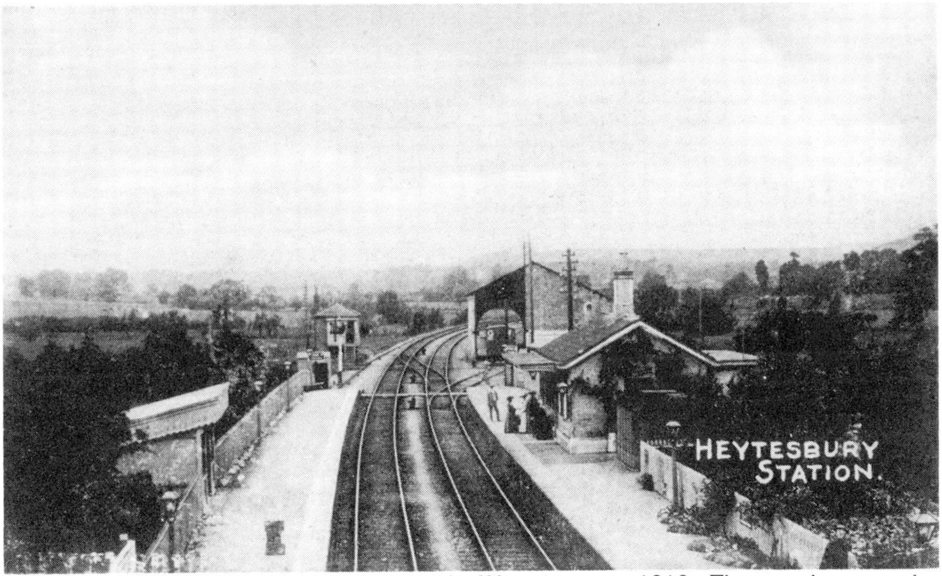

HEYTESBURY STATION, looking west towards Warminster, c.1910. Flowers decorate the platforms. At the far end of the station you can see the signalbox on the left and a goods shed on the right. The station building, like others on the line in the Valley, was designed by R.P. Brereton.

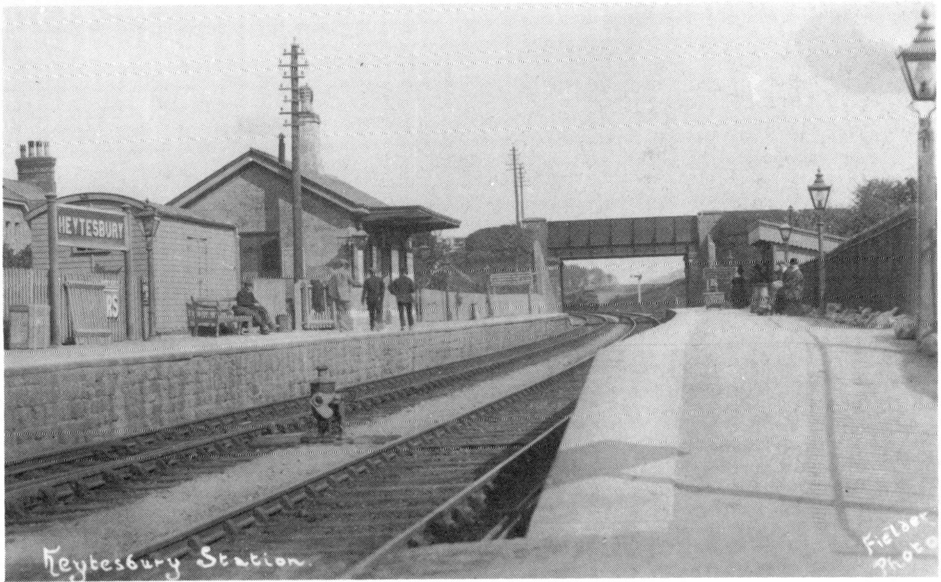

HEYTESBURY STATION, looking east, c.1920. In its early days Heytesbury only had a platform on the Down side. The bridge in the background carries the Heytesbury/Tytherington road over the rails. The people on the platform have not got long to wait, a train is approaching (just visible beyond the bridge).

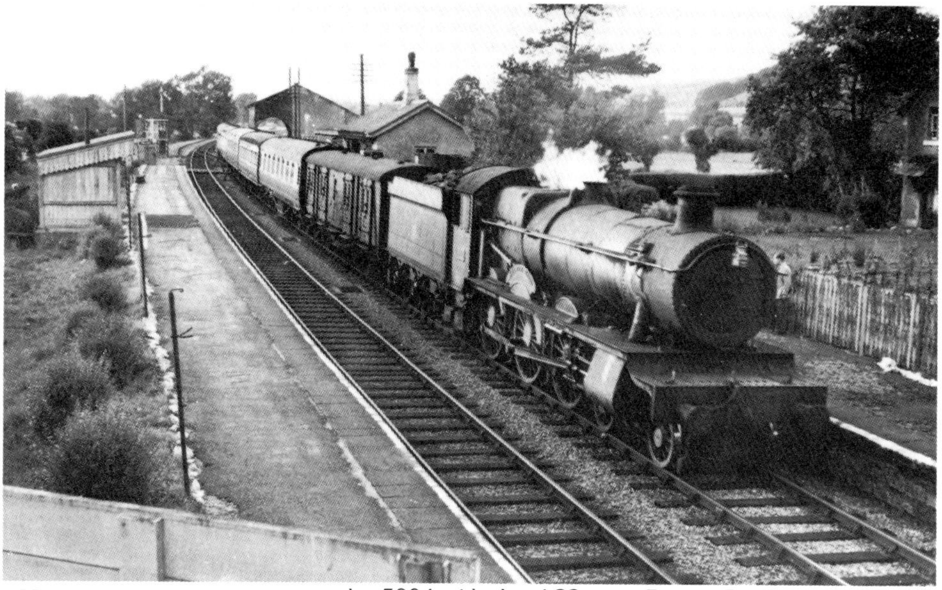

ARRIVING AT HEYTESBURY STATION, the 5904 with the 4.32 p.m. Bristol–Portsmouth train, 17 September 1955.

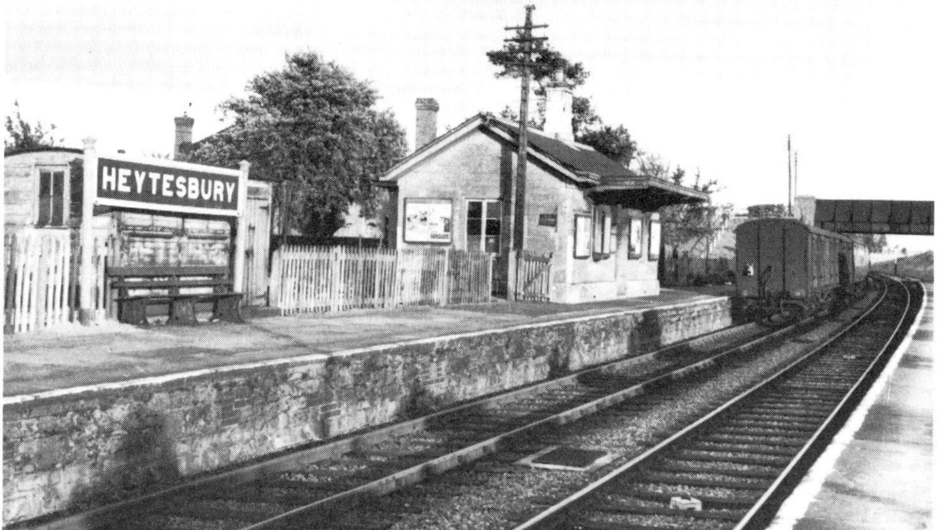

LEAVING HEYTESBURY, the 4.32 p.m. Bristol–Portsmouth train, 17 September 1955 (this was one of the last Down trains to call at the station – it closed for passenger traffic shortly afterwards).

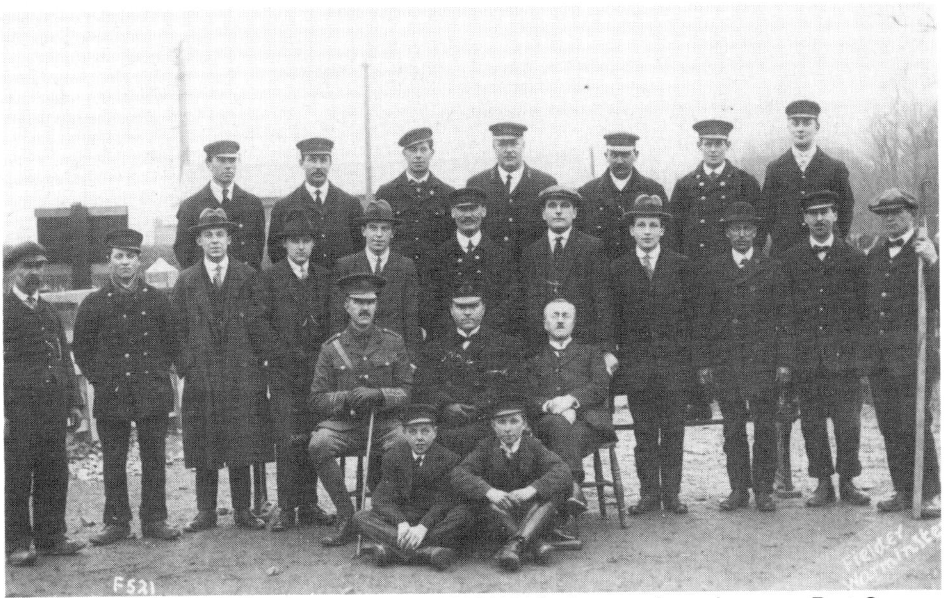

STAFF AND PORTERS AT CODFORD STATION, 1918/1919. Among those here are Bert Sparey, Sam Carpenter and Lance Lovet. During the First World War the station staff consisted of a station master, two booking clerks, one chief goods clerk, three goods clerks, two foremen, one goods checker, one mileage checker, one shunter, two goods porters, two parcel porters, two porters, two lad porters and three signalmen.

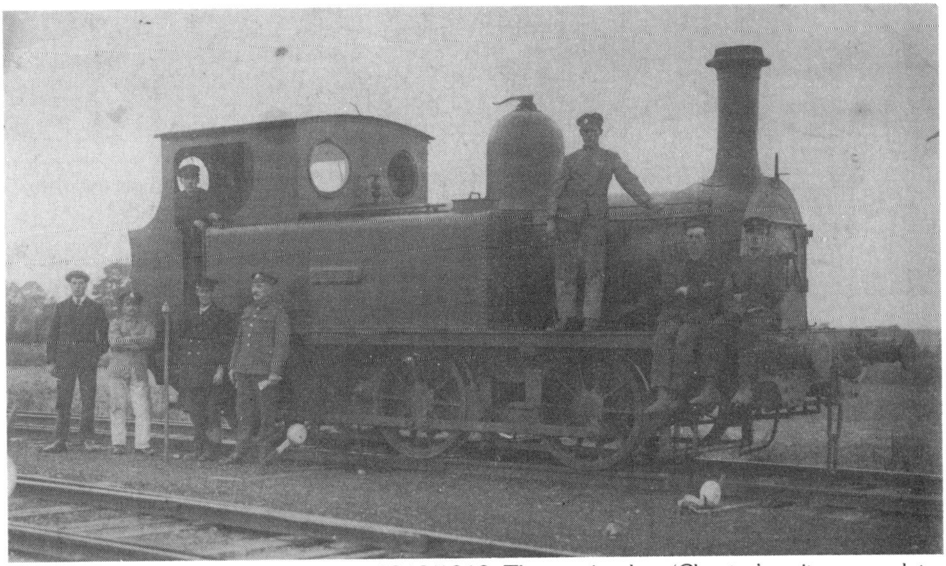

A SCENE AT CODFORD STATION, again 1918/1919. The engine has 'Chester' on its nameplate. The man holding the pole is Sam Carpenter, a member of the Codford railway station staff.

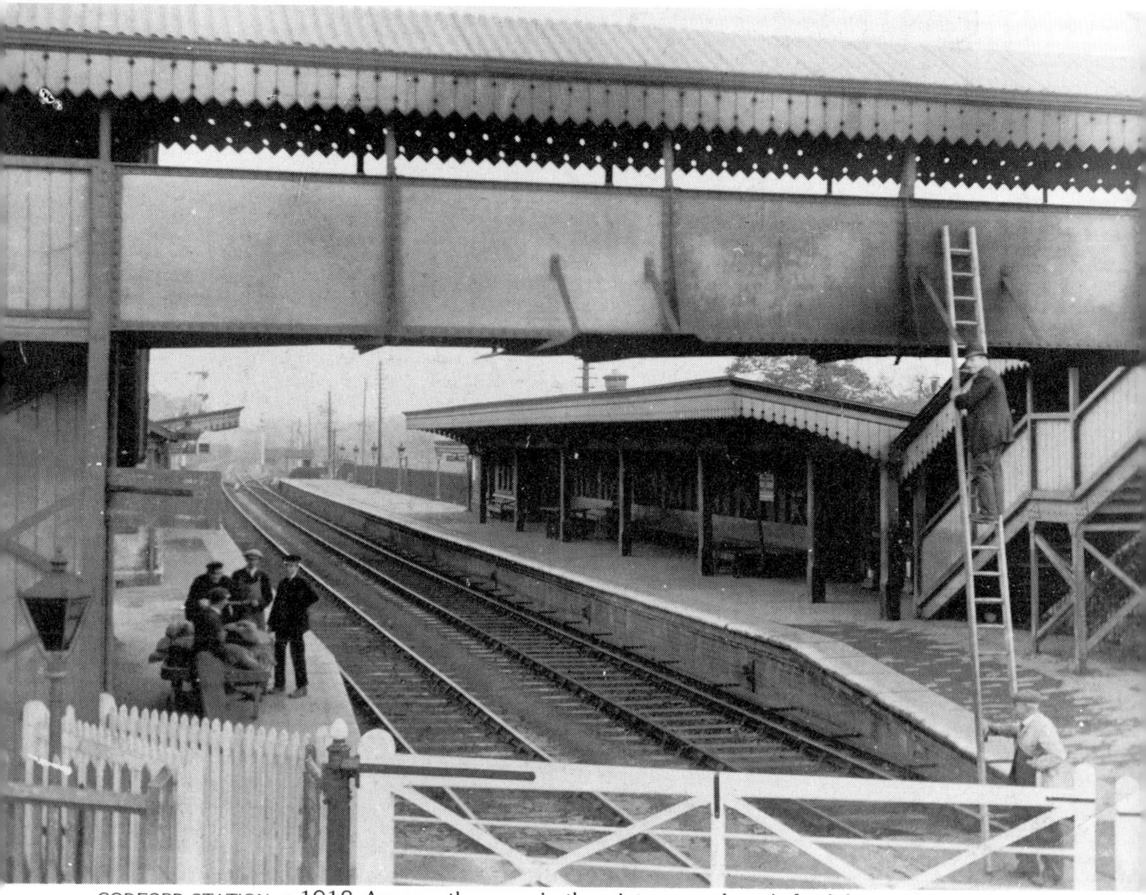

CODFORD STATION, *c*.1918. Among the men in the picture are Len Axford, Lance Lovet, Jack Fleming and Mr Stevens.

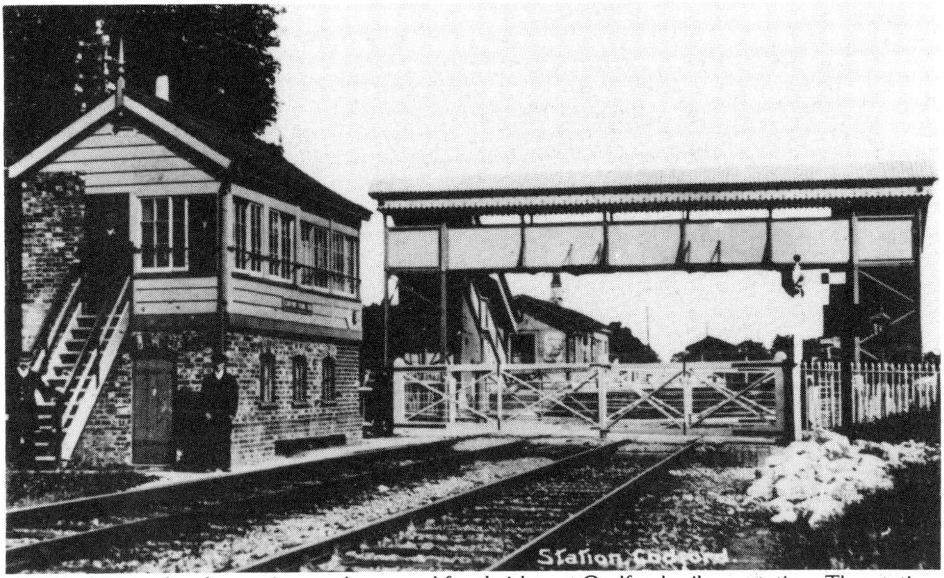

THE SIGNAL BOX, level crossing and covered footbridge at Codford railway station. The station closed for passenger traffic in September 1955 and for freight in 1960.

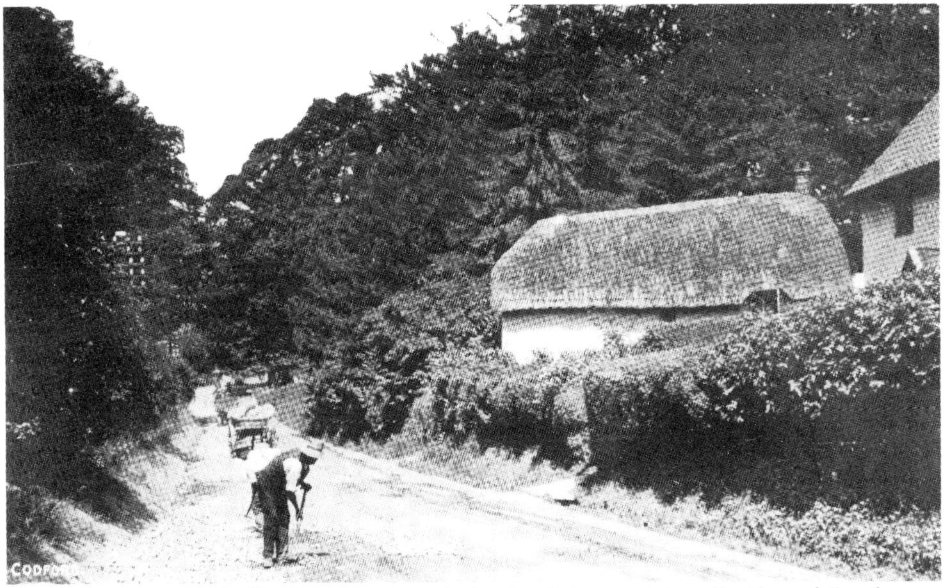

AT FIRST GLANCE it looks like these men are trying to pick up potatoes that have fallen from a passing cart. They are, in fact, spreading stones about to fill the ruts in the road. The photograph was taken at Codford, *c*.1920.

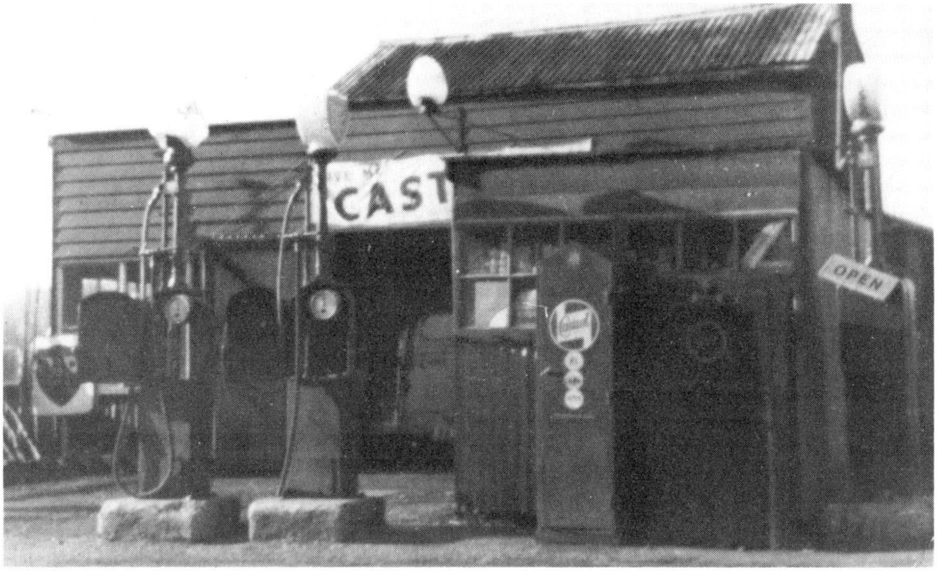

A PICTURE OF THE GARAGE on the south side of Codford High Street taken soon after Paul Cole succeeded Mr Dewey as the proprietor. Mr Cole ran the garage from 1 September 1950 until 1973. There was no water or electricity at the garage until 1952. The petrol pumps seen here, standing immediately next to the main road, were pumped by hand.

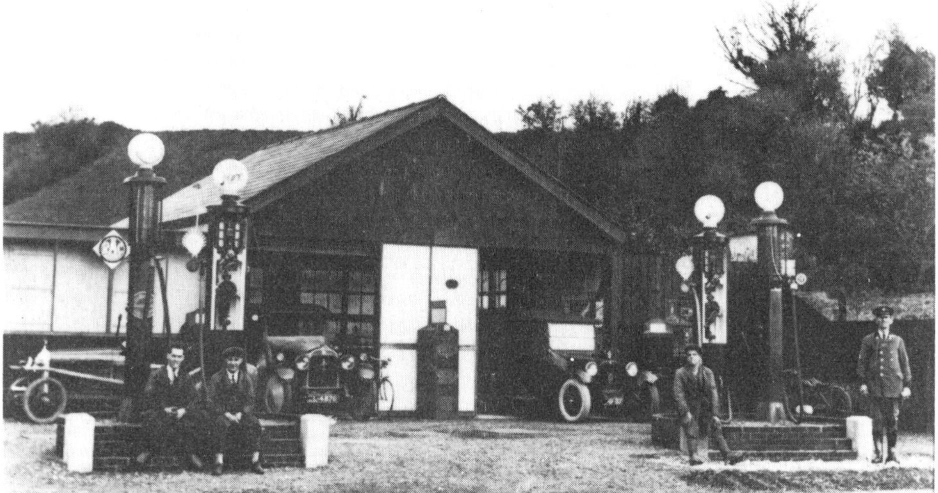

THE GARAGE AT DEPTFORD, on the A36 Warminster to Salisbury road, near Wylye, 1937.

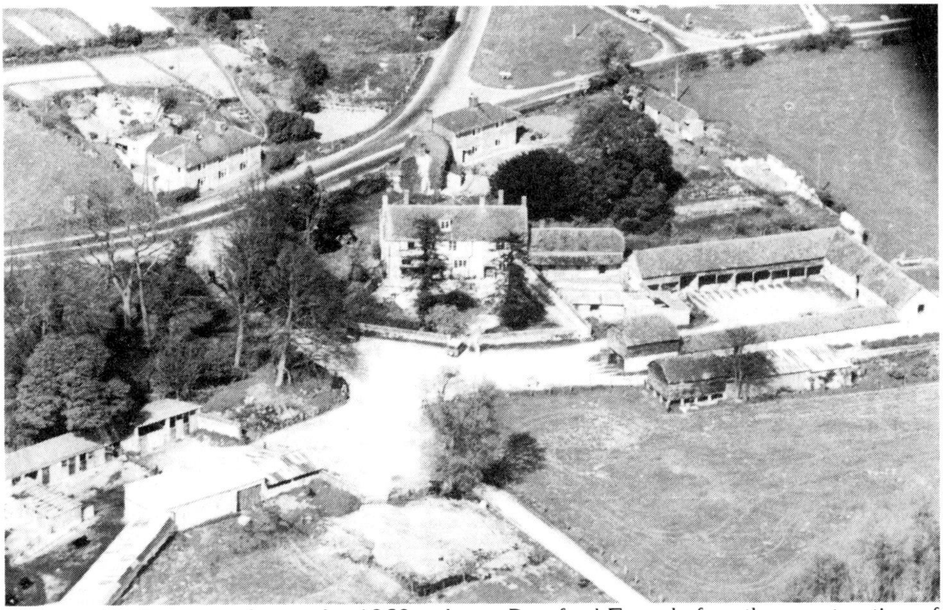

THIS AERIAL VIEW, taken during the 1960s, shows Deptford Farm before the construction of the Wylye Bypass. The houses near the top left of the picture were demolished to make way for the bridge which now carries the A36 Warminster–Salisbury road over the A303 Exeter–Andover road. The construction of the bypass and the dual carriageway at Deptford has made Wylye peaceful once again, and the holiday traffic which always came to a standstill at Deptford has no longer to be endured.

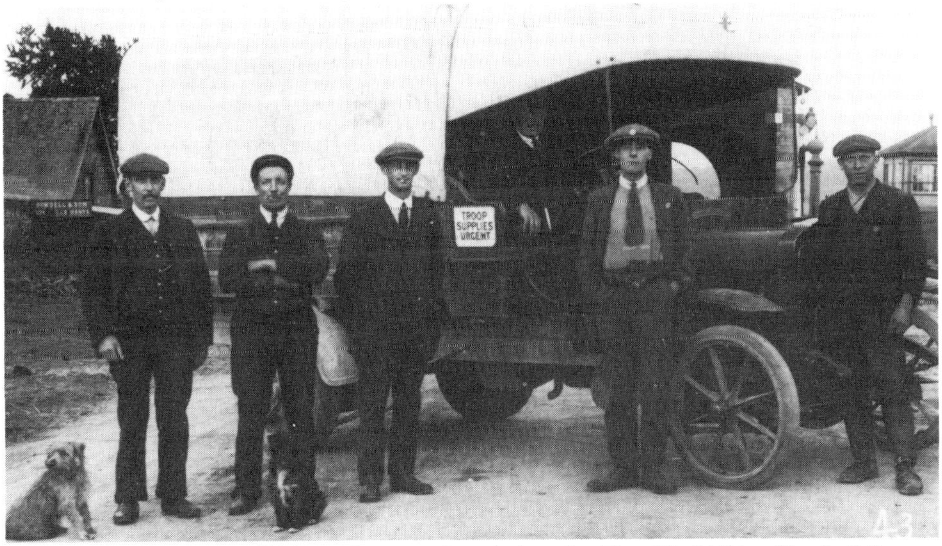

TROOP SUPPLIES TRUCK at Wylye railway station during the First World War. The building on the left has a sign advertising 'Dowdell & Son, Coal Merchants'.

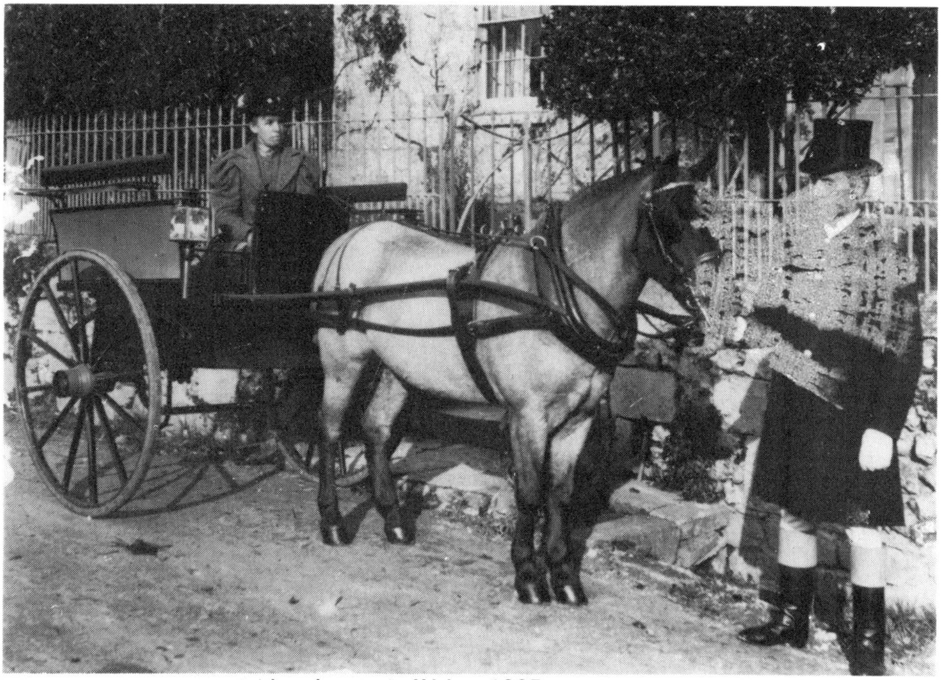
HORSE AND CARRIAGE outside a house in Wylye, 1905.

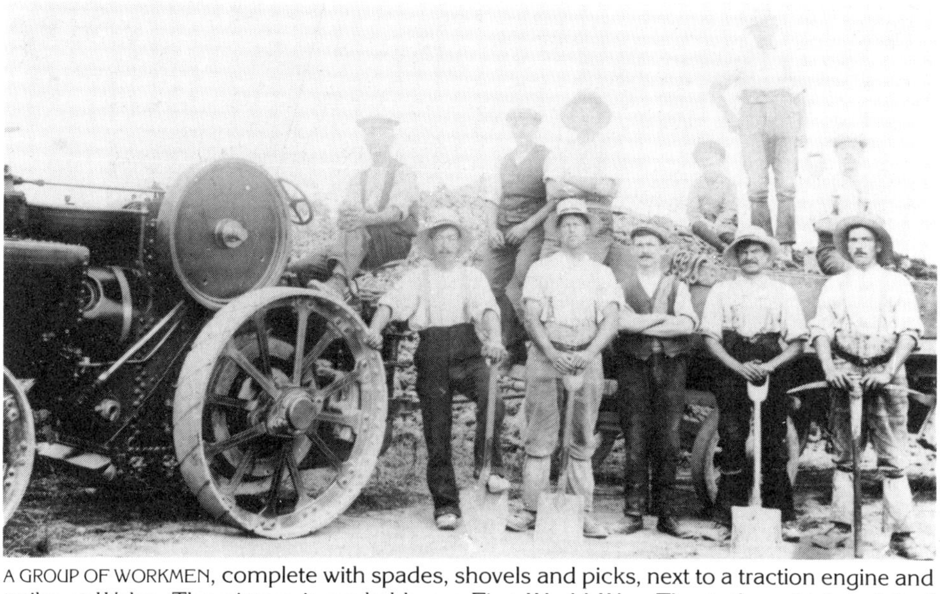
A GROUP OF WORKMEN, complete with spades, shovels and picks, next to a traction engine and trailer at Wylye. The picture is probably pre-First World War. The trailer, which is full of rubble and has a few chains hanging over the headboard at the front, has wooden blocks for brakes.

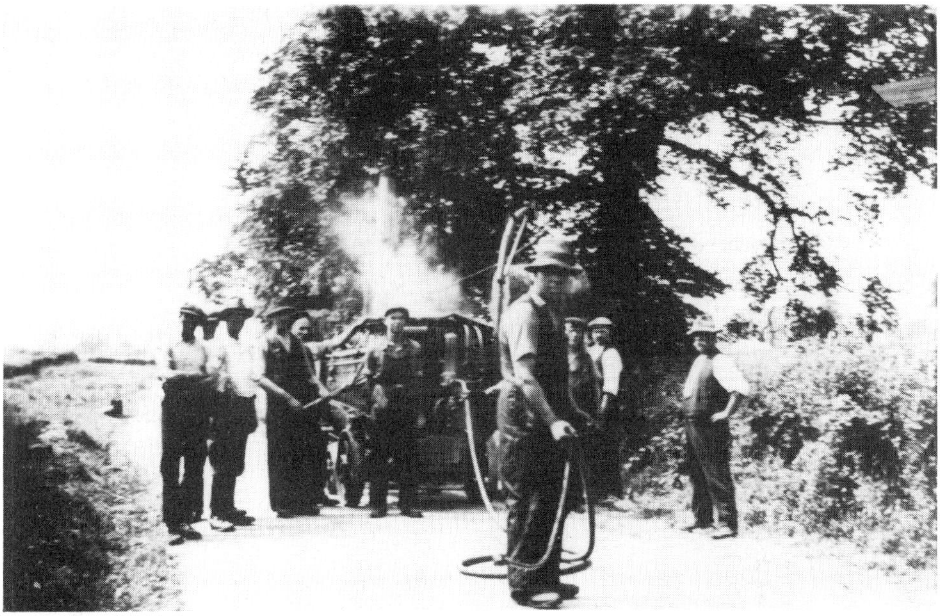

ROAD GANG WITH A TAR BOILER at Wylye during the 1920s.

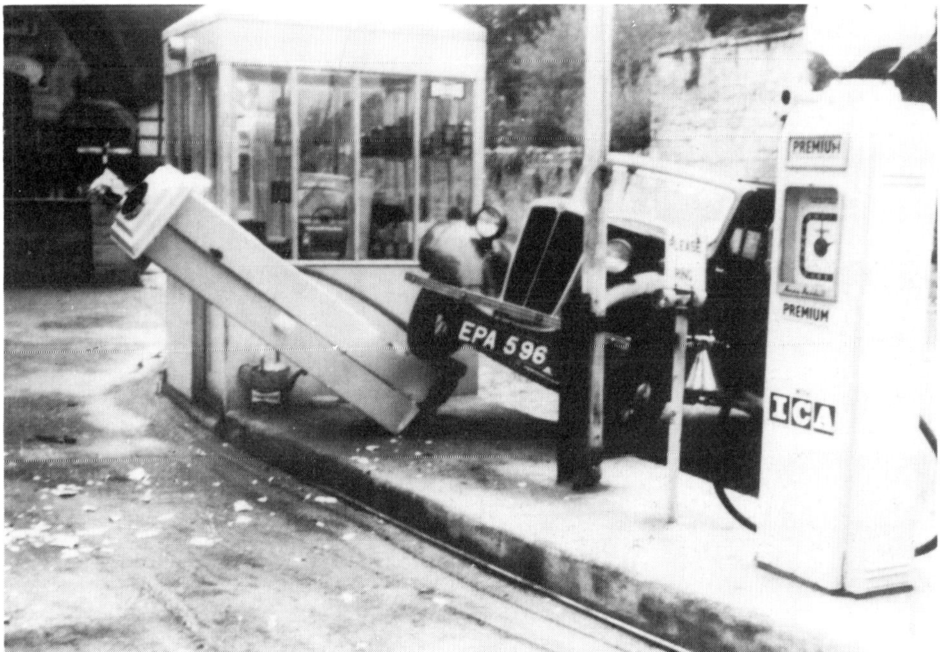

CAR CRASH at Smith Bros' Garage, High Street, Wylye, in 1956.

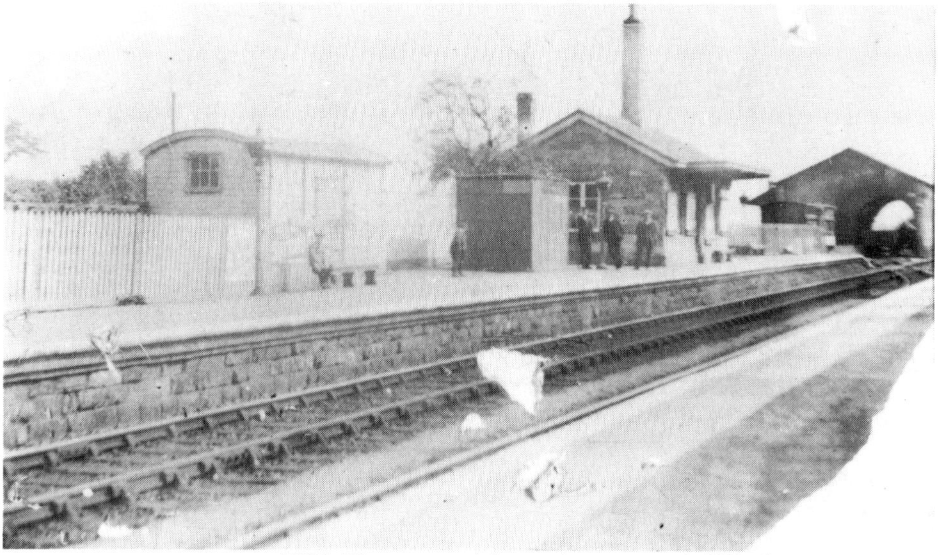

THE GWR STATION AT WYLYE, 1920. The name of the station was spelt 'Wiley' up until August 1874.

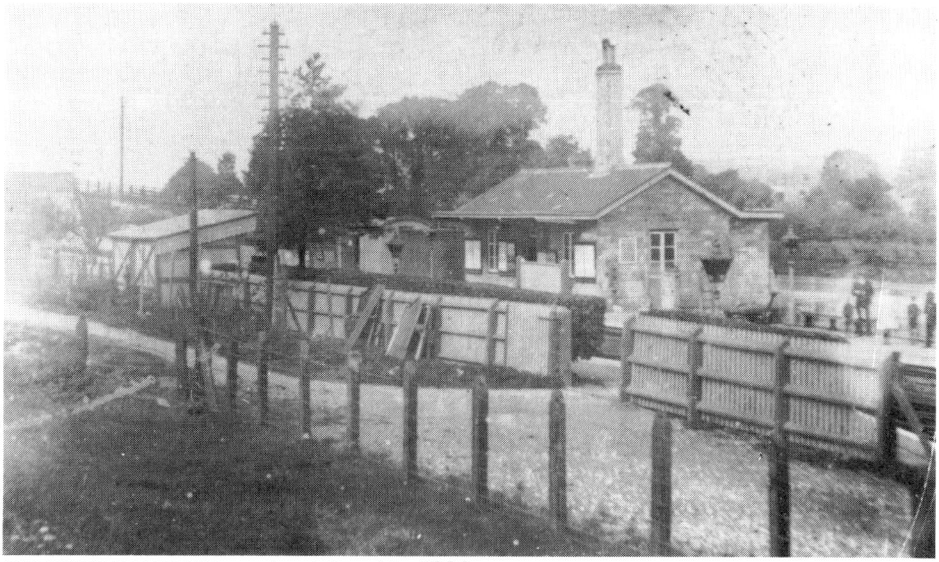

GWR STATION AT WYLYE, again pictured in 1920.

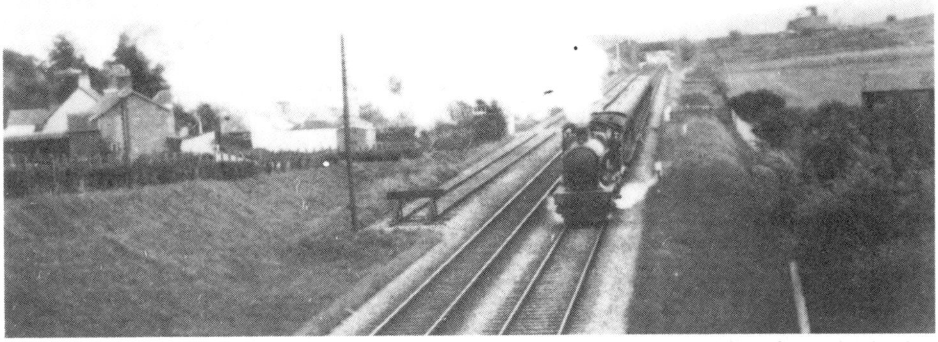

A STEAM TRAIN LEAVING WYLYE STATION in 1933. The photograph was taken from the bridge that carried the old London–Exeter road over the railway, west of the village.

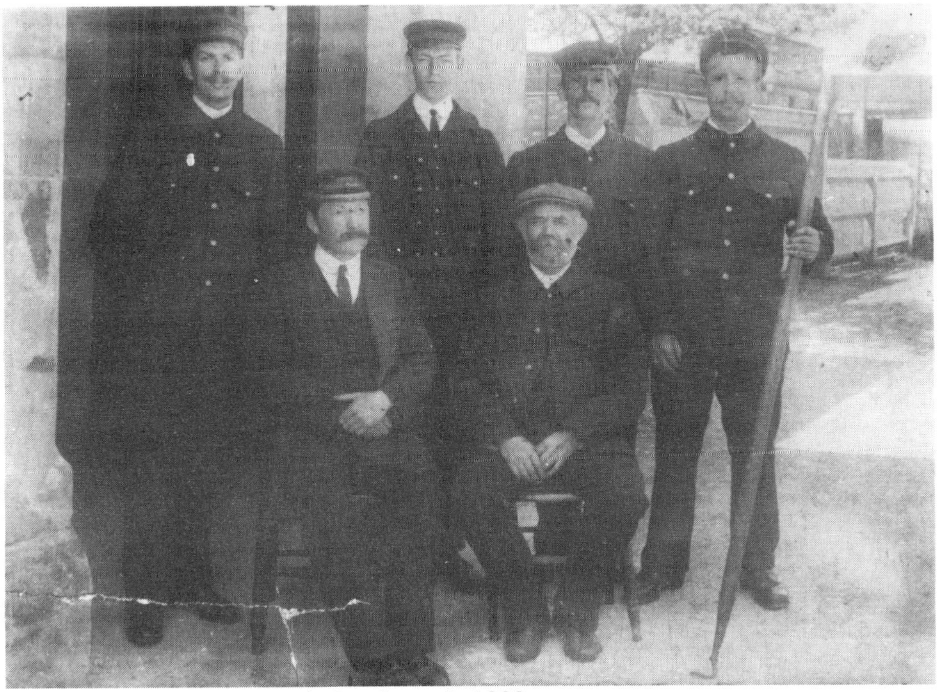

GWR STAFF AT WYLYE STATION during the early 1900s.

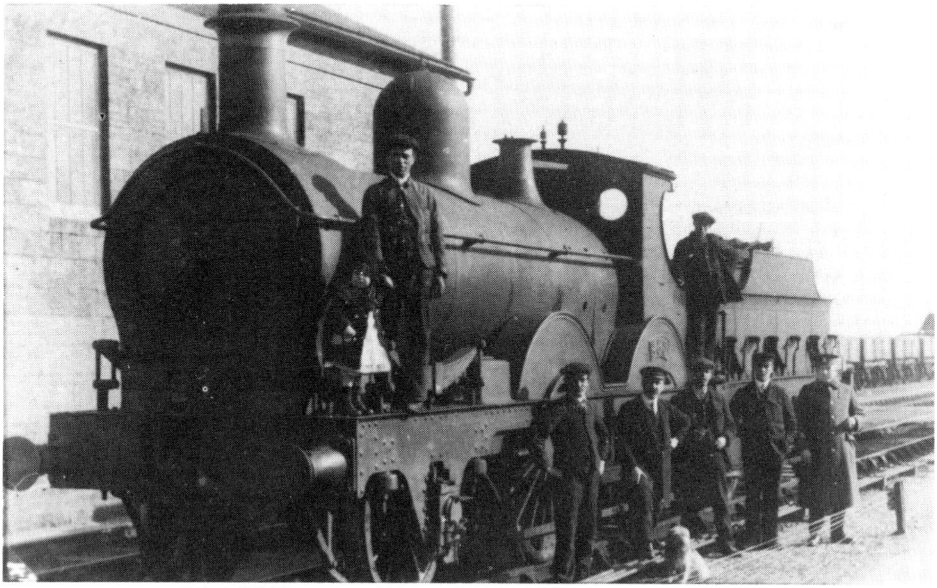
MEN AND ENGINE at the GWR station, Wylye, 1914–1918.

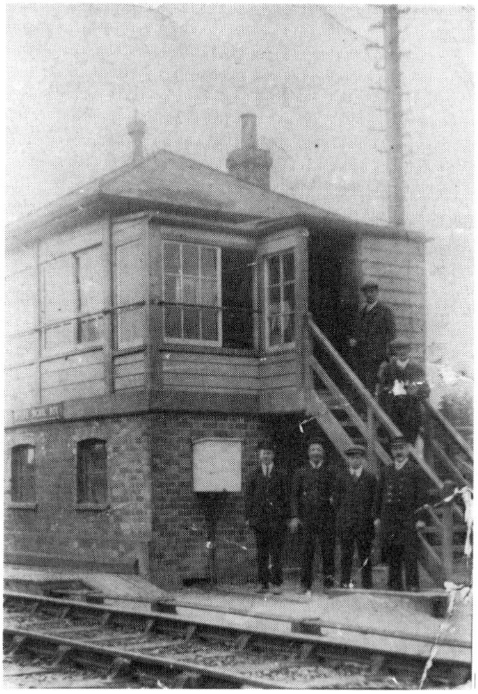
RAILWAYMEN OUTSIDE THE SIGNALBOX at GWR station, Wylye, during the First World War.

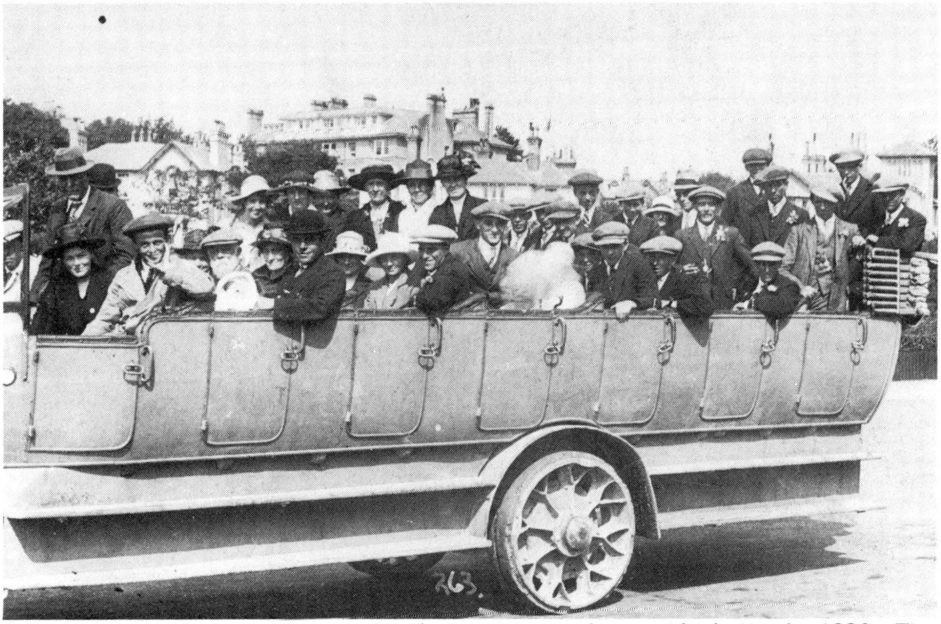

HANGING LANGFORD RESIDENTS on a charabanc outing to the seaside during the 1920s. The charabanc, belonging to Hall & Son of Shrewton, had solid tyres and a hood (folded up at the rear) in case of inclement weather.

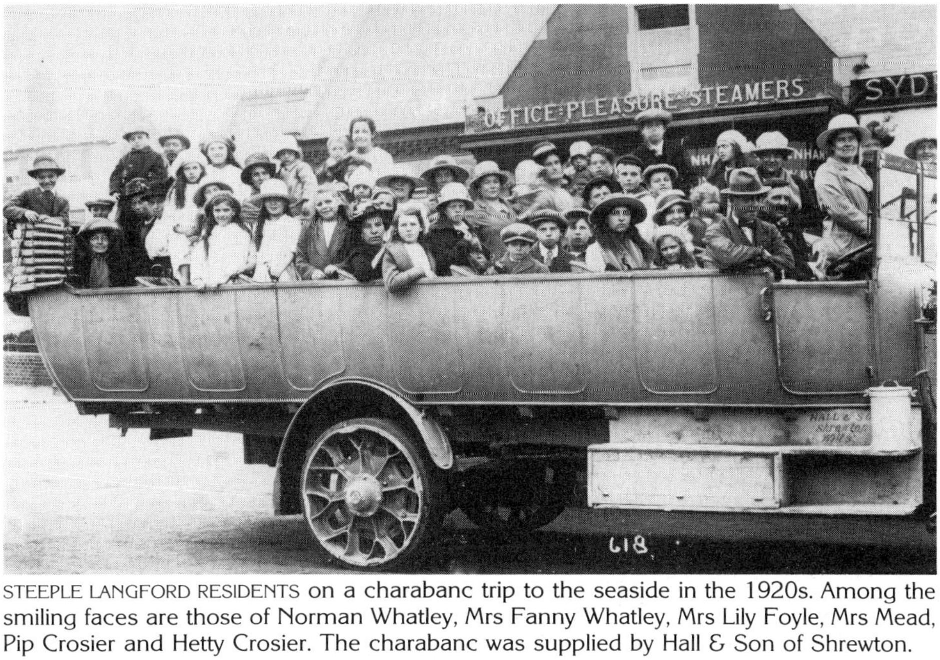

STEEPLE LANGFORD RESIDENTS on a charabanc trip to the seaside in the 1920s. Among the smiling faces are those of Norman Whatley, Mrs Fanny Whatley, Mrs Lily Foyle, Mrs Mead, Pip Crosier and Hetty Crosier. The charabanc was supplied by Hall & Son of Shrewton.

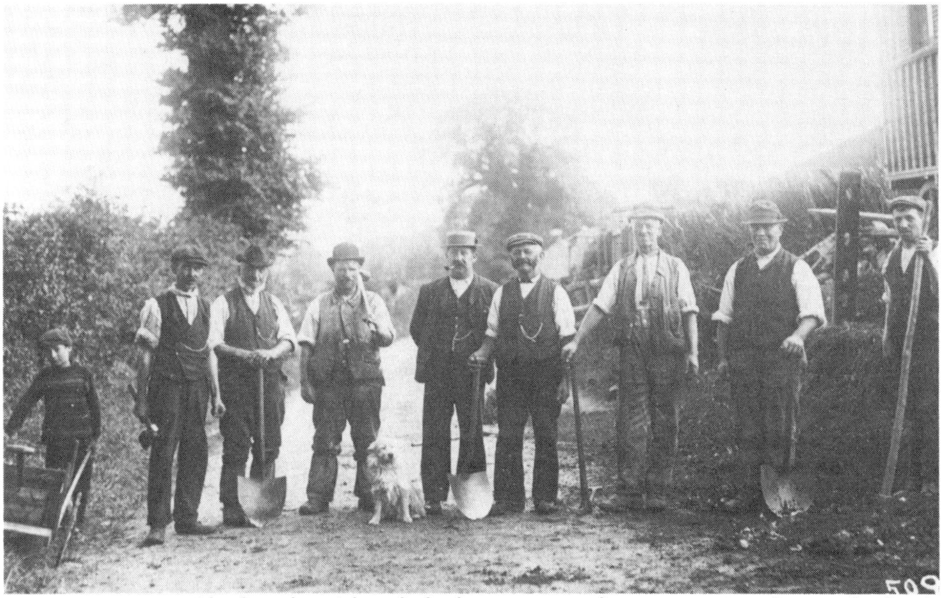

THESE WORKMEN, with shovels, picks, sledgehammers and axes, are attending to the bank and the fence beside the road at the rear of Wishford station, c.1903. The men include Harry Davis, Mr Hesbridge, A.E. Scott (behind the dog), Bill West, Mr Pile, and H. Newton. The little boy on the left with the barrow is unknown.

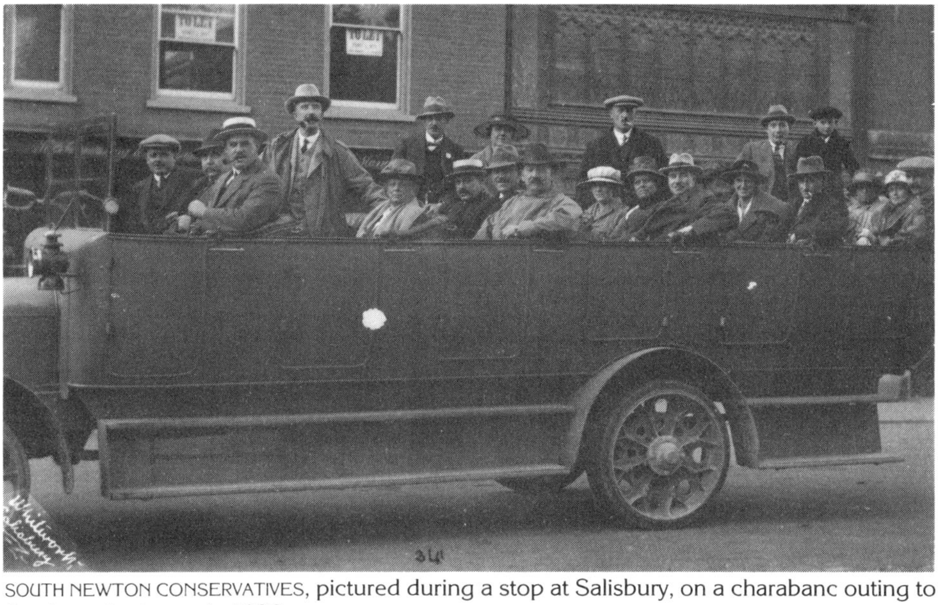

SOUTH NEWTON CONSERVATIVES, pictured during a stop at Salisbury, on a charabanc outing to Southsea in the early 1920s.

SECTION FIVE

Soldiers

During the First World War the way of life in the Wylye Valley changed considerably when the area became one of several places chosen for the assembly and training of soldiers. The first troops arrived in Sutton Veny on 27 April 1915. At one point over 35,000 men were in camp at Codford, nearly half as many again at Sutton Veny and about 5,000 at Longbridge Deverill. These soldiers included Australians and New Zealanders (Anzacs) and Canadian troops, plus Scottish and other regiments. Many were under canvas to begin with, until the building of huts was organised, and conditions were far from satisfactory. Mud was the biggest problem, and it affected not only camp life, but also the village communities.

The soldiers were instructed for combat and practised the art of trench digging, ready for the hostilities in France. For them, poor rations and regular route marches around the Wylye Valley became part of the normal routine. Eager to defend king and country, fathers and sons left homes and families, not knowing the terrible slaughter to come in the Somme. Many never returned from the battlefields abroad, and those who did were lucky to come back in one piece. Many lost limbs or suffered mental damage, and the post-war years offered them no consolation – even those who were able and fit for work found themselves unemployed because of the depression during the 1920s. Some soldiers, still in camp when the end of the war was nigh, thinking the worse was over, succumbed to an epidemic of Spanish flu that swept through the Wylye Valley. The First World War was not a happy time.

One good thing to come out of it all was a boom in the local economy. Many small shops sprang up to cater for the soldiers' needs and local traders flourished. Some of the local civilian population found work with hut building and our photographers cashed in on a golden opportunity, supplying the all-important postcards for those gallant lads to send home. Printers and stationers produced souvenir booklets of the men and the camps, and these provide us with a wealth of pictorial material. The photographs in the first part of this section are all reproduced from the huge stock of postcards and booklets that survive. I hope this selection portrays something of what life was like for the soldiers in camp in the Wylye Valley during the First World War. To close this section I have included pictures of local lads and others who, during the Second World War, served on Home Guard and other duties.

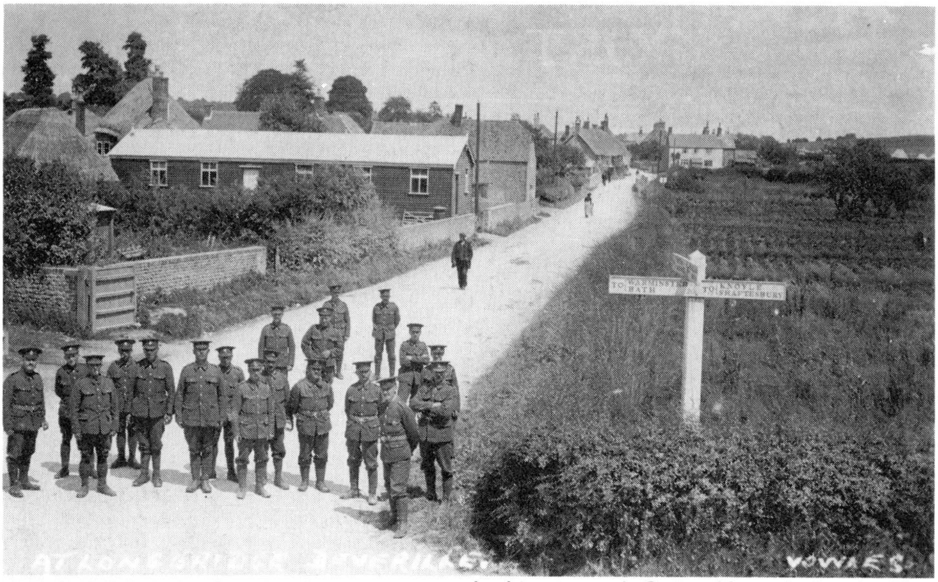

FROM THE CROSSROADS IN LONGBRIDGE DEVERILL, looking towards Sutton Veny, during the First World War. The soldiers were probably based at Sandhill Camp, near the village, or the camp on the way to Sutton Veny (some of the tents are just visible top right). The area in the lower left of this photograph, next to the signpost, is now occupied by Cripps & Devereaux' Garage.

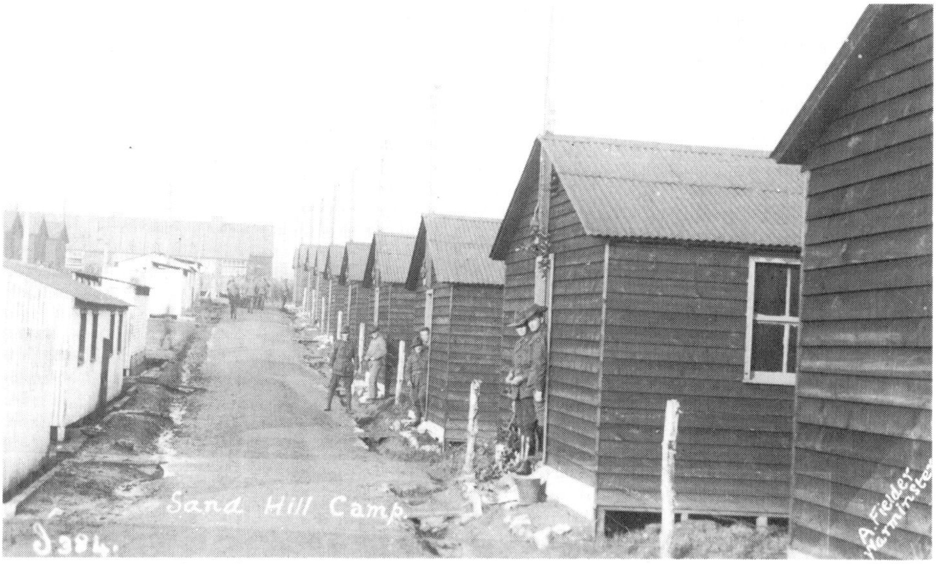

SANDHILL CAMP at Longbridge Deverill during the First World War. There was accommodation for 5,000 men here. The hats and uniforms of the soldiers identify them as Anzac troops. The hut at the far end of the path has a map of Australia painted on its external wall.

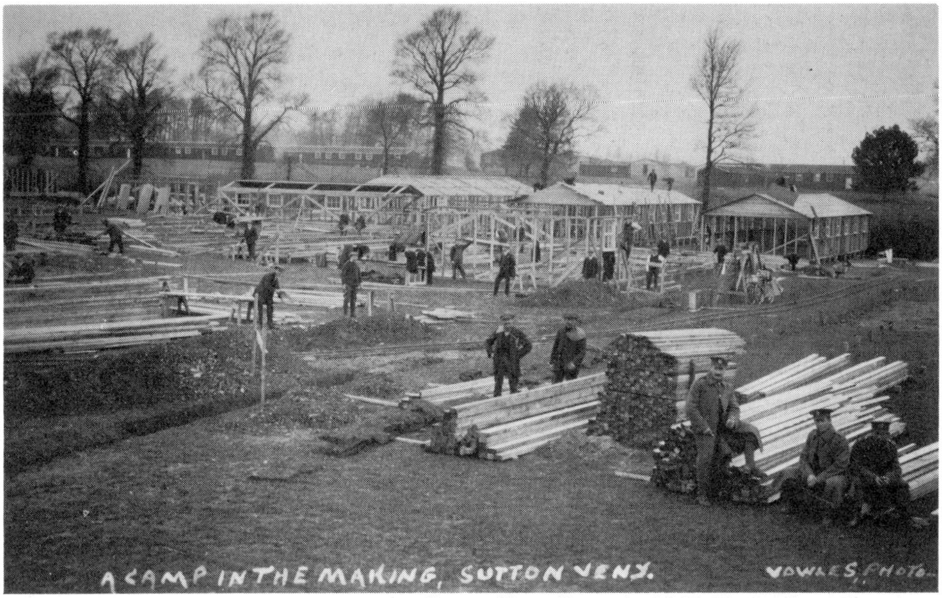

ERECTING HUTS, NORTH OF FIVE ASH LANE, at Sutton Veny Camp in 1915. Notice the railway line, specially built for easy delivery of timber and other supplies. This connected the camp with the main line at Heytesbury station. Close inspection of the photograph reveals 32 civilians on construction work.

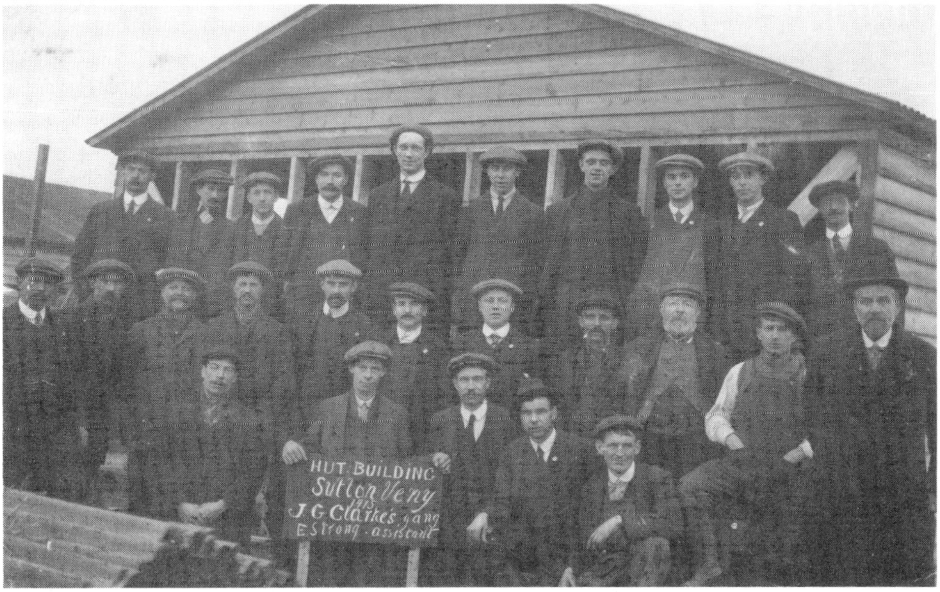

A GROUP OF HARD-WORKING HUT BUILDERS pose for the camera at Sutton Veny Camp in 1915. The sign in the foreground tells us this is J.G. Clarke's gang, and that E. Strong is the assistant.

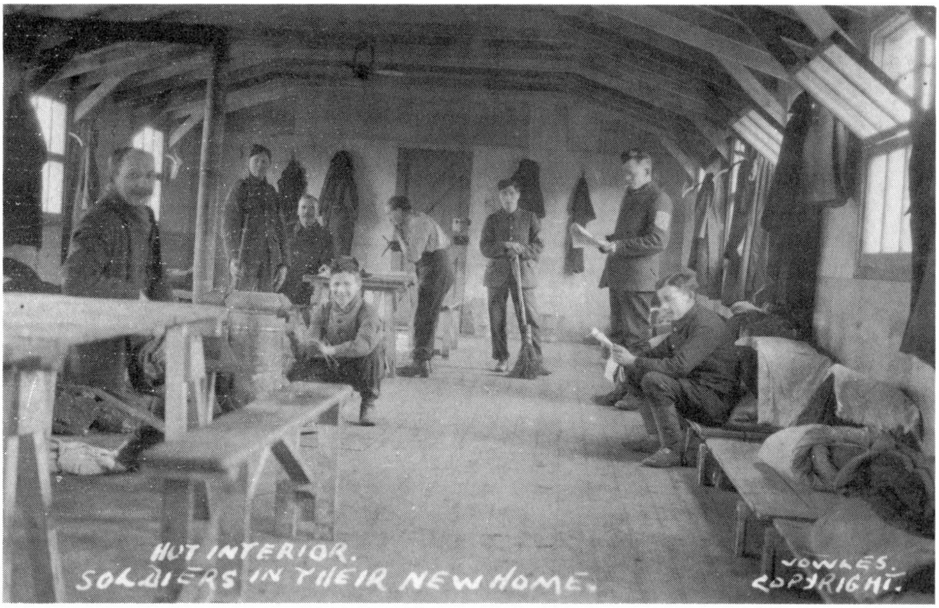

INTERIOR OF ONE OF THE HUTS at Sutton Veny, as depicted on a postcard. The sender, Jim, writing on 16 July 1915 to a Miss Netta Thomson in Glasgow, commented 'This is what the inside of our huts are like; notice our beds'. The beds are nothing more than planks of wood on legs, with palliasses for the men to lay on.

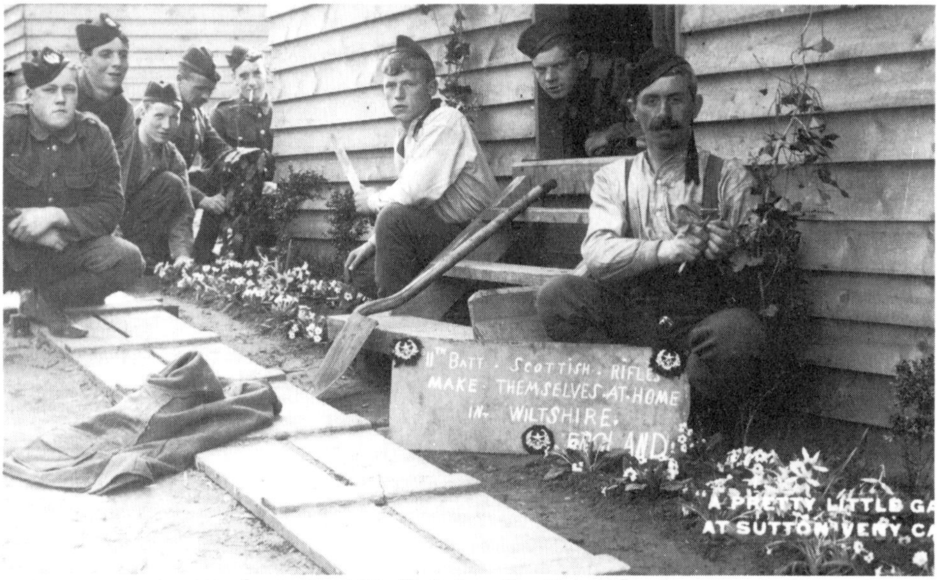

THESE YOUNG SOLDIERS from the 11th Battalion Scottish Rifles have made themselves at home at Sutton Veny Camp by planting primroses and other flowers around their hut.

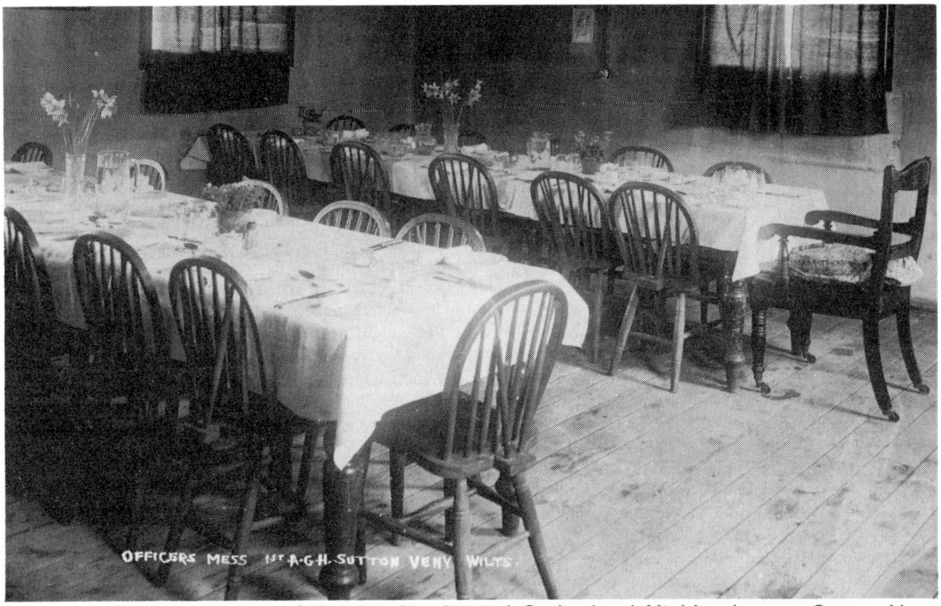

INSIDE THE OFFICERS' MESS of the 1st Argyle and Sutherland Highlanders, at Sutton Veny Camp, 1915. Vases of daffodils and pot plants decorate the tables, which are laid for a meal. Note that the chair, complete with castors, at the head of the table is the only one with a cushion!

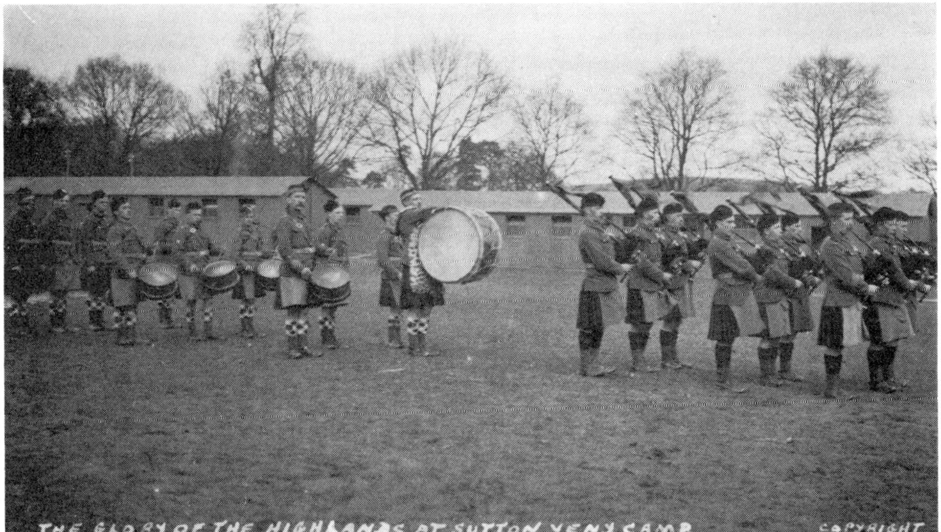

The photographer, A. Vowles, titled this picture for a postcard 'THE GLORY OF THE HIGHLANDS AT SUTTON VENY CAMP'. Jim, the sender, writing again to Netta, on 22 July 1915, noted 'This is an old photo of our band, taken last January . . . The weather we are getting down here is rotten but it makes no difference . . . wet or dry, parades go on as usual'.

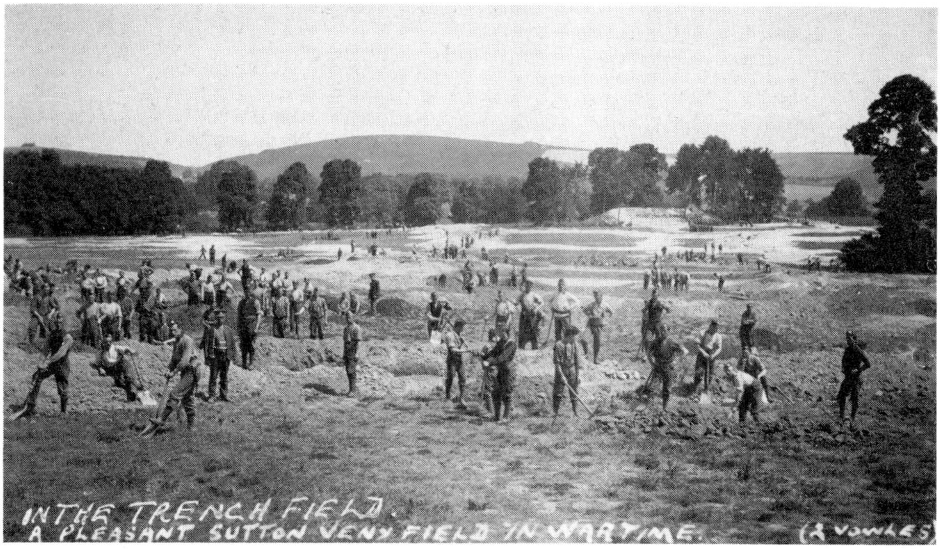

THESE SOLDIERS ARE PRACTISING TRENCH DIGGING at Sutton Veny Common in 1915, before going to France. Middle Hill (distant left), Scratchbury Camp (centre) and Cotley Hill (right) break the skyline and enable easy location of this scene. The picture looks north-east from the Five Ash Lane area. The line of trees, stretching across the middle of this picture, border Eastleigh Lane. Today the Warminster Bypass dissects the far end of this field, this side of the trees, running parallel with Eastleigh Lane.

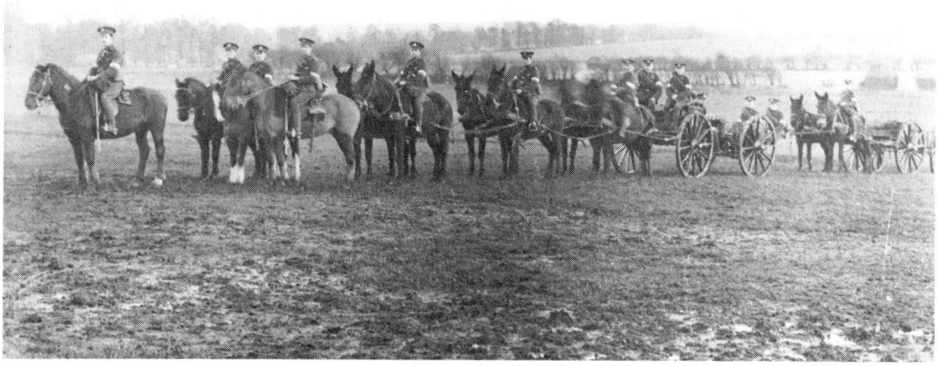

MULE TEAM WITH GUN AND AMMUNITION WAGON at Sutton Veny during the First World War. This particular field is currently farmed by David Eyres (of North End Farm) and is situated south-west of what is now the Walnut Close residential estate in the village. The view looks south-east, down the Wylye Valley, with Haycombe Hill off the right of the picture. The spire of St John's Church can just be seen rising up behind the trees on the far left.

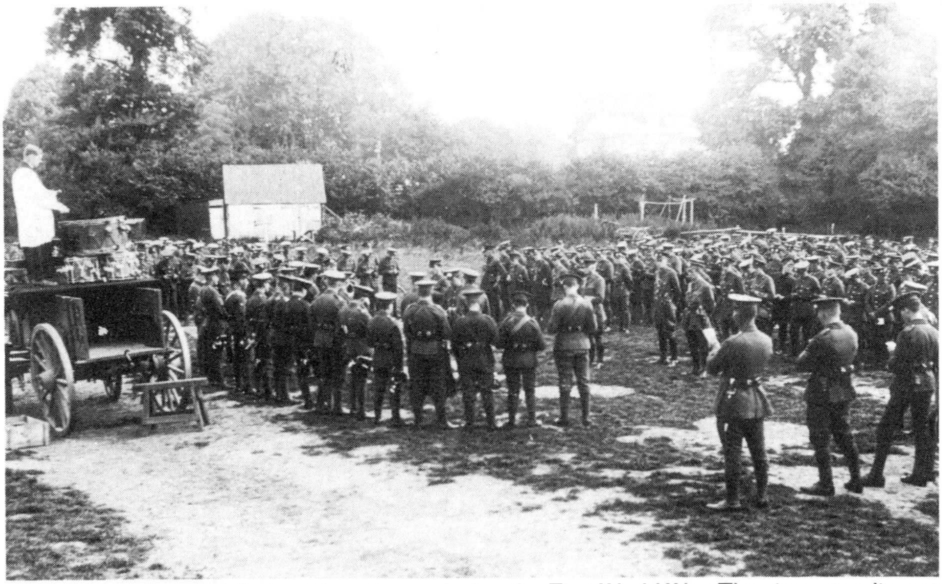

A DRUMHEAD SERVICE at Sutton Veny Camp during the First World War. The vicar, standing on the cart, behind the drum, preaches to the soldiers. The scene is near Greenhill House, which is situated in the distance behind the hedge in the background.

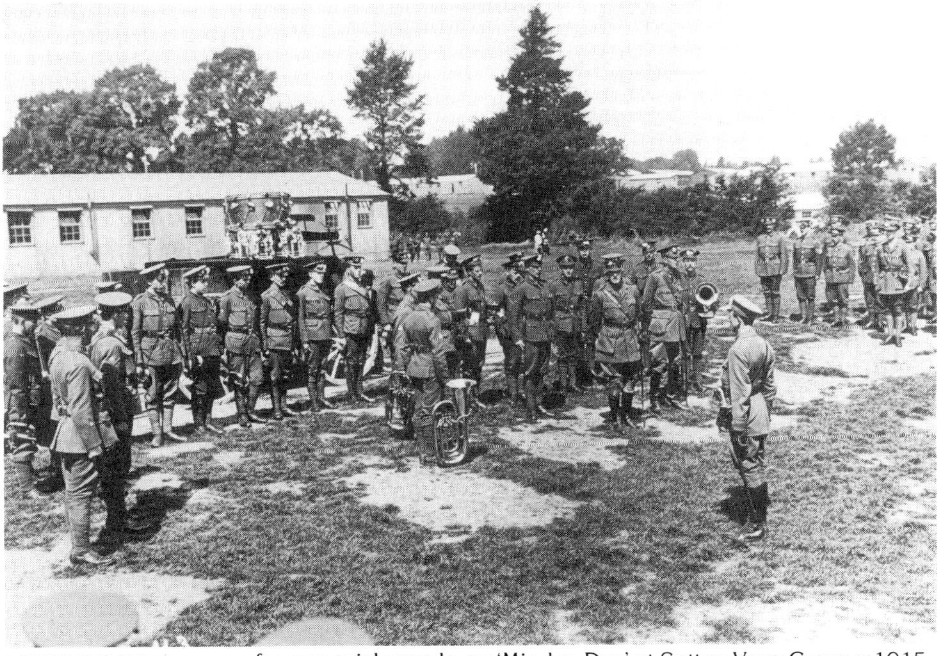

A MILITARY BAND prepares for a special parade on 'Minden Day' at Sutton Veny Camp c.1915.

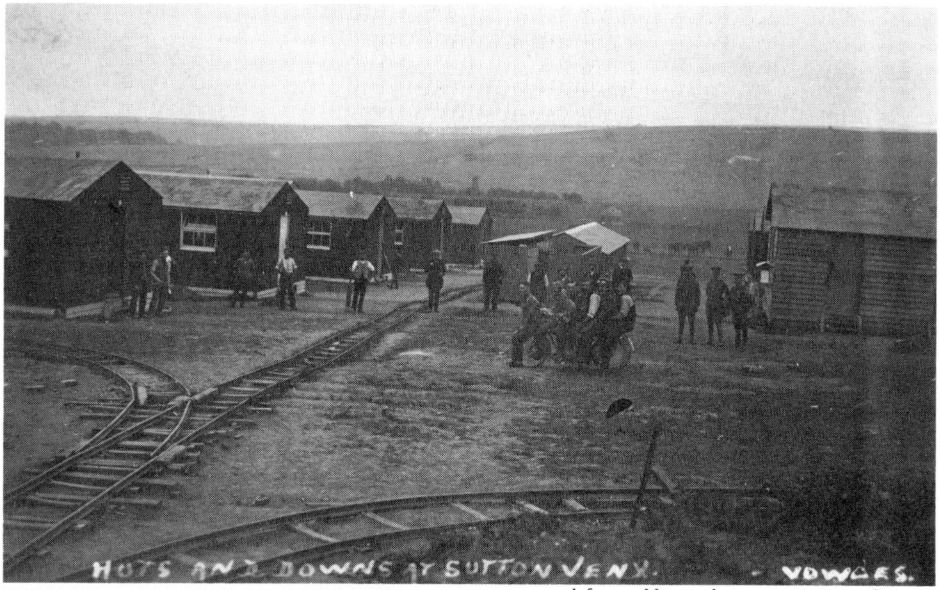

THREE AND A HALF MILES OF RAILWAY LINE was constructed from Heytesbury station to Sutton Veny Camp and it ended by branching three separate ways south of the Deverill Road. The men seen here (civilians employed with hut construction) are having a moment of fun for the camera. Six are riding on one bicycle, while the man standing immediately left of the middle rails is holding a cricket bat. The building in the centre looks like a washroom, showers and toilets. The hill in the background is the eastern end of Cow Down.

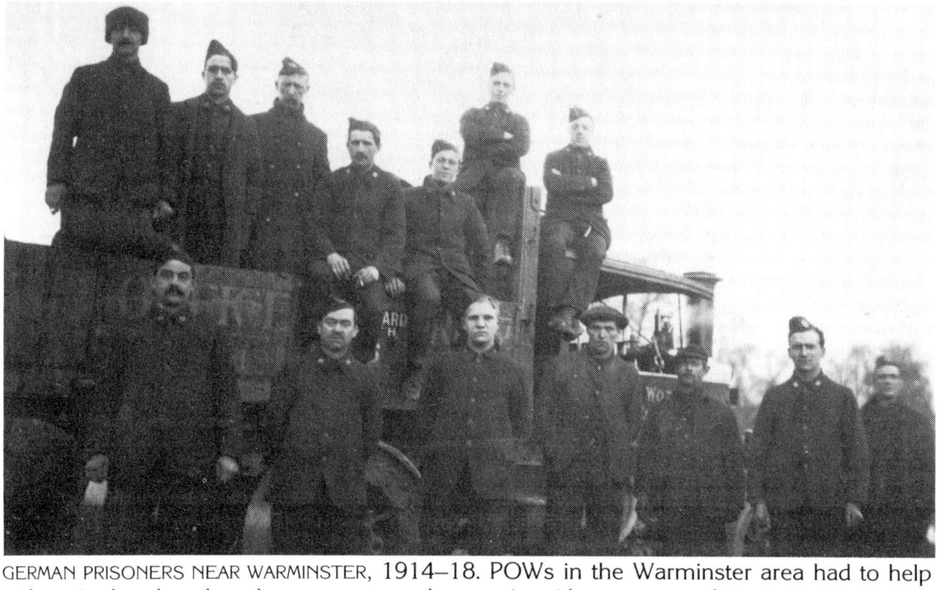

GERMAN PRISONERS NEAR WARMINSTER, 1914–18. POWs in the Warminster area had to help with agricultural work and some were made to assist with sewerage schemes in the villages.

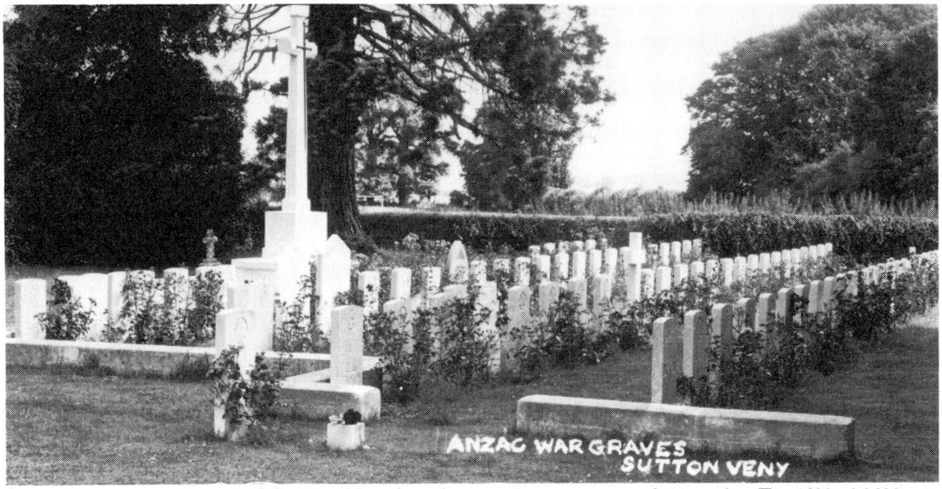

A PERMANENT REMINDER of Sutton Veny's role as a troop camp during the First World War is the Anzac War Cemetery, in St John's churchyard. Buried here are 169 soldiers who died of a mass flu epidemic that swept through the area in 1918. Other Anzac troops are buried at Codford and Baverstock. 39 German prisoners buried at St John's, Sutton Veny, were transferred in 1963 to a German war cemetery in Staffordshire.

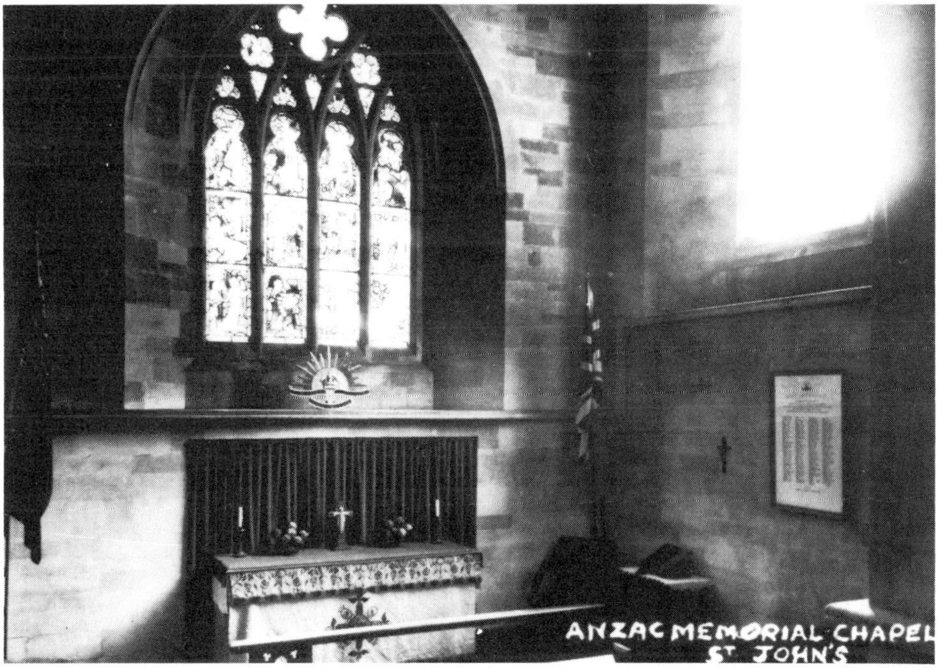

THE ANZAC MEMORIAL CHAPEL inside St John's Church at Sutton Veny. An Anzac Day Service is held annually. Nearly 90,000 Anzac troops were in camp or passed through the Wylye Valley during the First World War.

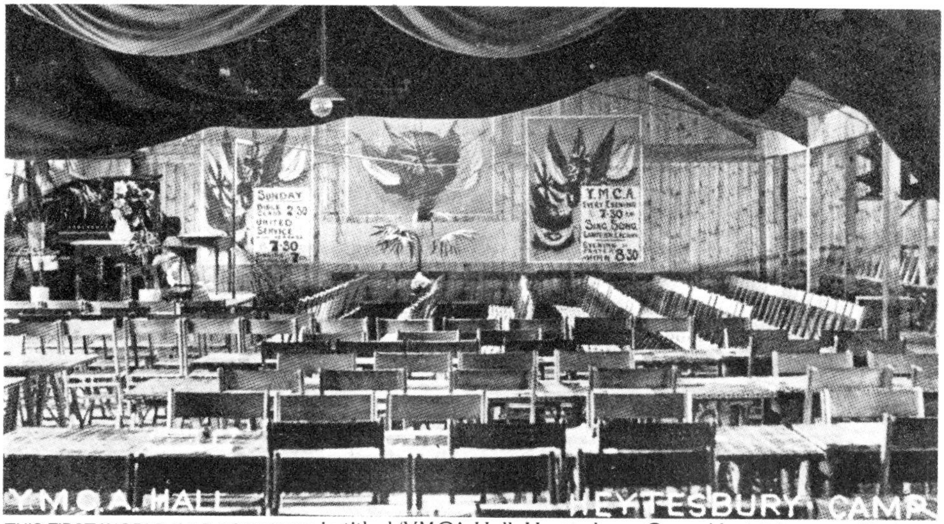

THIS FIRST WORLD WAR POSTCARD is titled 'YMCA Hall, Heytesbury Camp' but it is more likely to be at nearby Knook. A piano can be seen on the left and posters showing the Union Jack, Australian, Canadian and other flags, decorate the walls. The notices advertise Sunday bible classes at 2.30 p.m., followed by a United Service at 7.30 p.m. A sing-song is advertised for every evening, except Sundays, at 7.30 p.m., followed by a lantern lecture. Evening prayers are at 8.30 p.m.

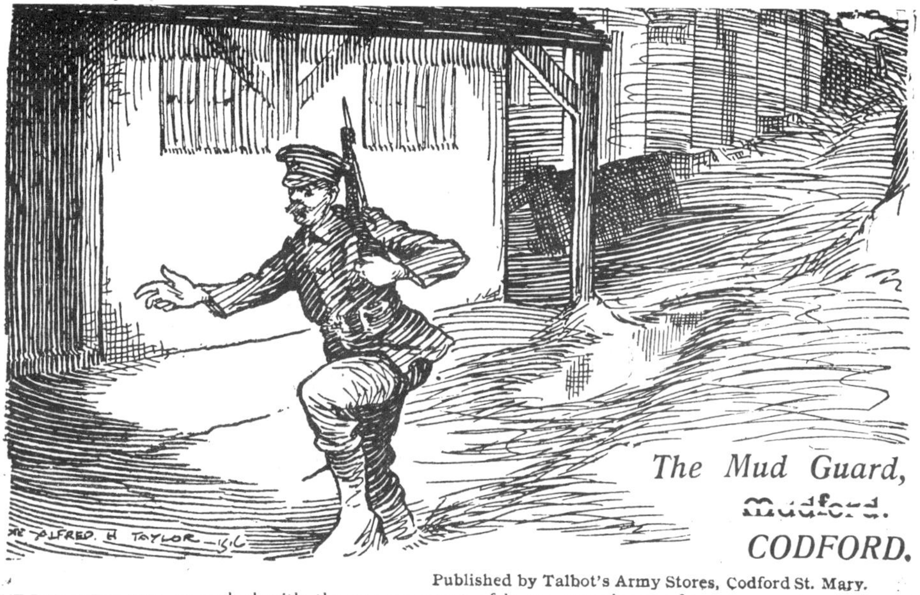

THE BAD WEATHER, coupled with the movement of large numbers of troops and supplies at Codford, turned it into a muddy place. So much so that the place was nicknamed 'Codford-on-the-Mud' or 'Mudford'. This postcard, of a drawing by Alfred H. Taylor, portrays 'The Mud Guard at Mudford/Codford' *c*.1916.

W.H. MALCOLM, the Trowbridge and Codford tobacconist, published several 'humorous' postcards showing what life was like for the thousands of poor souls in camp at Codford. Here are just a few – the pictures and the words say it all. This one is titled 'Abandon All Hope Ye Who Enter Here'. Troops are shown marching towards the camp and a church surrounded by tombstones. A chicken wanders aimlessly, a man's head lays on the ground, a soldier has a medicine chest on the back of his bike and a sign says 'Danger, Mud'. The scene is watched over by an angel with a magic wand!

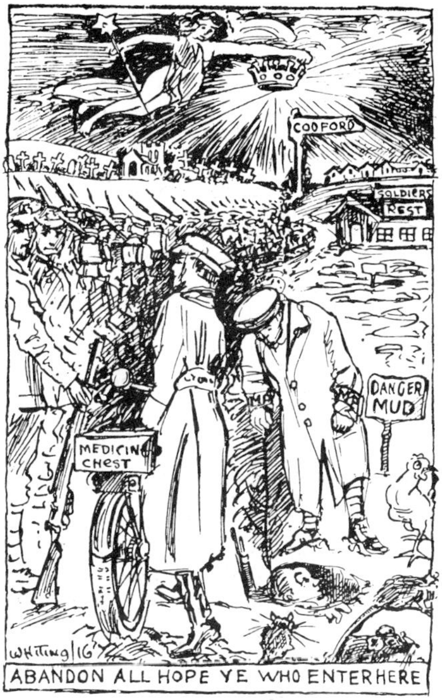

Published by W. H. Malcolm, Tobacconist, Trowbridge and Codford.

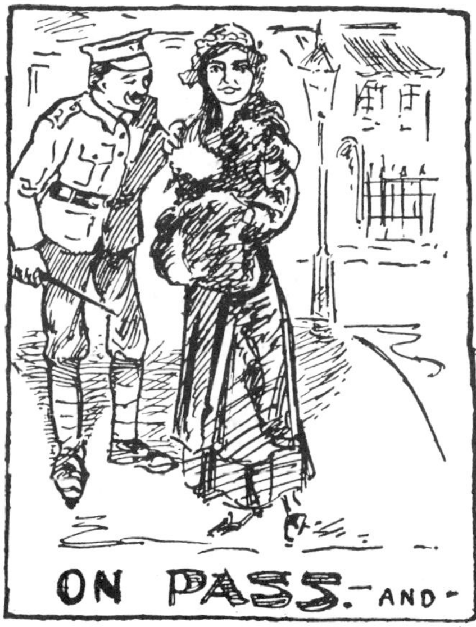

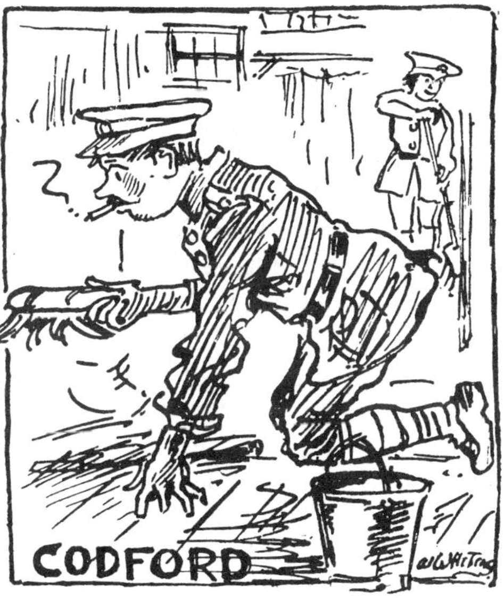

'ON PASS' shows a soldier walking with his sweetheart along a city street; meanwhile at 'Codford' it's forever scrubbing mud off the floors inside the huts. How the men must have dreamed of being on leave from that muddy camp!

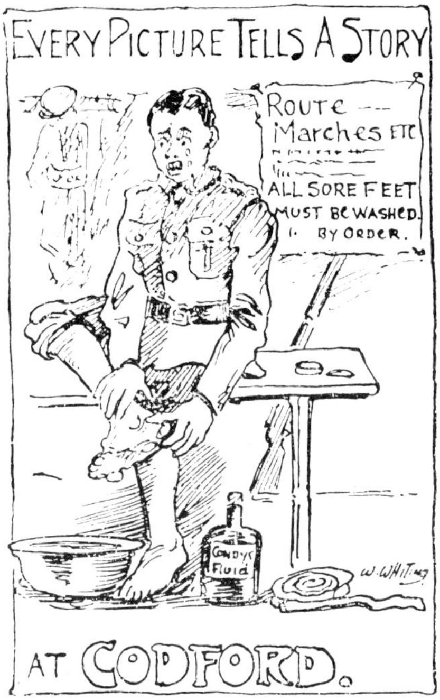

Published by W. H. Malcolm, Tobacconist, Trowbridge and Codford.

'EVERY PICTURE TELLS A STORY'. This one certainly does! Route marches obviously left their toll, and a sign declares that 'All sore feet must be washed by order'. A bowl of water, a bottle of Conby's Fluid and a roll of bandages did little to ease the pain – this poor devil is crying large tear-drops down his cheeks!

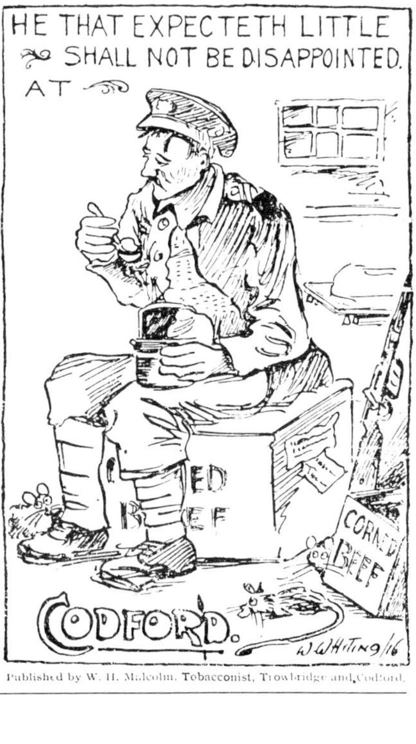

Published by W. H. Malcolm, Tobacconist, Trowbridge and Codford.

'HE THAT EXPECTETH LITTLE SHALL NOT BE DISAPPOINTED AT CODFORD'. Judging by the size of the crate of corned beef this soldier is sitting on, it would appear that corned beef was the only ration available, day after day. Things must have been bad for the rats too – the artist has drawn three of them, thin specimens at that, looking on, waiting for something better to drop.

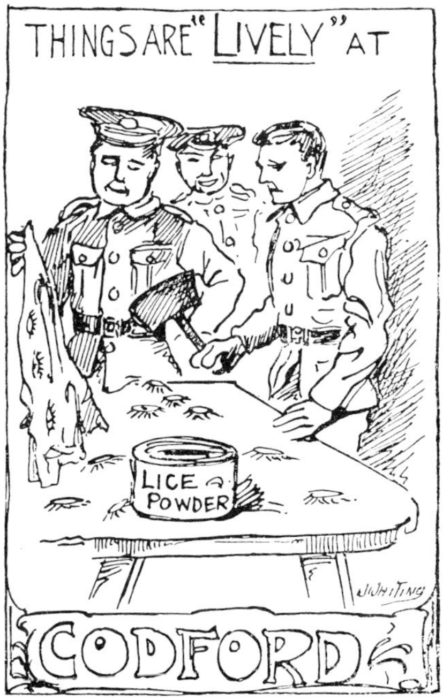

Published by W. H. Malcolm, Tobacconist, Trowbridge and Codford.

'THINGS ARE "LIVELY" AT CODFORD'. According to this picture, there were other livestock in camp – lice! A soldier shakes the little creatures from his tunic, so that a colleague can deal with the problem. It looks like they have forsaken the tin of lice powder, and are using a hammer to get rid of their unwanted guests.

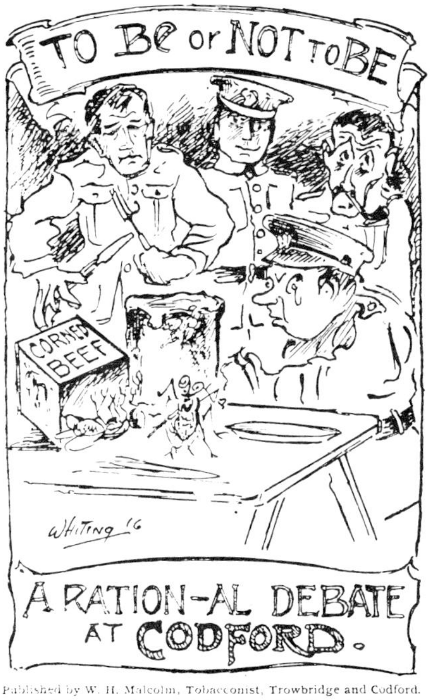

Published by W. H. Malcolm, Tobacconist, Trowbridge and Codford.

'TO BE OR NOT TO BE, A RATION-AL DEBATE AT CODFORD'. These soldiers are portrayed as having to choose between corned beef again, or the huge flys that co-exist in the camp. Some choice of ration! No wonder the men have glum faces.

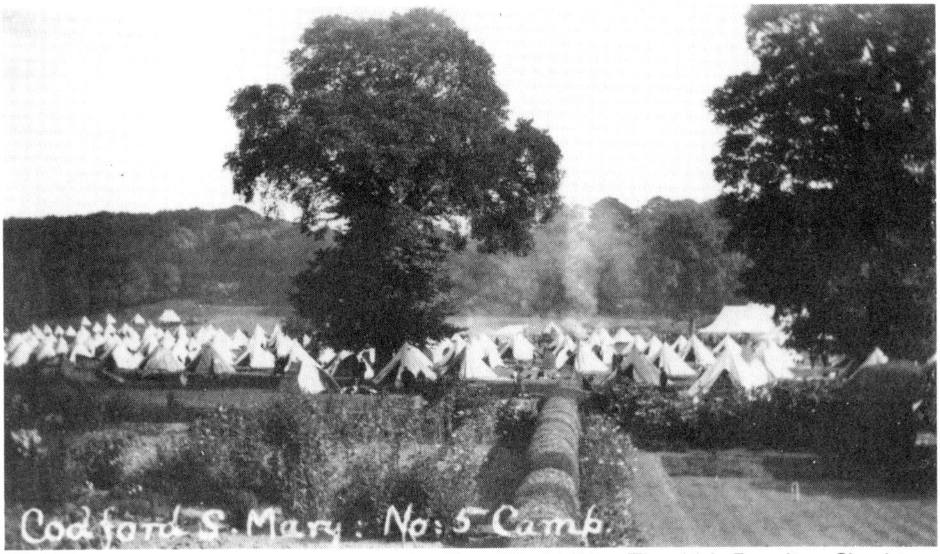

NO. 5 CAMP AT CODFORD ST MARY during the First World War. The 11th Battalion Cheshires were stationed under canvas here. Each camp at Codford 'housed' one battalion, which numbered 1,100 men.

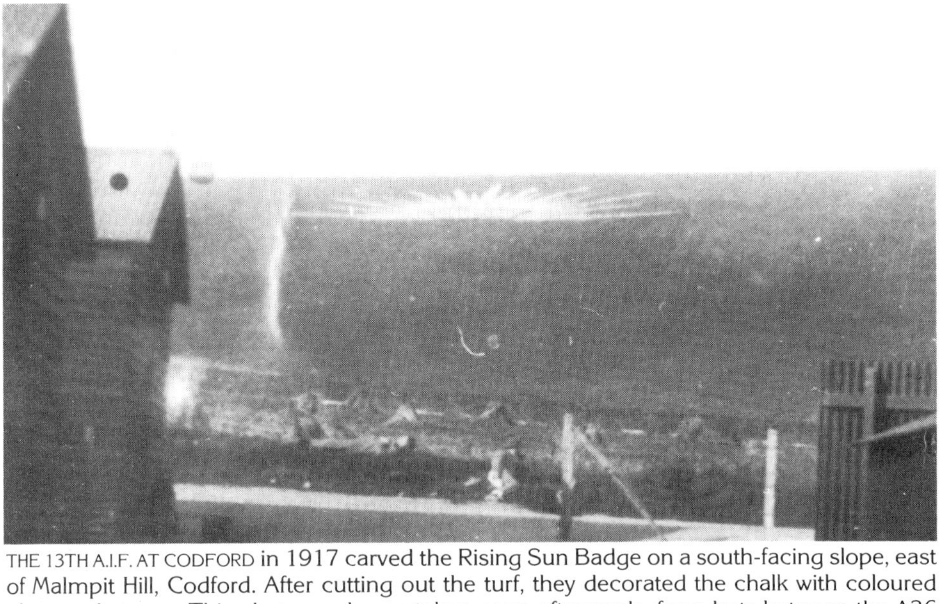

THE 13TH A.I.F. AT CODFORD in 1917 carved the Rising Sun Badge on a south-facing slope, east of Malmpit Hill, Codford. After cutting out the turf, they decorated the chalk with coloured glass and stones. This photograph was taken soon afterwards, from huts between the A36 road and the River Wylye below. The badge is 175ft. in length and 150ft. high. The soldiers nicknamed the slope 'Misery Hill', on account of having to run up and down it with packs on their backs, as part of their training. The badge can still be seen today. Since the First World War it has been periodically maintained by Boy Scouts and Venture Scouts.

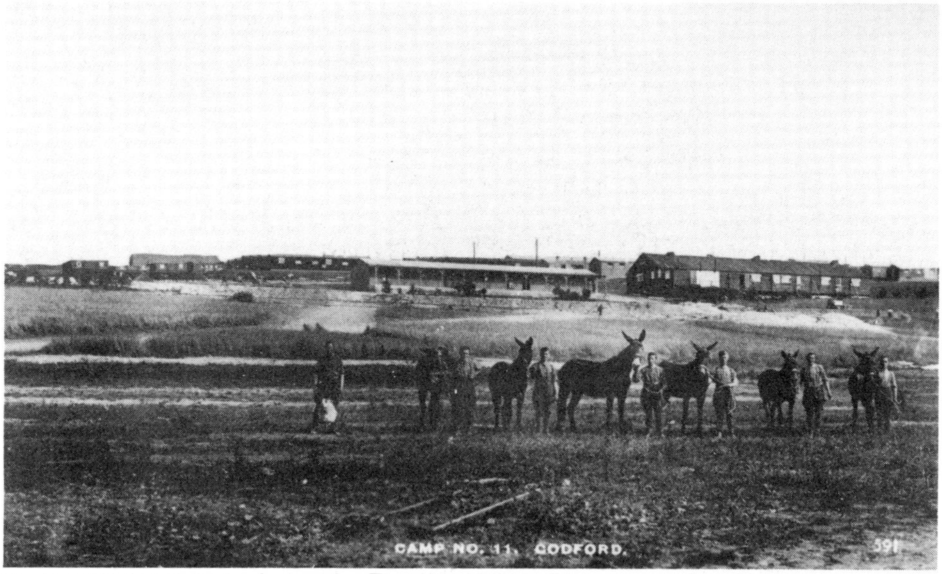

NO. 11 CAMP AT CODFORD during the First World War. The men are handling mules and the soldier on the left has a sheep trapped between his legs. The buildings in the background are serviced by a railway line, from Codford station. Close inspection reveals trucks of the Great Western and London Midland railways, stationary on the tracks.

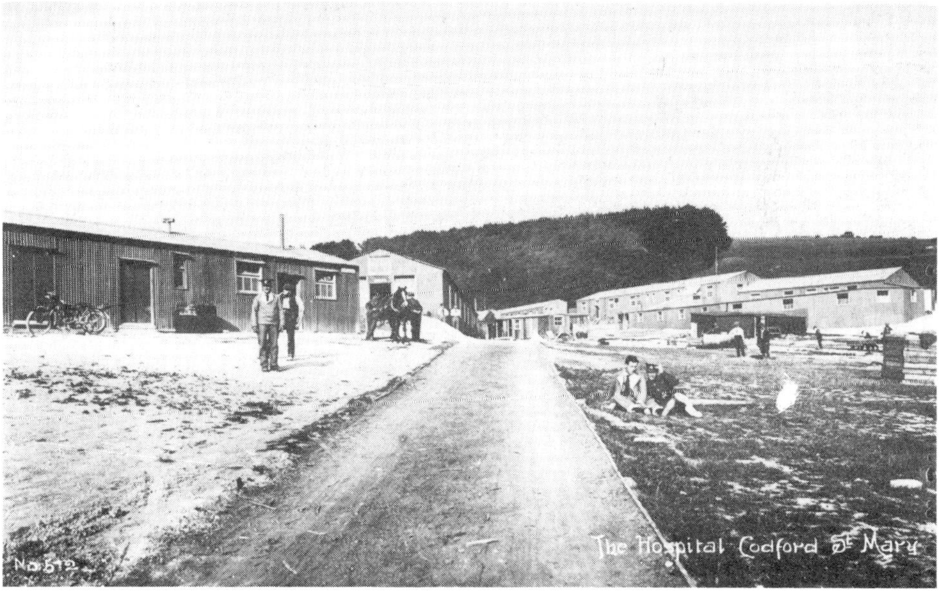

THERE WERE 15 CAMPS AT CODFORD, plus a Hospital Camp. This photograph shows the Camp Hospital at Codford St Mary, c.1916.

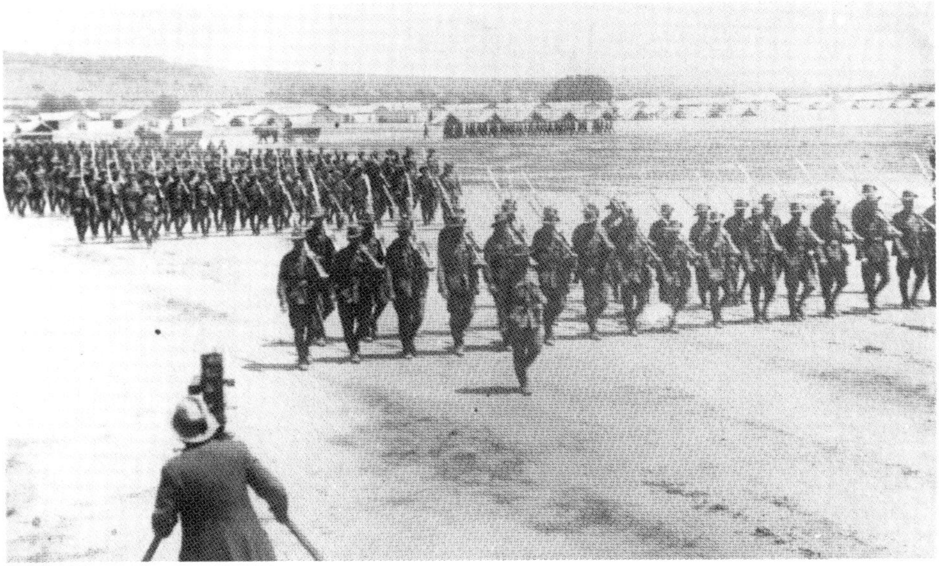

THESE ANZAC TROOPS, on parade at Codford, are being filmed by what looks like a movie camera. Perhaps this scene of our gallant comrades was shown in local and other cinemas to boost morale?

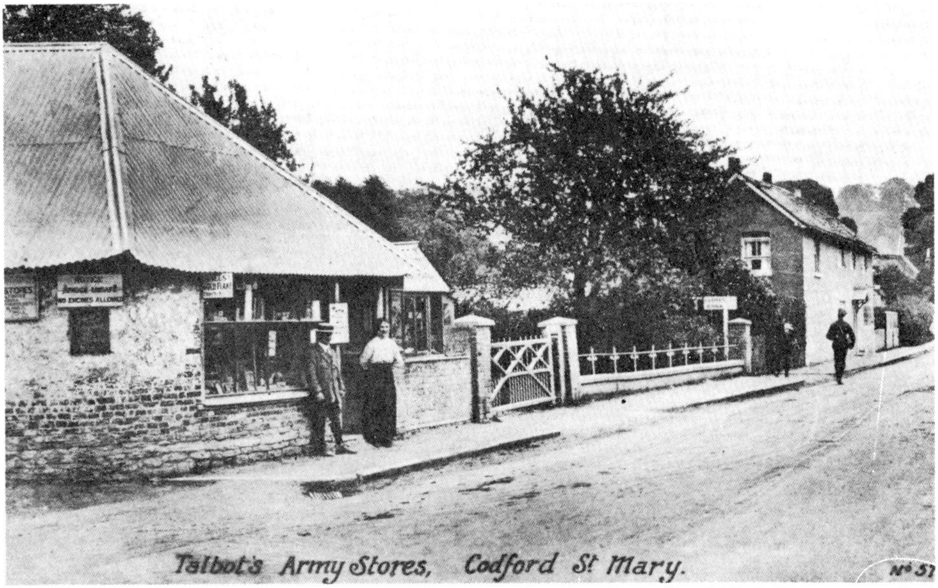

TALBOT'S ARMY STORES, at the junction of Chitterne Road with Codford High Street, supplied everything from postcards and tobacco to gloves and handkerchiefs. A sign on the wall declares the bridge at Codford as unsafe and forbids engines upon it. The house further down the street (the home of Mr Paul Cole today) is seen here when it was in use as Lloyds Bank.

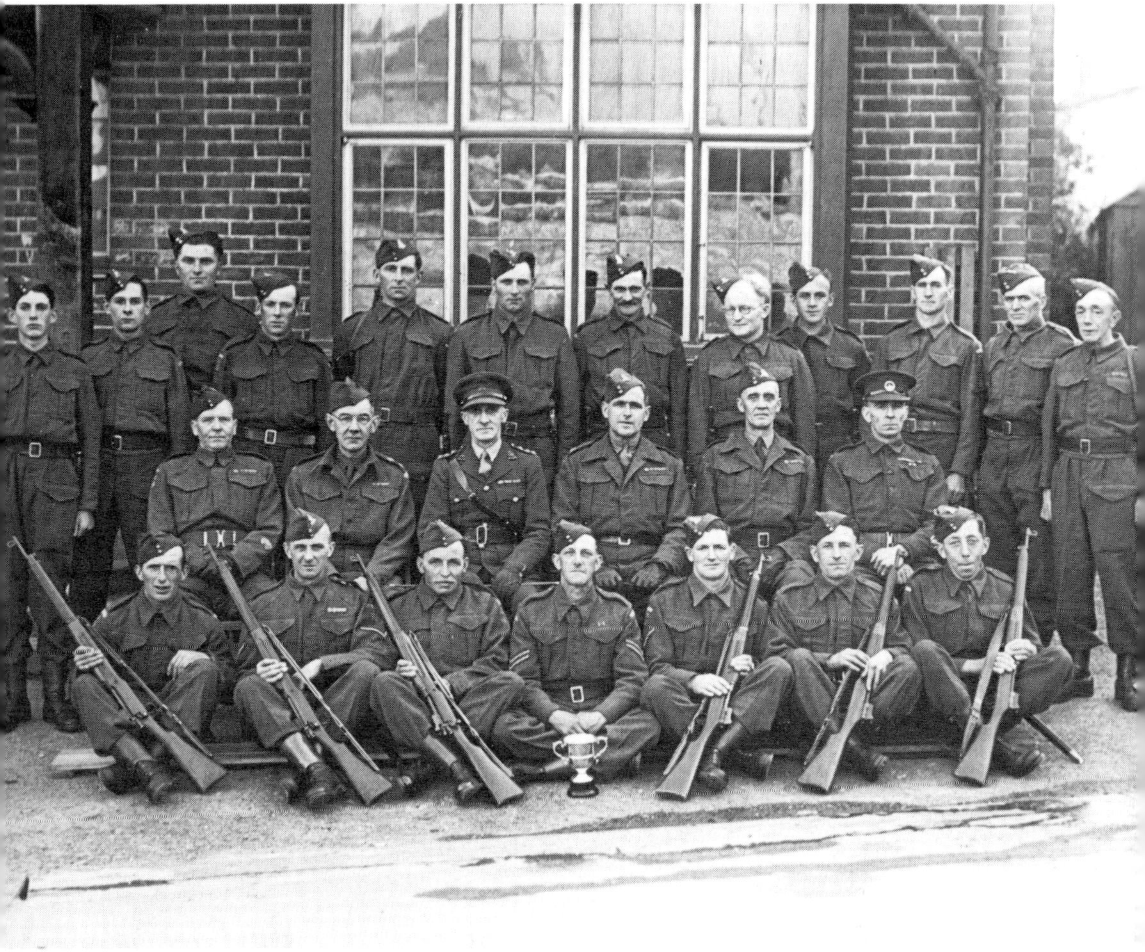

SUTTON VENY PLATOON OF THE HOME GUARD pictured outside the Woolpack in the village, c.1943/44. Among the familiar faces here are Pete Fuller, George Beach, Jack Eyres, Percy Banbury, Albert Eyres, Harold Long, Bobby Clark, Jim Mitchell, George Franklin, Mr Harris, Howard Cant, Bill Snelgrove, Fred Curtis, Lofty Everett, RSM Thomson (regular), John Everett, Henry Smith, Howard Beach, Albert Down, Len Sims, Jack Payne, Vic Coward and Percy Eyres.

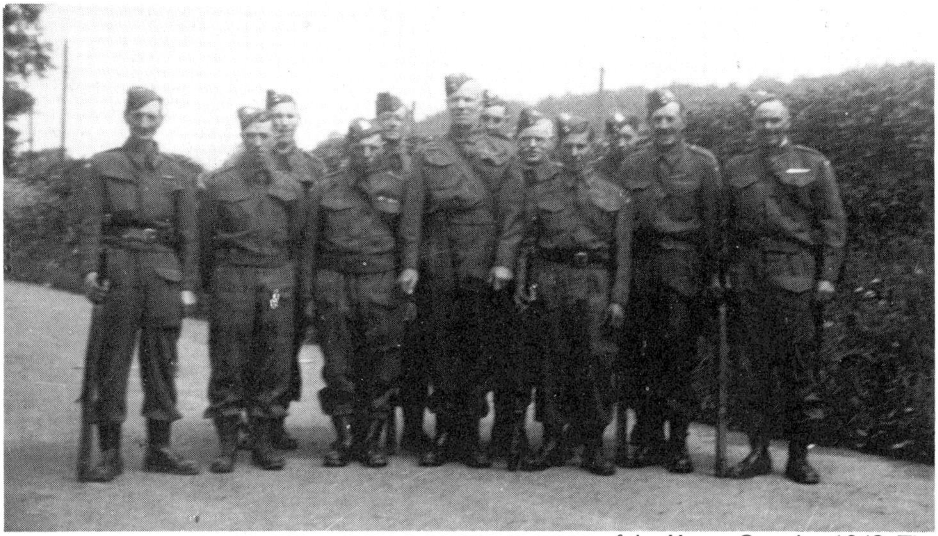

SOME OF THE MEMBERS OF UPTON LOVELL & CORTON PLATOON of the Home Guard, *c.*1943. The platoon, made up of men mostly from the local farming community, included Reg Blake, Alec Trollope, Bob Ball, Billy Day, Mr Gurney, Albert Trollope, Mr Witt, Leslie Bourne, Mr Pottow, Jack Sharp, Bill Bailey, Sgt. Polden, Commander Jeans, David Smith, Joe Day, Arthur Powell, Frank Poolman, Henry Paulter, Sonny Grant, Bill Morgan, Ben Williams, Tom Rugg, Reg Macklin, Fred Seviour, Mr Gage, Bill Smith and Mr Ruddick. They were often accompanied by Dennis Smith (who was in the Army Cadets). They met on alternate weeks at Upton Lovell Hall and Corton Hall. Some of the men mentioned above are in this picture.

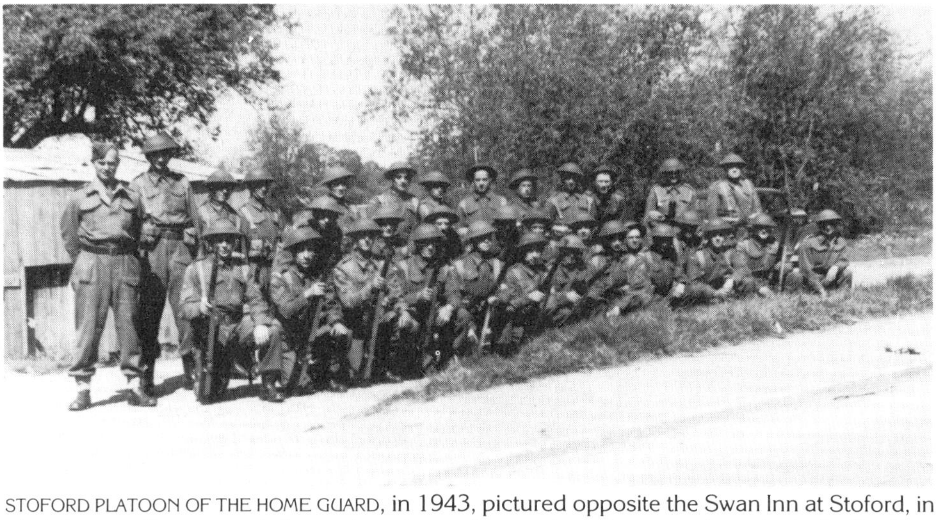

STOFORD PLATOON OF THE HOME GUARD, in 1943, pictured opposite the Swan Inn at Stoford, in what is now the car-park for pub patrons. Remembered names here include Geoffrey Parsons, Cyril Shergold, H.O. Edwards, Sidney Harrison, Percy Dewey, Stan Ransome, Sam Petty, Jim Harrison, Fred Shergold, Frank Jeans, Eric Mundy and Alec Moulding.

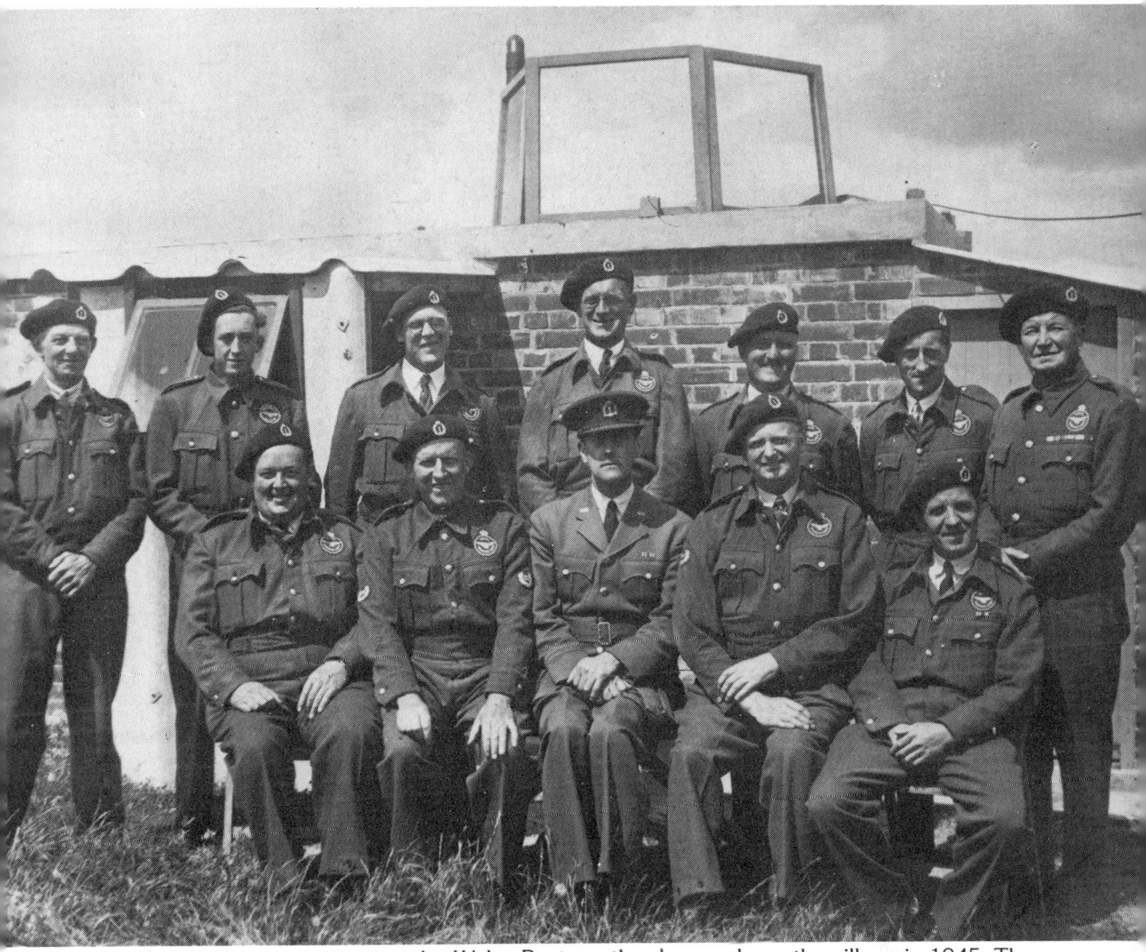

THE ROYAL OBSERVER CORPS at the Wylye Post, on the downs above the village in 1945. They were on look-out for enemy aircraft 24 hours-a-day. The men include Alan Vallis, Norman Barnard, Mr Barter, Jim Miles and Mr Griffiths.

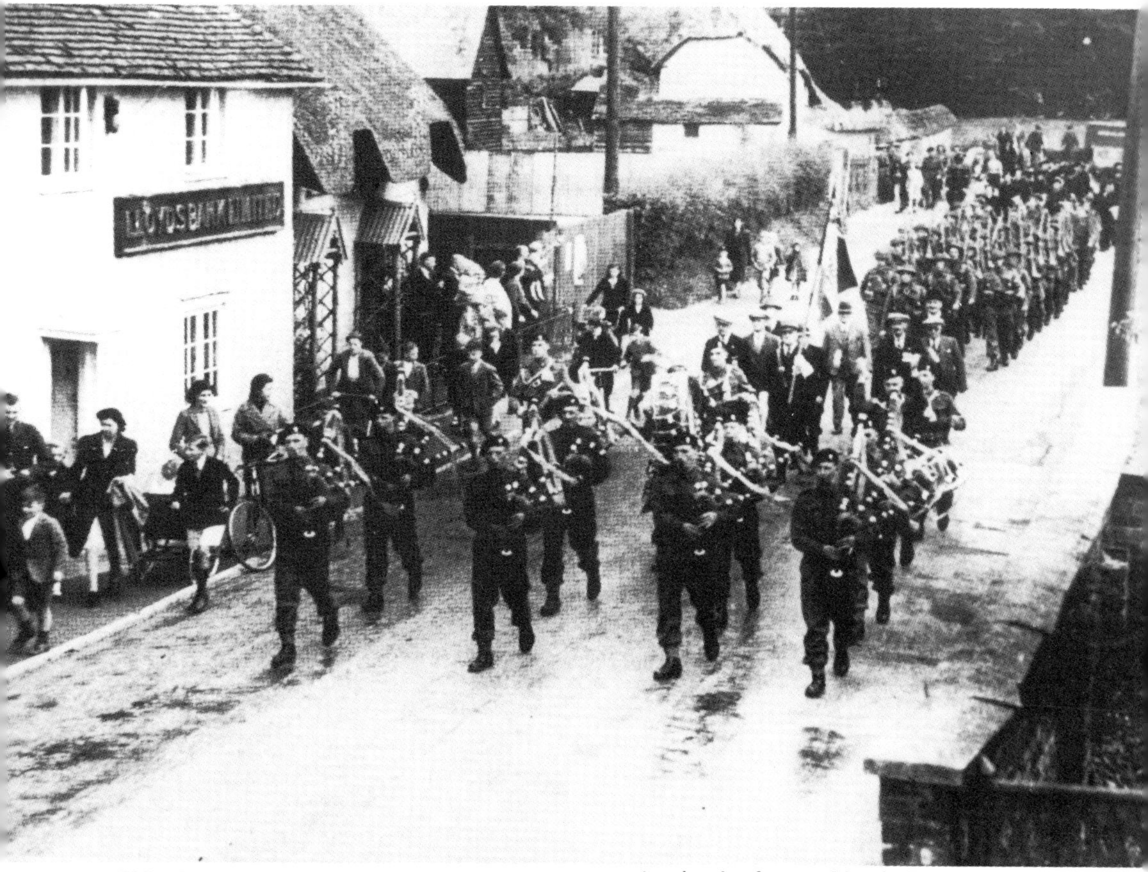

HERE WE SEE THE 11 NOVEMBER ARMISTICE PARADE passing by the former Lloyds Bank (now a private residence) at Codford High Street, after the Second World War. The British Legion Standard Bearer, almost centre of the picture, is Albert Sheppard, one of the gentlemen on the left of the picture is Bert Hart, on the right is Bill Feltham and the gentleman wearing the dark glasses, also on the right, is Charlie Bacon. Among the soldiers following behind are Ron Candy, Guy Wood, Howard Case, Percy Harvey, Maurice Carter, Frank Phelps, Ron Harvey, Maurice Ferber, Neville Rhodes, Ron Sutton, Arthur Bray and Walter Conduit.

SECTION SIX

When we were Young

They say your schooldays are the best years of your life. Tell that to any youngster currently at school and nearly all will find it hard to believe. And it is probably true for any schoolchild during any period of time. Years ago, for the working class, school was something to be endured and the majority of pupils could not wait to leave – anxious to get out to work and earn some money to boost their family's meagre income. There were few opportunities compared with today, but those who were fortunate to pass an exam went on to higher education, if funds allowed, and subsequently better prospects afterwards. The rest finished their schooling with no qualifications but made good in later life. 'Strict but fair' is how many senior citizens remember their teachers in retrospect. 'They had a job to do and what they taught us held us in good stead for our future lives' is another well-used sentence. Discipline and good manners were instilled from an early age and there was the cane and worse for those who begged to differ. Those who remember the cane tell me now that it did them no real harm and they are thankful for their upbringing in such fashion. It seems to them that society is lacking in discipline today and children have no respect for their elders. The three 'Rs', reading, writing and arithmetic, were the backbone of the curriculum, but there were also other subjects, like needlework for the girls and carpentry for the boys. For most, a school uniform was unheard of – it was everyday clothes and hobnail boots for both boys and girls to go to school in. Still, everyone was in the same boat and it was useless to complain to teachers or parents in any case. I have named as many children as could be identified in the photographs which follow. Those who are still alive will recognise themselves and their contemporaries, and I shall be pleased to hear from anyone who can put a few more names to faces for future reference.

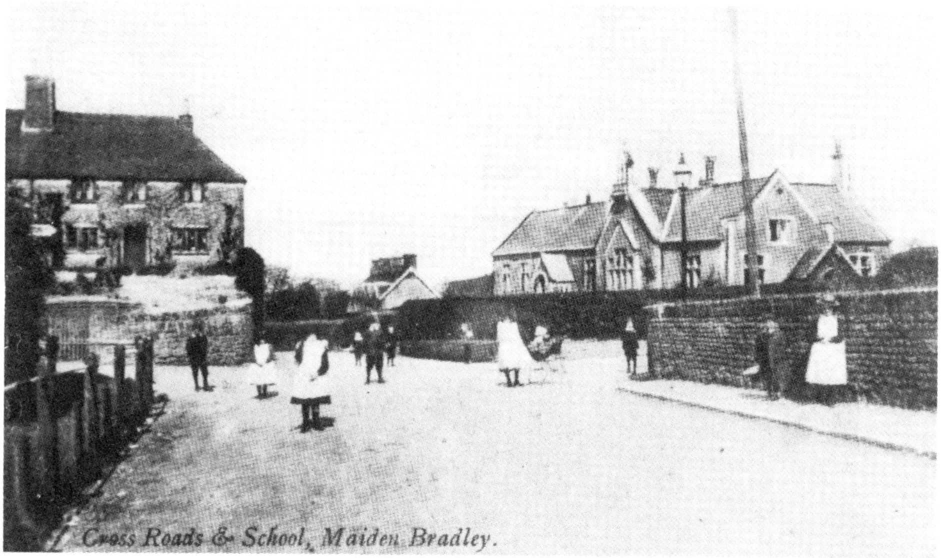

IT WOULD BE DANGEROUS FOR CHILDREN TO PLAY IN THE STREET at Maiden Bradley today, but there was little in the way of traffic at the turn of the century when this photograph was taken. The school at Maiden Bradley was enlarged and improved in 1888 at a cost of £310. It could take up to 162 children. During the early 1900s, when John Scanes was the master, the average attendance was 110.

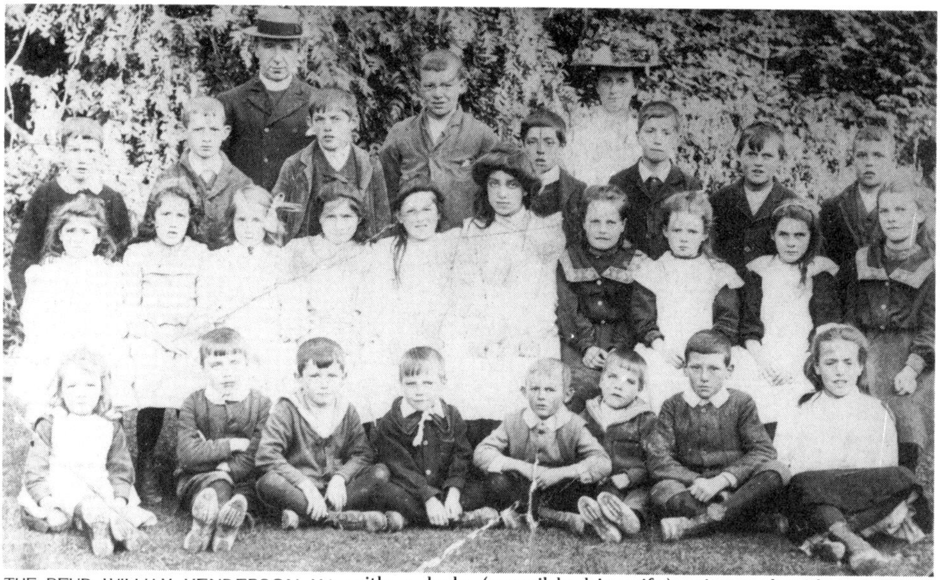

THE REVD WILLIAM HENDERSON MA with a lady (possibly his wife), pictured with pupils of Kingston Deverill Elementary School, *c*.1910. Notice the hobs in the soles of the boots worn by the boys and girls. The school, built in 1853, could accommodate up to 71 pupils. The schoolmaster (not in this picture) in 1910 was Mr A. Elliott.

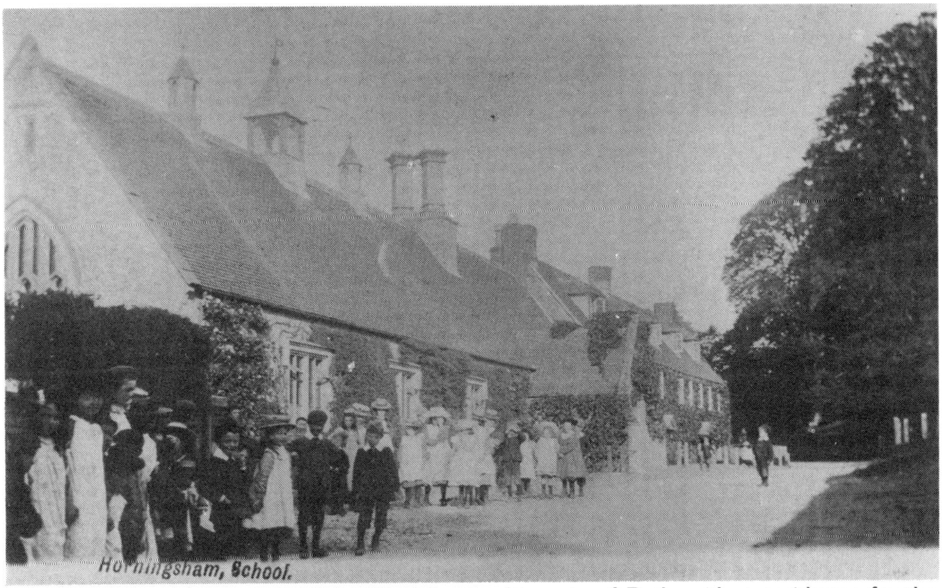

HORNINGSHAM SCHOOL was built in 1844 by the Marquis of Bath, with a residence for the master. The school was enlarged in 1892 and could take up to 200 children. Thomas Welbourn was the master when this picture was taken just after the turn of the century. The average attendance at that time was 130.

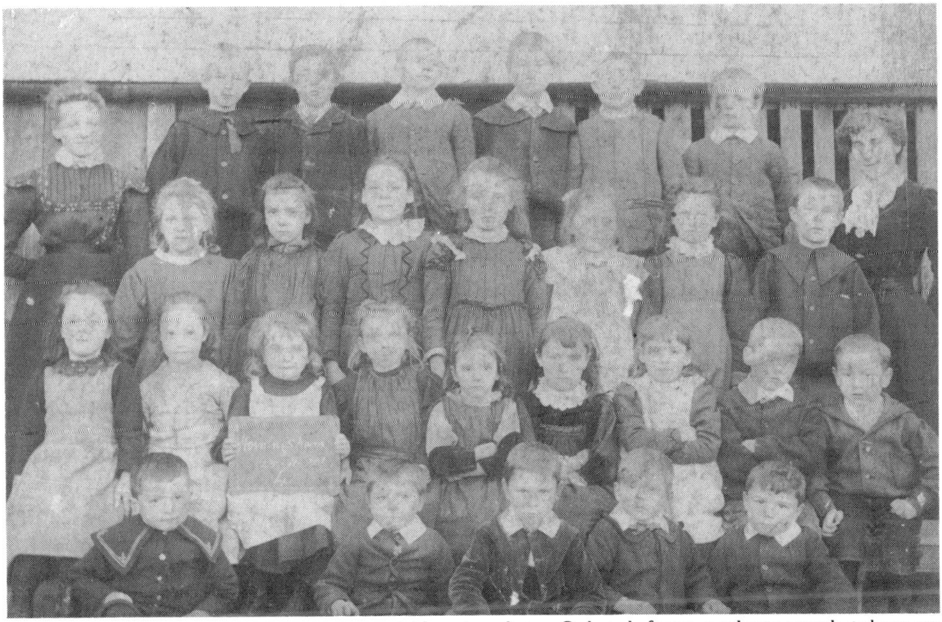

TWO TEACHERS AND A CLASS OF PUPILS at Horningsham School, from a photograph taken on 25 November 1901.

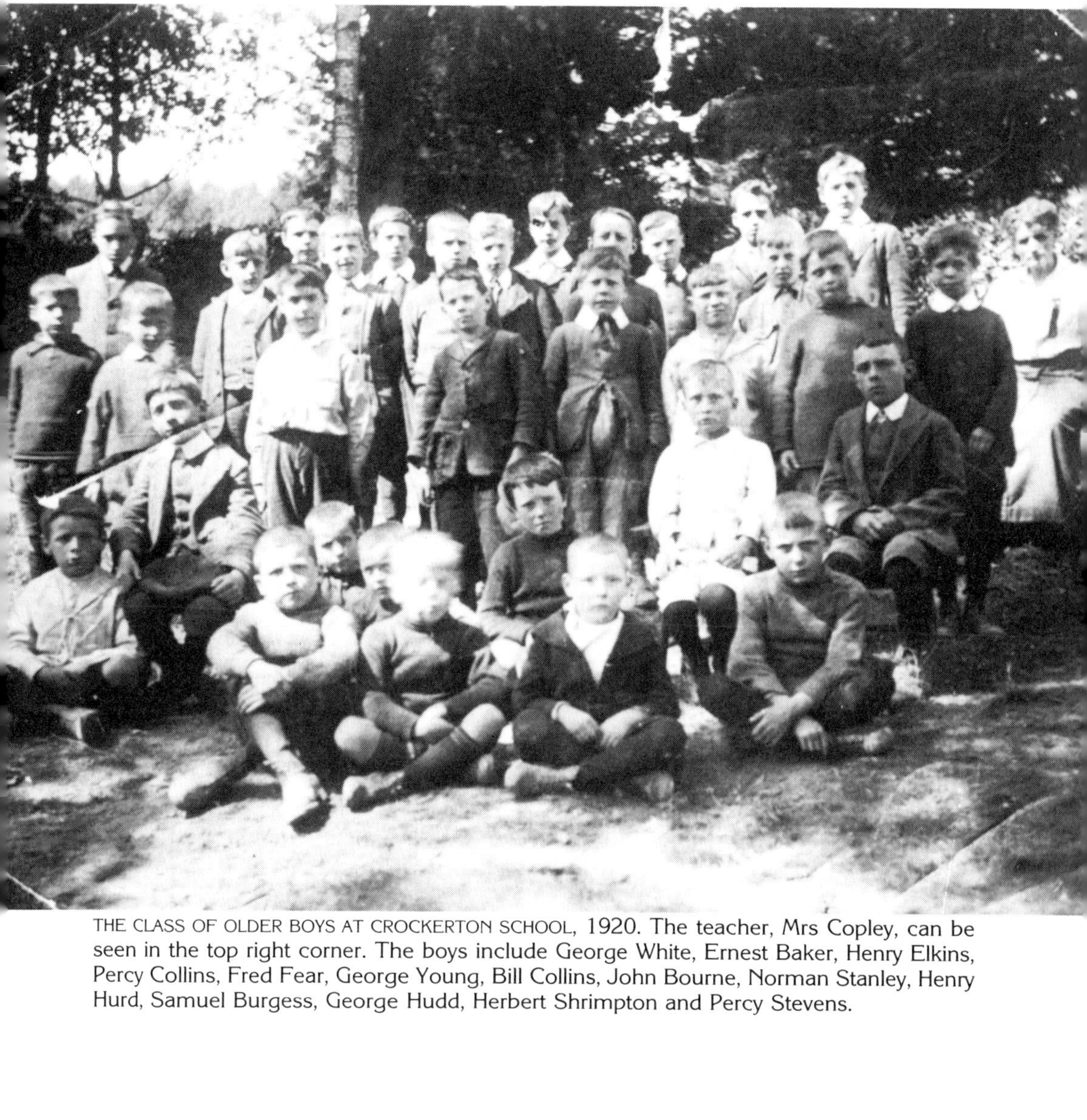

THE CLASS OF OLDER BOYS AT CROCKERTON SCHOOL, 1920. The teacher, Mrs Copley, can be seen in the top right corner. The boys include George White, Ernest Baker, Henry Elkins, Percy Collins, Fred Fear, George Young, Bill Collins, John Bourne, Norman Stanley, Henry Hurd, Samuel Burgess, George Hudd, Herbert Shrimpton and Percy Stevens.

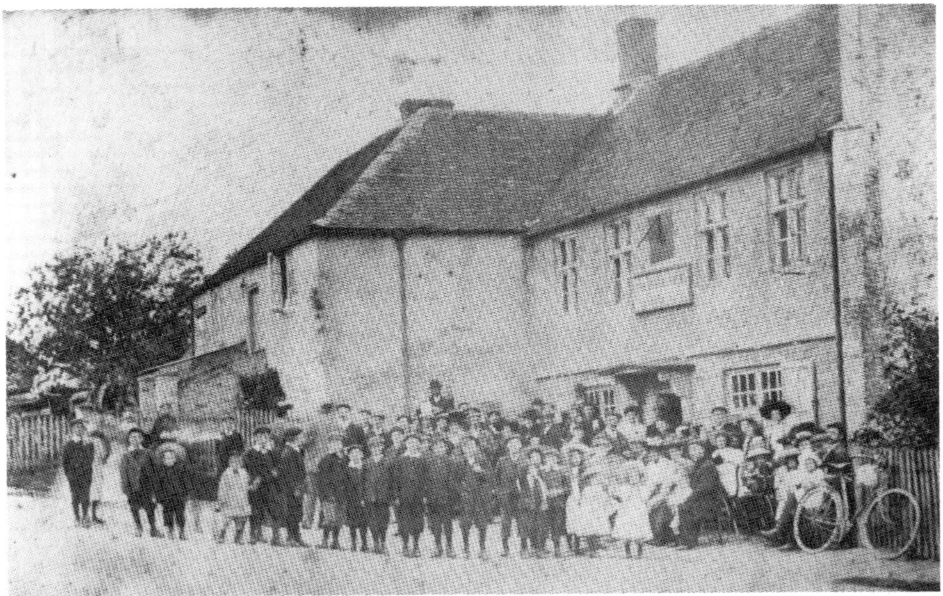

PARENTS AND CHILDREN assembled outside the Bath Arms, Crockerton, for the annual Crockerton Revels, c.1906.

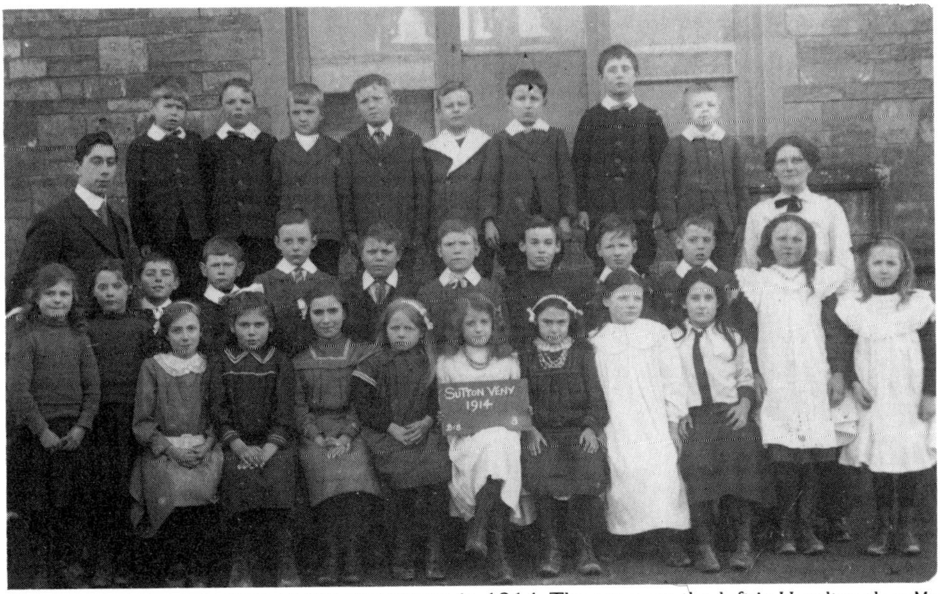

TEACHERS AND PUPILS AT SUTTON VENY SCHOOL in 1914. The man on the left is Headteacher Mr Thomas. The lady on the right is possibly Miss Smart. Because of the food shortages during the First World War, some of the older pupils were excused attendance by the Board of Education to assist with agricultural work.

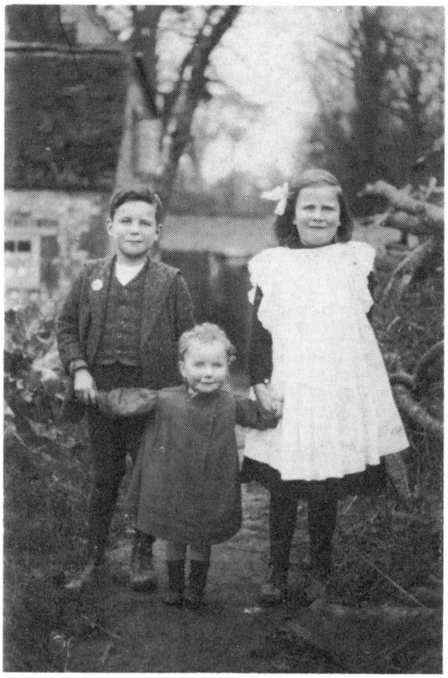

URIAH WHITE with his sisters, Emma and Pheobe, at Heytesbury, *c.*1910.

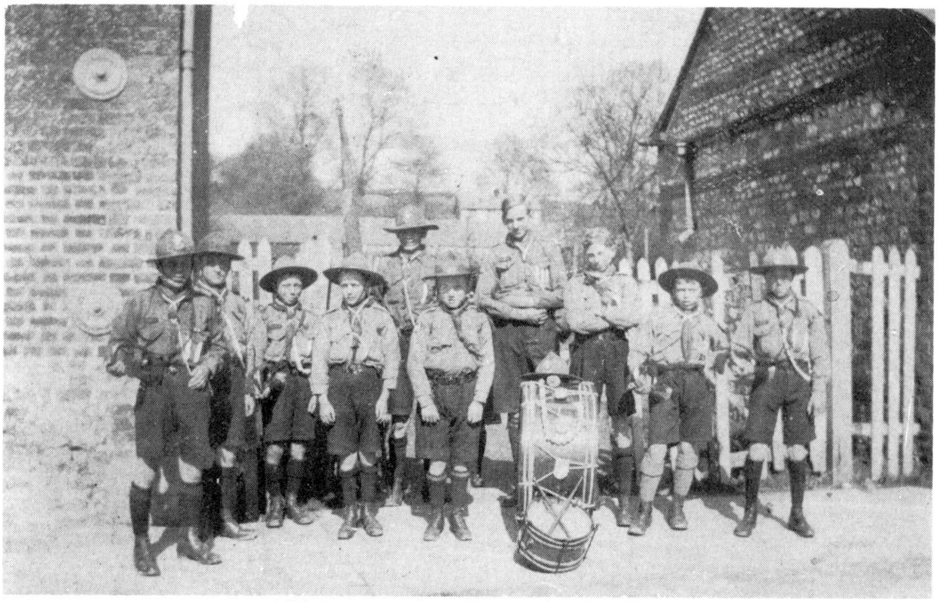

HEYTESBURY BOY SCOUTS, *c.*1914, pictured on the north side of the High Street, opposite the church. The Scouts include Uriah White, on the far left, holding the bugle, and Chris Kitley, the Scoutmaster, fourth from right, behind the drums.

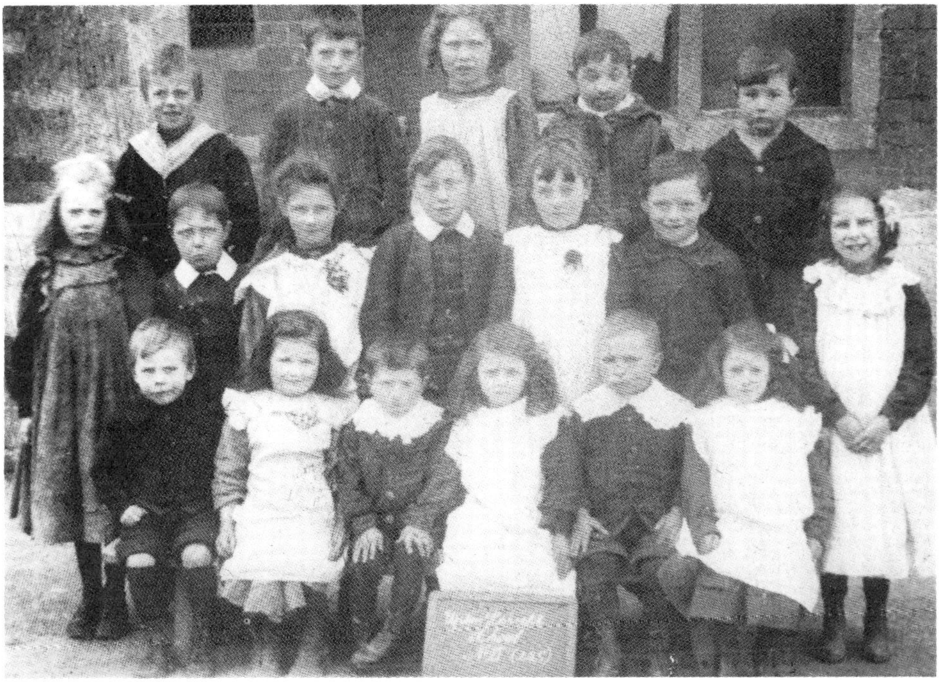

CHILDREN AT UPTON LOVELL SCHOOL, c.1912. The girl standing in the centre of the back row is Lily Dredge.

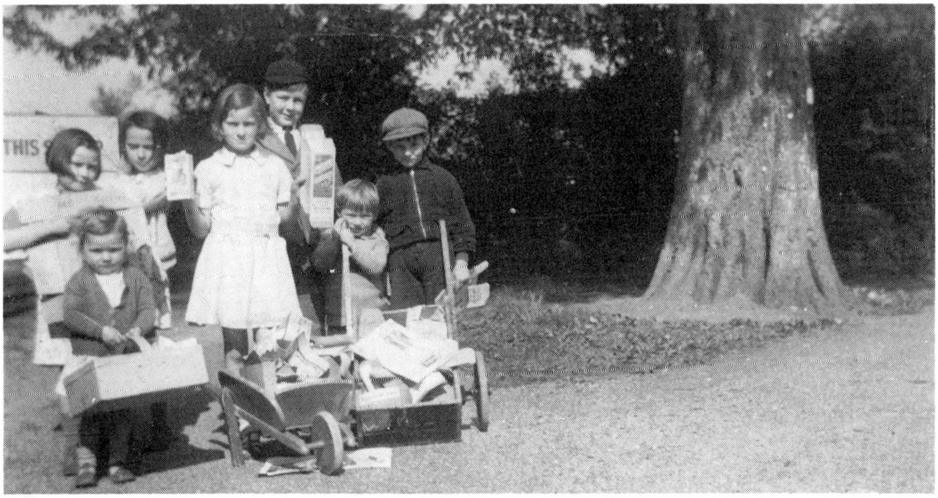

HERE WE SEE SOME OF THE CHILDREN OF UPTON LOVELL, c.1941/42, next to the chestnut tree in the village, where many happy childhood hours were spent. The children collected waste paper every Saturday morning during wartime as their part towards the war effort. Pictured here are Valerie Macklin, Jean Feltham, Jean Butler, Norman Gage, Ted Day, Ena Macklin and Bob Parkins.

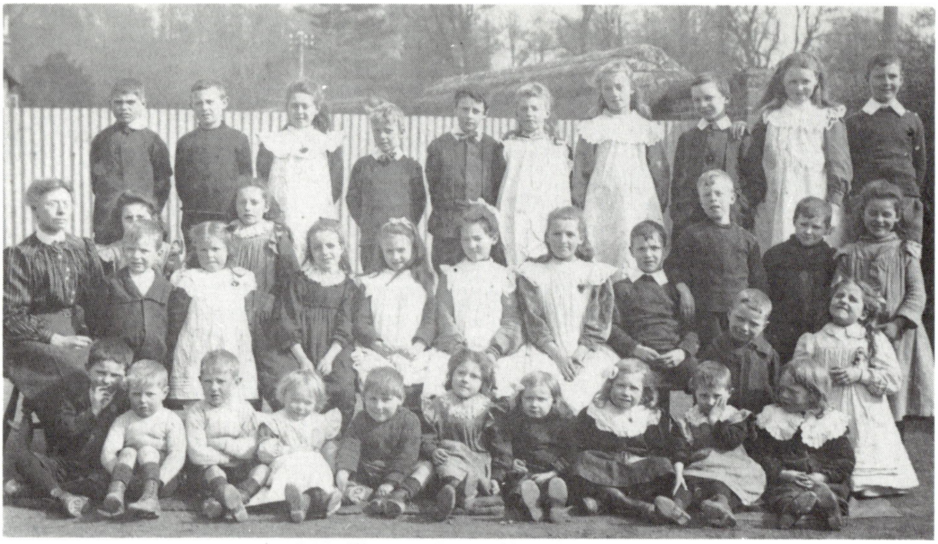

CODFORD ST MARY'S SCHOOL, 1912. The teacher is Miss Weston and the pupils, seen here, are Eddie Ford, May Conduit, George Fleming, George Tucker, Lily Blake, Walter Fleming, Amy Sanders, Barney Matthews, Laura Matthews, H. Bowden, Dorothy Roskelly, Ethel Moon, Amy James, Horace Matthews, Cooper, Grace James, John James, Nora Mizen, Renee Whale, Lily Whale, Turner and Freda Mizen.

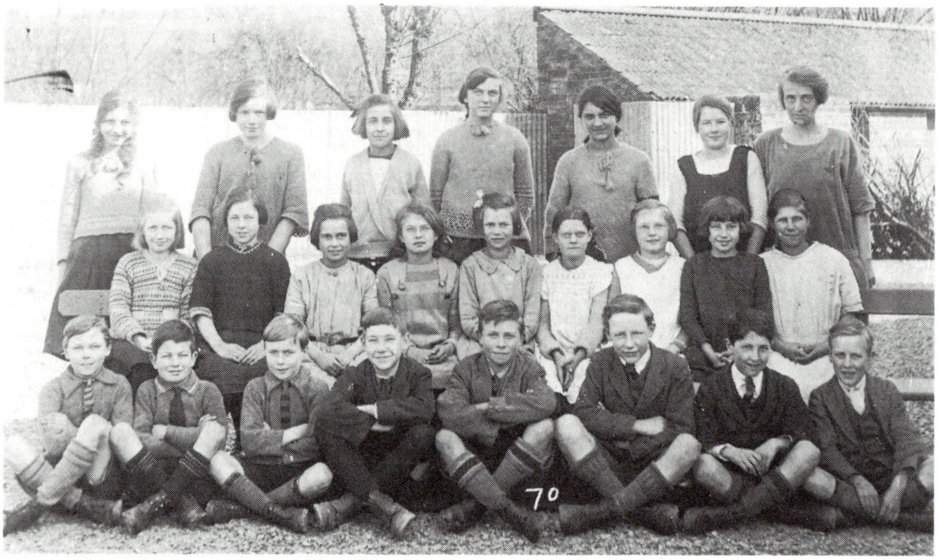

CODFORD ST MARY'S SCHOOL, 1924. The teacher is Miss Scull and the pupils, pictured here, include Kathleen Rogers, Mary Stone, Kitty Bevis, Charlotte Boulter, Dorothy Thomas, Gwen Vane, Evelyn Carpenter, Gwen Davis, Francis Earney, Janice Poolman, Gertie Day, Major Whale, George Fry, Hedley Spiller, Willie Cooper, Kenneth Green, Ronald Churchill and Oswald Grant.

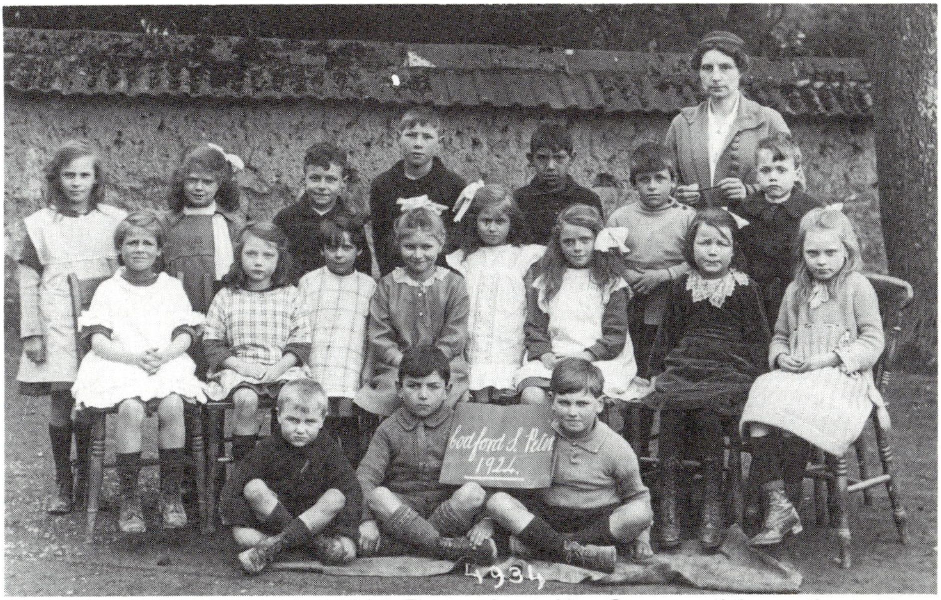

CODFORD ST PETER'S SCHOOL, late 1924. The teacher is Miss Cooper and the pupils seen here include Bridget Grant, Dorothy Davis, Teddy James, Ron Scard, George Thomas, Paul Cole, Jo Imber, Doreen Cole, Rose James, Gwen Cole, Thyra Tokley, Rose Jeffries, Joyce Bell, Mary Goodenough, Charlotte Imber, Bert Whatley, Malcolm Davis and Charlie Cull.

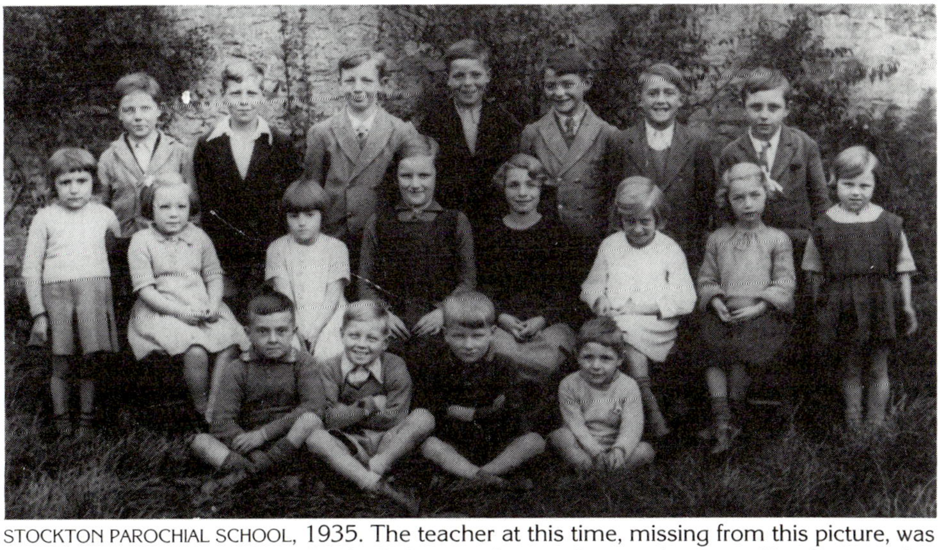

STOCKTON PAROCHIAL SCHOOL, 1935. The teacher at this time, missing from this picture, was Miss Bosworth who lived at Codford. Among the pupils seen here are Alan Bennet, Jim Goodenough, John Fawcett, Stan Moaby, Arthur Gilbert, Norman Barnard, Audrey Pearce, Edna Jebb, Iris Potter, Joan Nash, Chrissie Potter, Doreen Goodenough, Fred Nash, Ron Goodenough and Jack Webb.

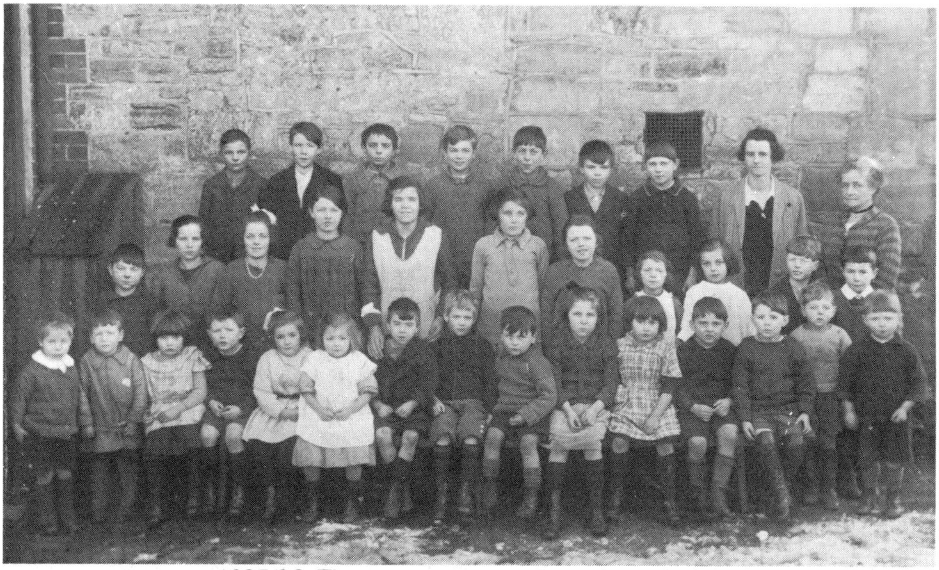

STOCKTON SCHOOL, *c*.1925/26. The two teachers at the right end of the back row are Miss Elworthy (left) and Miss Giles (right). The pupils include Ted Mills, George Pike, Stan Feltham, Jim Wootten, Reg Nash, Louis Pike, George Andrews, Billy Williams, Daisy Rhodes, Hilda Rhodes, Mabel Bennet, Vera Pike, Eddie Weston, Ivy Bennett, Violet Potter, Mary Gilbert, Jack Aldridge, Athol Rhodes, Jack Potter, Harold Bennett, Pearl Wootten, Nellie Gilbert, Syd Pike, Reg Cull, Painter, Willie Andrews, Norman Bartrum, Williams and Syd Andrews.

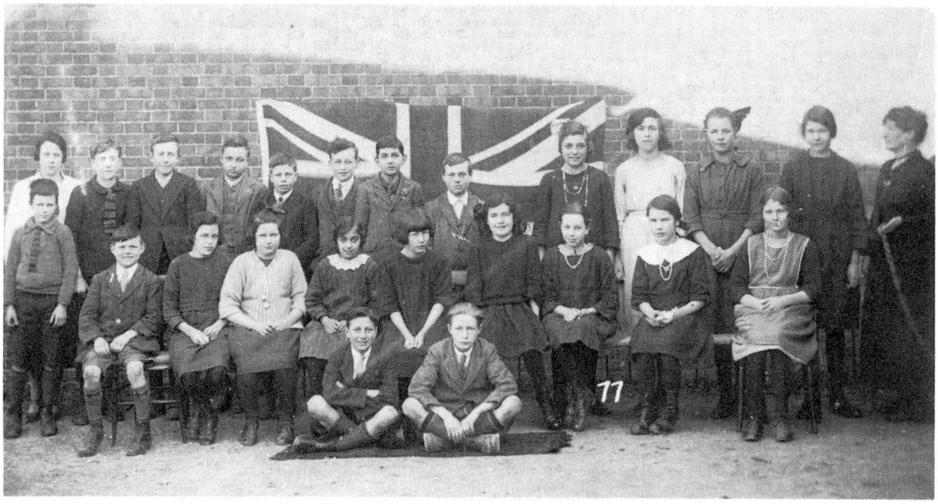

JUNIOR AND SENIOR CHILDREN at Wylye Church of England School, *c*.1925. The headmistress, Mrs Sobey, is on the far right, holding the chain of a dog. The assistant teacher, Miss Beaven, is on the far left, standing behind Ken Lovett. Norah Bull is sitting third from the right.

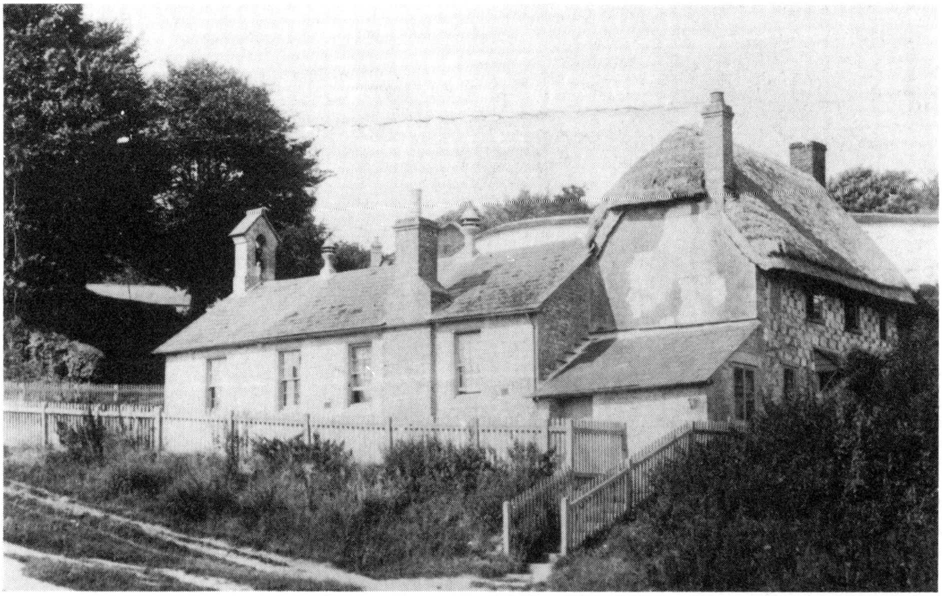

FISHERTON DE LA MERE SCHOOL, during the early 1900s. The school was built in 1865 for 60 children. It closed in 1921. Afterward these children had to go to the school in Wylye.

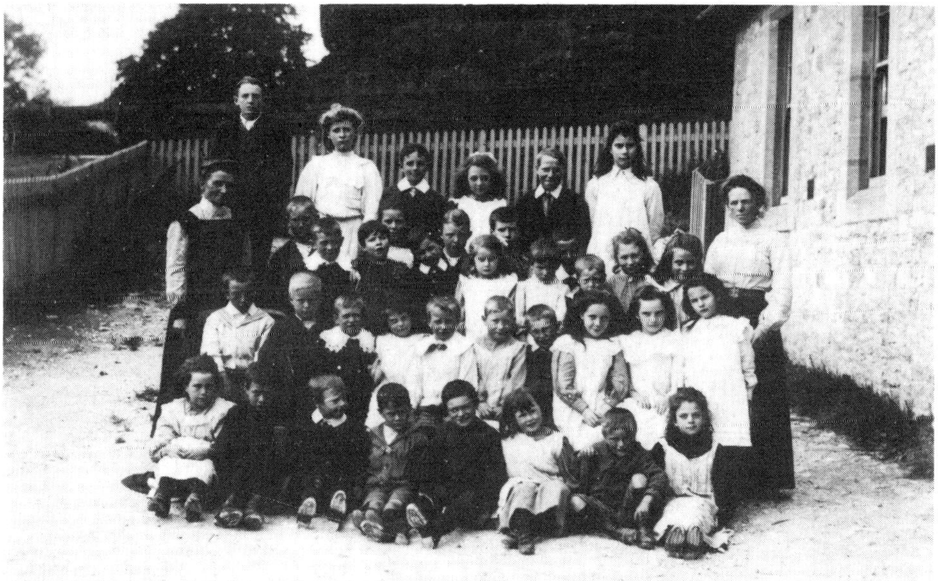

MISS CAROLINE HALL (schoolmistress) and her assistant teacher (name unknown) with pupils at Fisherton De La Mere School, during the early 1900s.

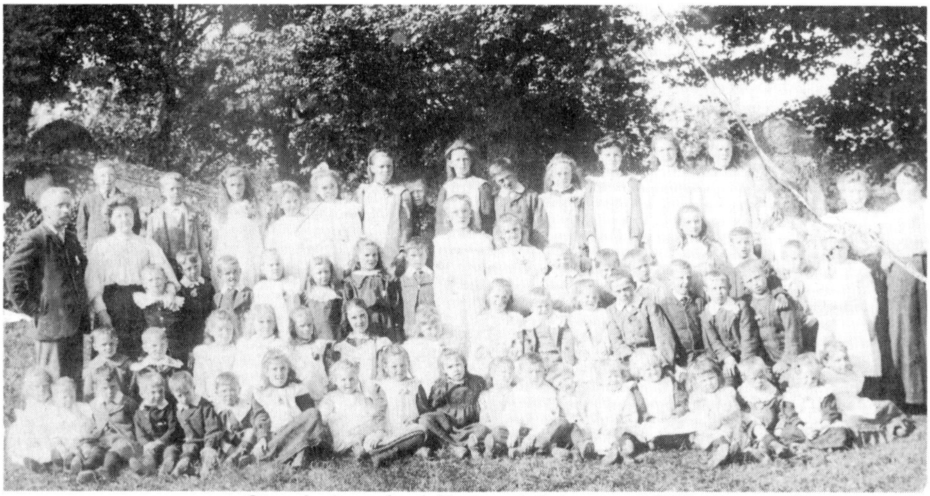

TEACHERS AND PUPILS at Steeple Langford National School, *c*.1900. George Hays was the master and Miss Margaret Davies was the schoolmistress. The school was built in 1860, complete with a master's house, and could accommodate 115 children. The average attendance in 1899 was 95.

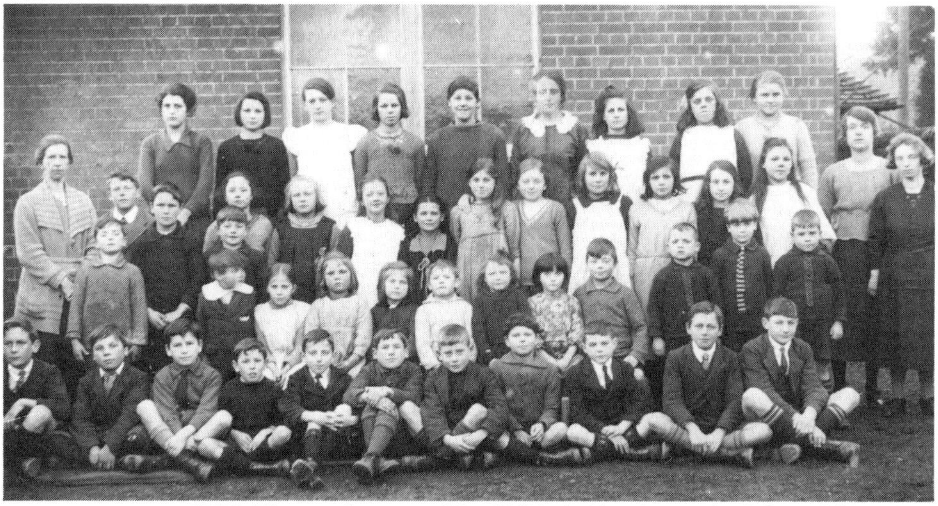

WISHFORD SCHOOL, 1923. The teachers are Miss Edith A. Mundy, on the left, and Miss Ada Scott (later Mrs L. King) and Miss C. Hand on the far right. The pupils from Great Wishford and also South Newton include Gertie Dimmer, Maggie Mills, Betty Carter, Florrie Mills, Gladys Smith, Marjorie Gurd, Doris Bennett, Elsie Smith, Elsie Kerby, Frank Shergold, Bill Stone, Emily Harrison, Jessica Herbert, Bessie Shergold, Christine Mundy, Elsie Banfield, Nelly Joiner, Winnie Hibberd, Arthur Davison, Fred Shergold, Leslie Shergold, Jane Bryant, Violet Shergold, May Thorne, George Truckley, Bessie Black, Joan Smith, Derrick Davison, Lionel Kerley, Jimmy Wootton, Stanley Kerley, Mary Carter, Rosa Butler, Rosie Bough, Eddy Stone, Frank Stone, Eric Mundy, Frank Truckle, Leonard Bryant, Victor Lampard, Ted Kerley, Jo Bough, Leonard Rowe, Ted Smith and Bill Rowe.

SECTION SEVEN

The Sporting Life

Those who work hard usually play hard, and Wylye Valley residents were, and still are, no exception. To conclude this book I have put together some aspects of the sporting life in the Wylye Valley during the first half of the twentieth century. I need say little here, for the photographs show what one would expect – hunting and shooting being the prerogatives of the gentry and the farmers, with football and cricket dismissing the class barriers and bringing together villagers from all walks of life. How well I remember as a child visiting Stockton and other villages, to watch my father and my uncle play cricket (they were in the Warminster Post Office team). Before the game one player (who shall remain nameless!), with the help of a small shovel and a sack, collected the sheep droppings from the wicket, to take home afterwards for his garden. The match would then commence, and I can remember the long shadows of the fielders created by the setting sun, and the echo of the noisy shouts of 'Howzat' as the friendly rivalry grew. I also recall helping the elevens to devour the ham sandwiches that were served in the pavilion (an old wooden shed), and I watched, spell-bound, as the tea was poured from the spout of a shining silver urn. How simple life was! I am pleased to say that cricket and football continue in the Wylye Valley today, and the good-natured competition between sides still provides amusement and friendship for both players and spectators.

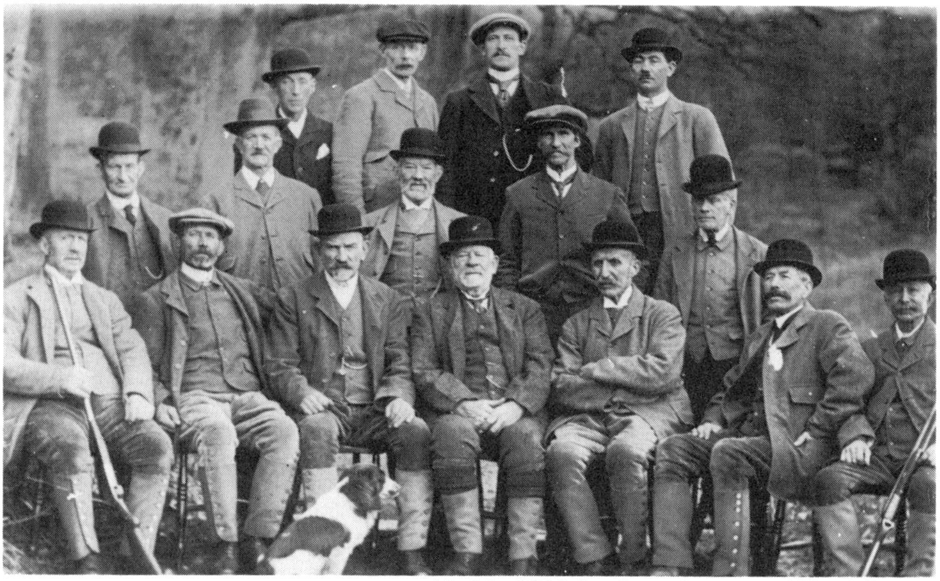

LONGLEAT KEEPERS AND FORESTERS, assembled in 1919 for the retirement of Head Keeper Peter Stockley. He is seated centre of the front row. Also identifiable are Jim Sims, first left, back row; Stuart Stockley, third left, back row; Mr Lucas, fourth left, middle row and Mr Bell, fifth left, middle row.

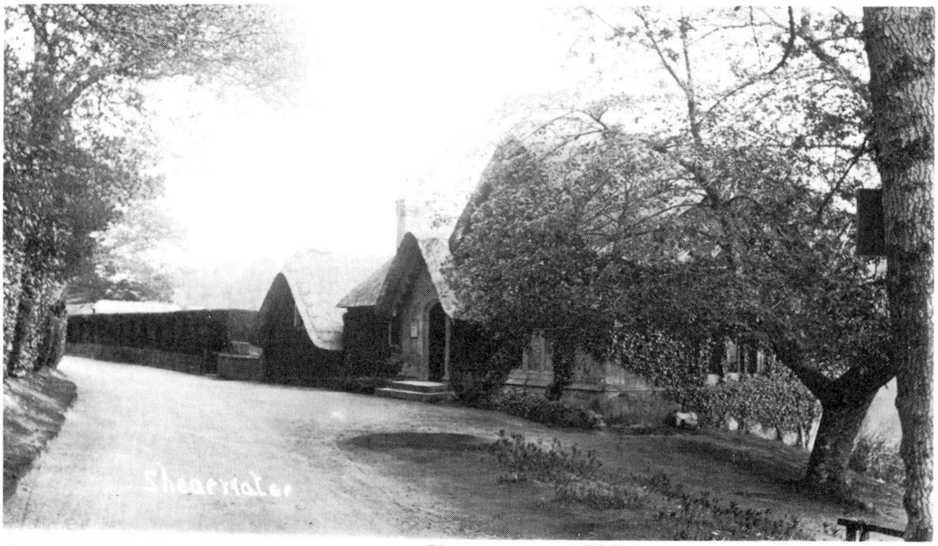

THE THATCHED BOATHOUSE AND COTTAGE at Shearwater, *c.*1930. A spectacular fire, watched by Whitsun holiday-makers, destroyed much of this picturesque building on the afternoon of Saturday, 4 June 1938. Mrs Penny, wife of the boathouse keeper, raised the alarm just after 2 p.m. The fire came only a month or two after the death of the previous boathouse keeper, Mr A. Trollope. He had been at the boathouse for over 50 years.

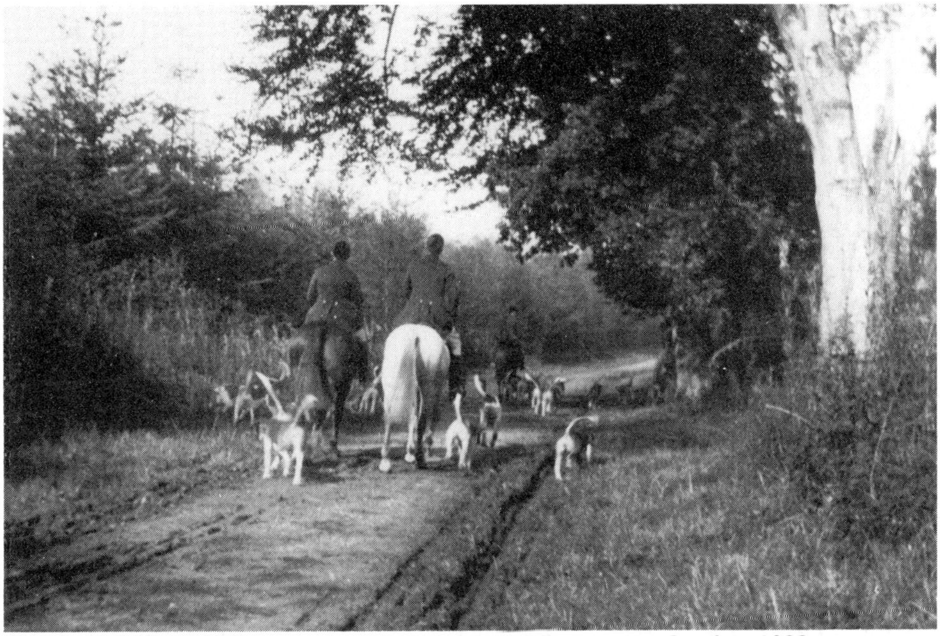

THE SOUTH AND WEST WILTS HUNT in the woods near Shearwater, October 1932.

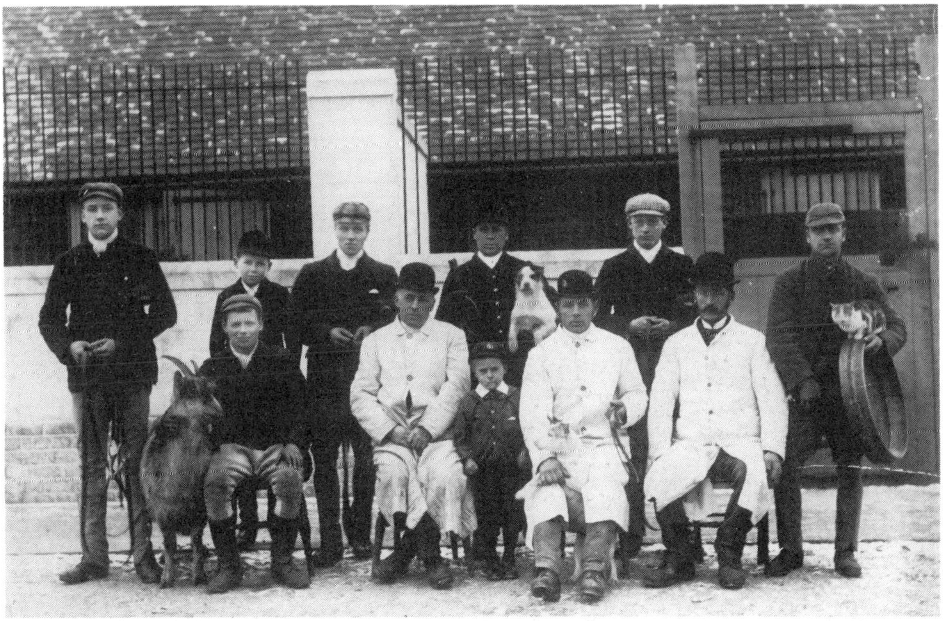

KENNELS STAFF at Greenhill House, Sutton Veny, *c.*1900/1920. The photograph, which also includes a dog, a cat and a goat, was taken by W.H. Croucher, who had studios at Warminster and Trowbridge.

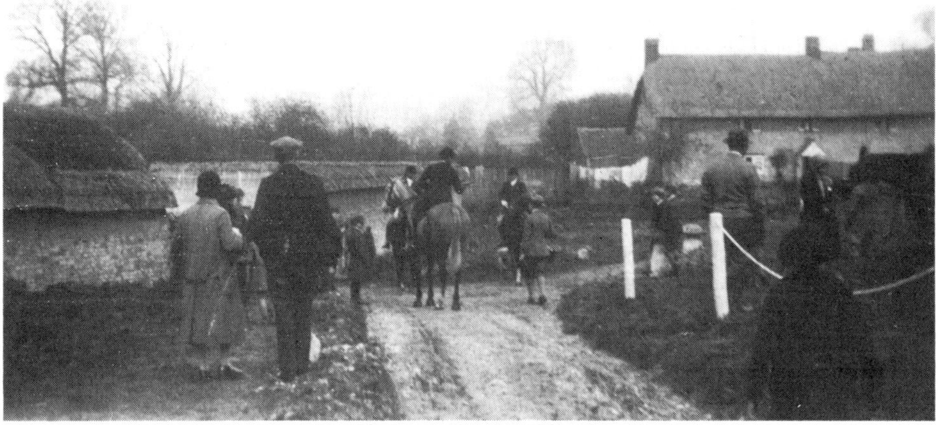

A MEET OF THE WYLYE VALLEY HUNT at Tytherington in 1924. The Master of the Hunt at that time was Mr R.H.H. Eden.

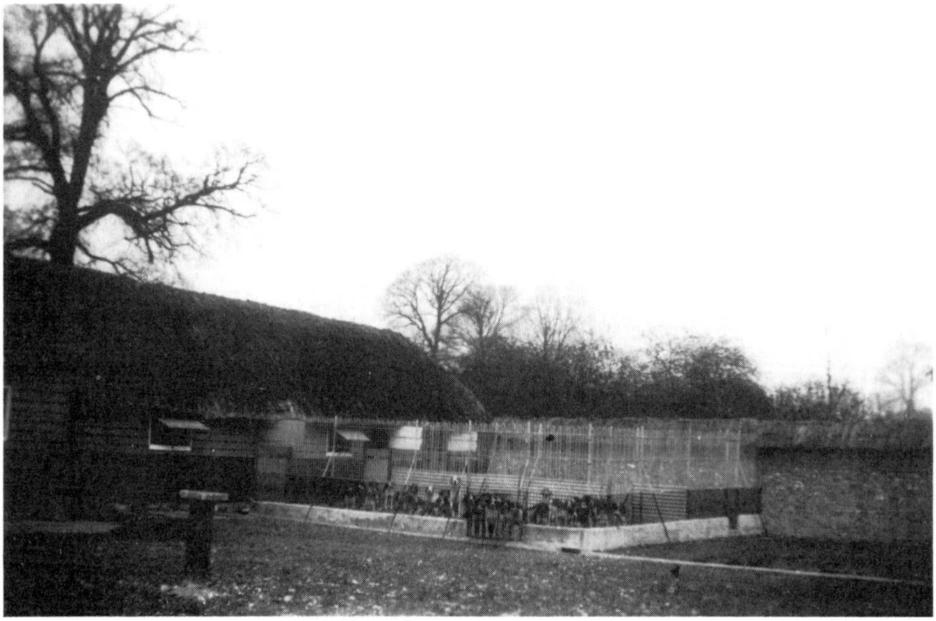

KENNELS OF THE WYLYE VALLEY HUNT at Tytherington, in 1924, when the Honorary Secretary was Captain Reid.

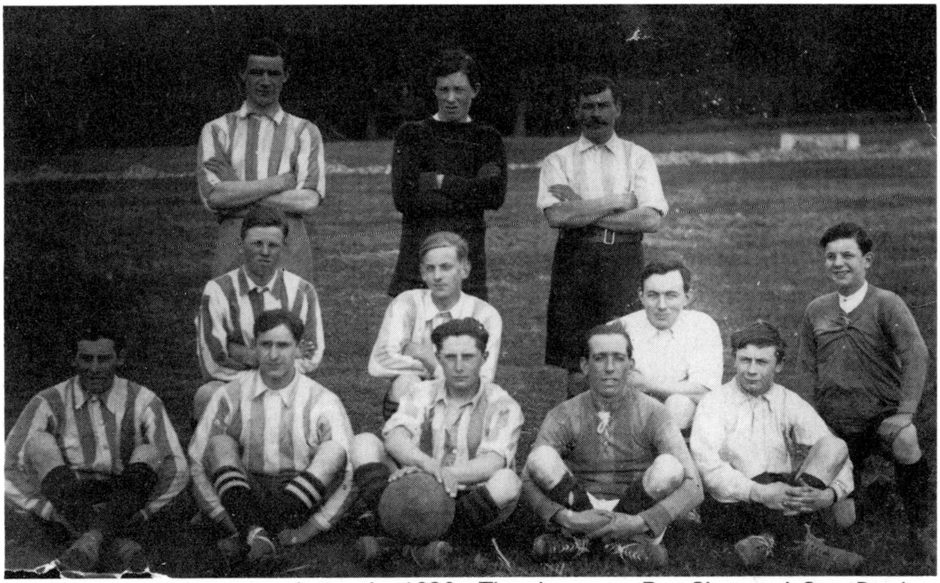

HEYTESBURY FOOTBALL CLUB, during the 1920s. The players are Bert Sheppard, Sam Dredge, Frank Pearce, Uriah White, 'Scout' Hancock, Jack Maslen, Arthur Pike, Chris Kitley, Mr Foot, Mr Ladd, Walt Cull and Fred Routley.

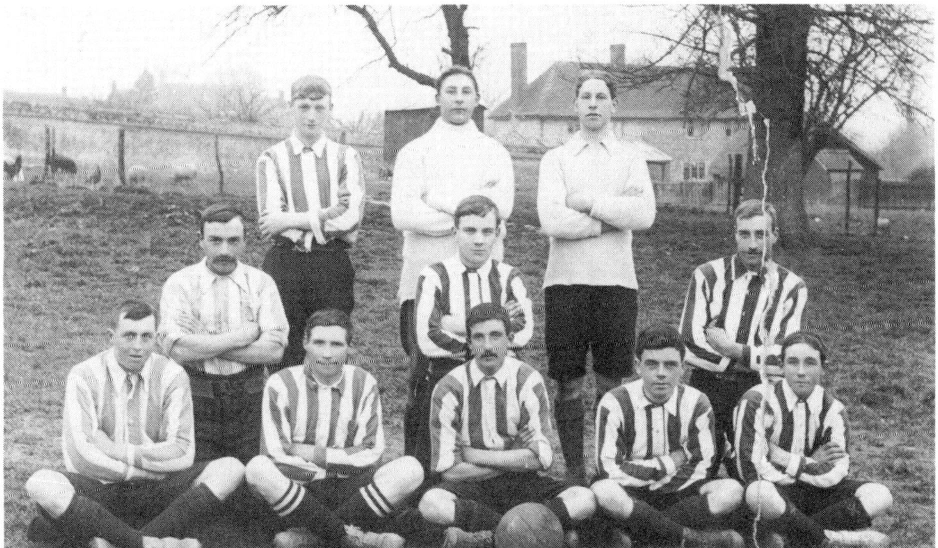

CORTON ROVERS FOOTBALL TEAM pictured at Corton, *c*.1912/14. The players seen here include Chick Sparey, Reg Gilbert, Stan Gray, Pat Sparey, Mr Imber, B. Shergold, H. Harvey, F. Axford, B. Sparey and F. Robbins. Obtaining proper football kit was a problem – two are without football shirts and it appears that only six could get shorts.

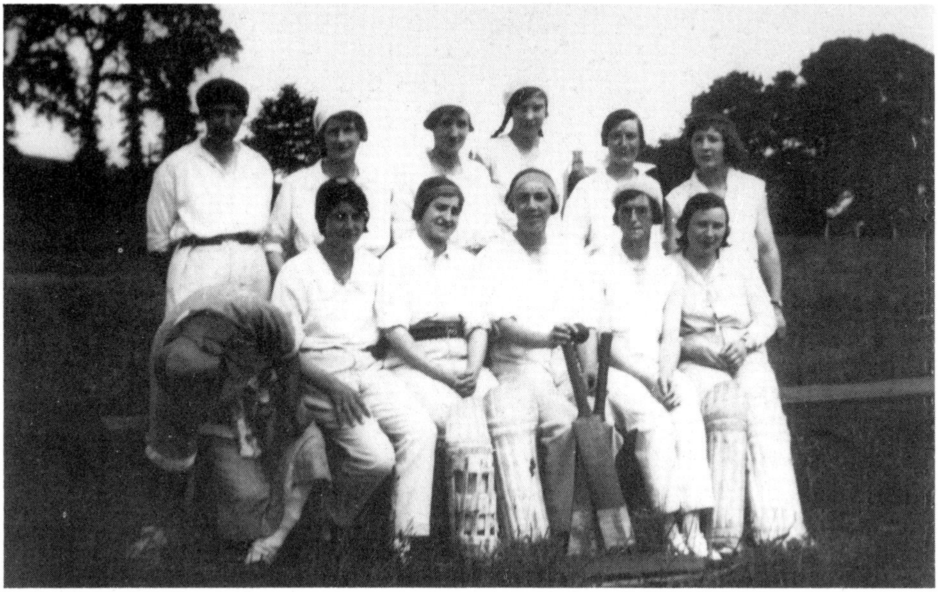

UPTON LOVELL LADIES CRICKET CLUB, in the 1930s. The players include Mrs N. Feltham, Mrs Bailey and Mrs B. Coward.

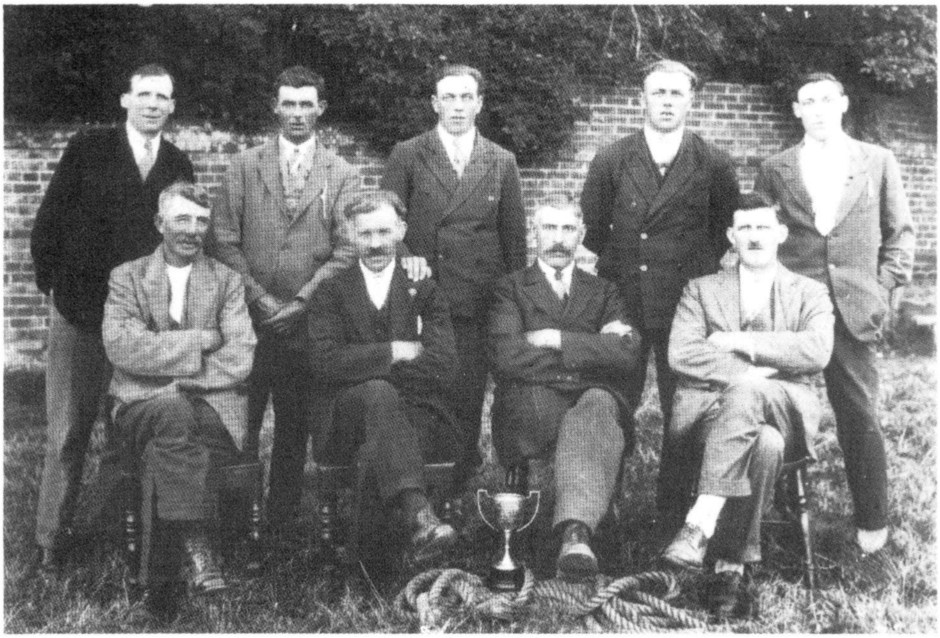

CODFORD TUG-OF-WAR TEAM, pictured in the late 1920s/early 1930s. Among the tuggers are Harold Harvey, Percy Pickford, Bert Pickford, Percy Harvey, Mr Jefferies, Bert Hart, Mr Trim and Nobby Clarke.

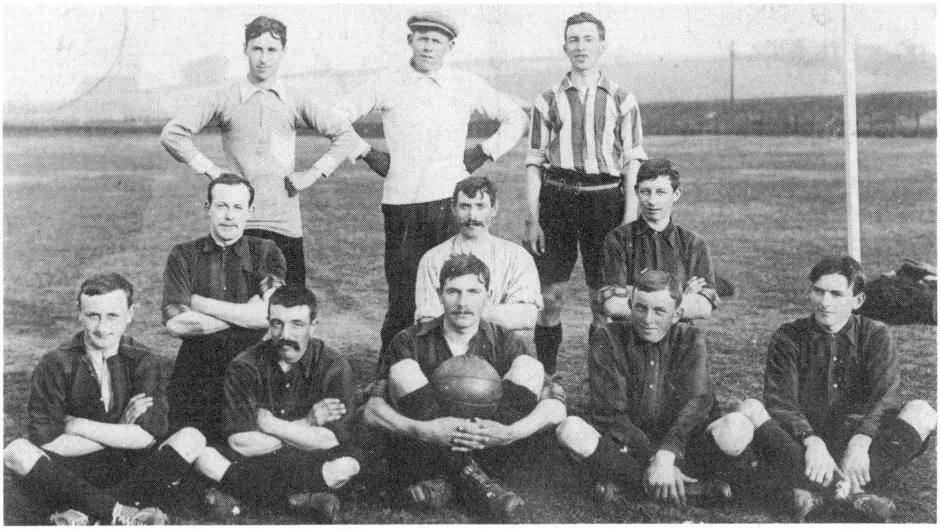

CODFORD FOOTBALL CLUB, *c*.1910/11, pictured behind the shop at Bapton, where they had their 'home ground'. The Warminster–Salisbury railway line is visible in the background. The club has continued intermittently over the years. After this picture was taken the club played in a field at Codford, which is now occupied by the Cherry Orchard housing estate, then opposite the Council Houses, later moving to a field behind Smith's Garage and finally to the centre of the village where the pitch is today. The players in this photograph include West, Conduit, J. Keele and Jack Robbins.

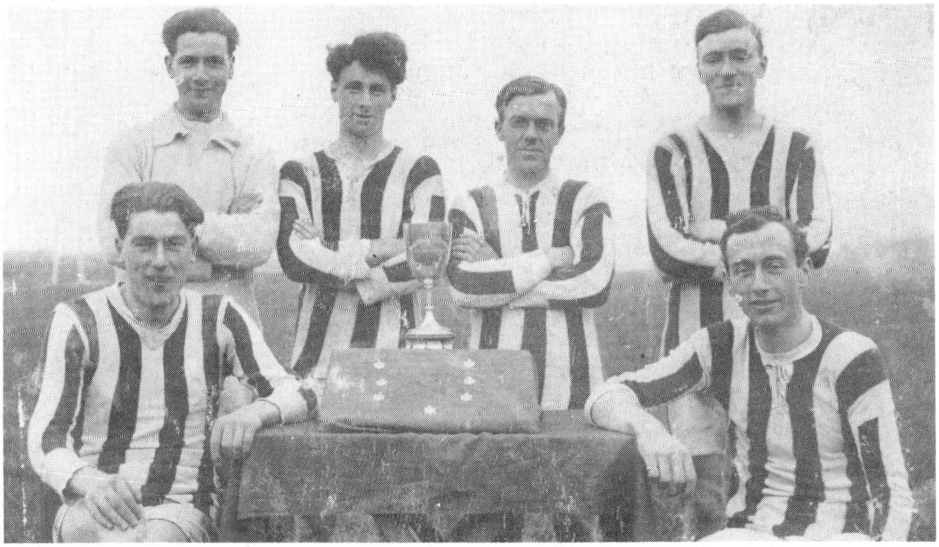

CODFORD SIX-A-SIDE FOOTBALL TEAM, pictured in the early 1920s with the cup and the medals they received after winning the annual Easter Monday Six-A-Side Tournament at Warminster. The players are Horace Matthews, Walter Fleming, Ernest Whitmarsh, Len Stacey, Harold Stacey and Harry Gregory.

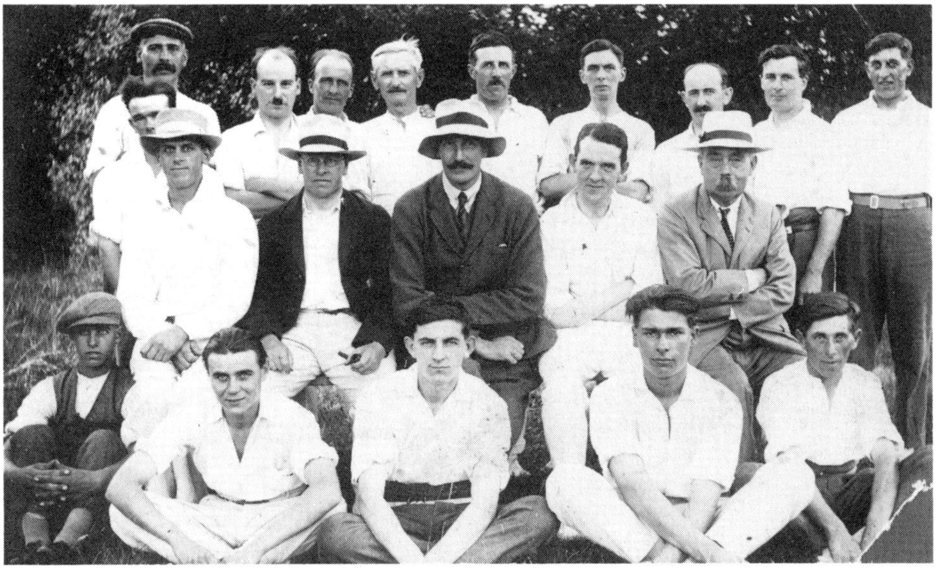

THIS IS BELIEVED TO BE THE FIRST-KNOWN PHOTOGRAPH OF STOCKTON CRICKET CLUB, and was taken *c*.1923/24. The club was founded in 1920 by Colonel Skeffington-Smythe, and the players came not only from Stockton but also from surrounding villages including Codford. Pictured here are Mr Trim (umpire), Jo Robbins, Stanley Parker, Norman Dewey, Bob Weare, Gilbert Gagen, Mr Burgess, Mr Symonds, George Nash, Frank Bartrum (secretary), Harry Cole (who took the photograph using a shutter delay), Revd Meyrick, Colonel Skeffington-Smythe, Mr Davenport, Mr Bartrum (another umpire), Jo Day, Percy Collier, Fred Courtney, Eric Trim and William Nash.

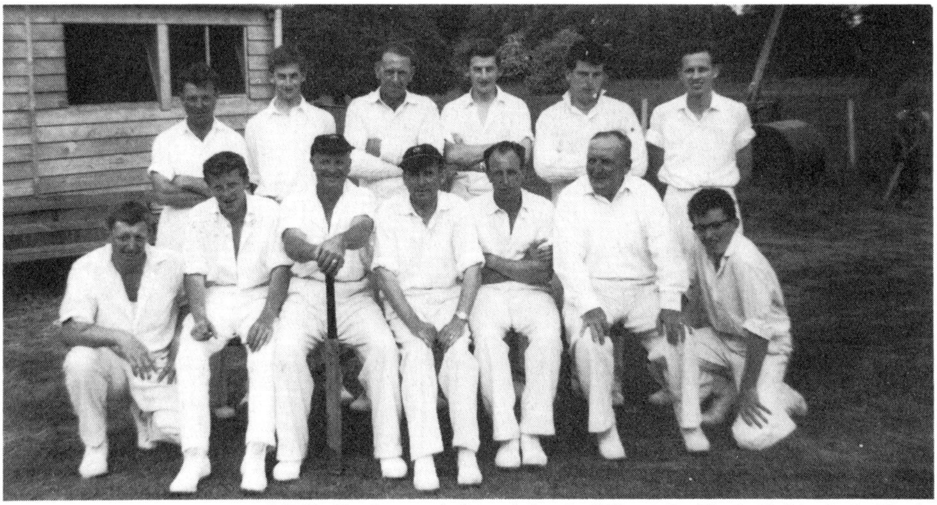

STOCKTON CRICKET CLUB, *c*.1953. Back row, left to right: A. Gilbert, D. Nash, R. Nash, A. Nash, R. Doughty and P. Marden. Front row: W. Meaden, R. Blanford, P. Bundy, N. Dawson, G. Conduit, A. Spratt and C. Wollard.

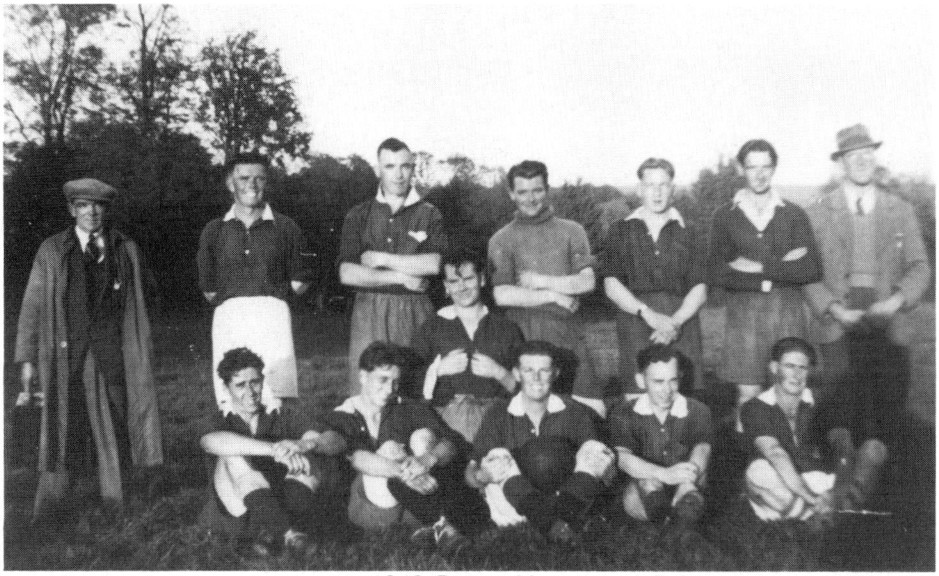

STOCKTON UNITED FOOTBALL CLUB in 1948. Pictured here are: J. Robins (trainer), H. Bennett, B. Bailey, A. Gilbert, R. Goodenough, P. Carter, A. Vallis (secretary), J. Barnard, L. Barnard, E. George, A. Bennett, Sgt. Grayson and W. Conduit.

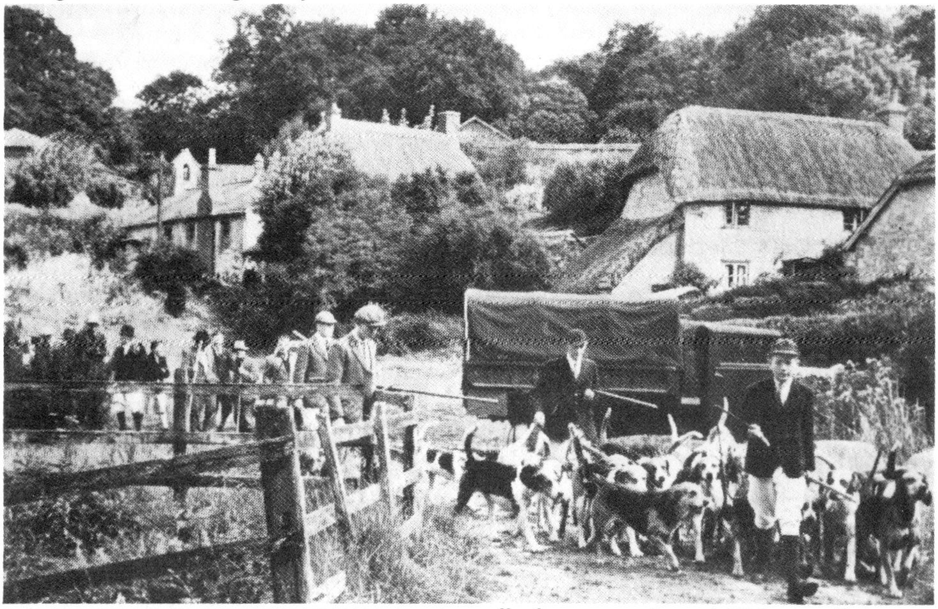

THE COURTENAY TRACY OTTER-HOUNDS moving off after a meeting at Fisherton Delamere during the early 1950s. The 1951 season was one of the best on record; the hounds went out on 60 days, found 40 otters and killed 25. Three otters weighed 28lbs each; one being killed on the River Frome, another on the River Wey and the third on the Wylye.

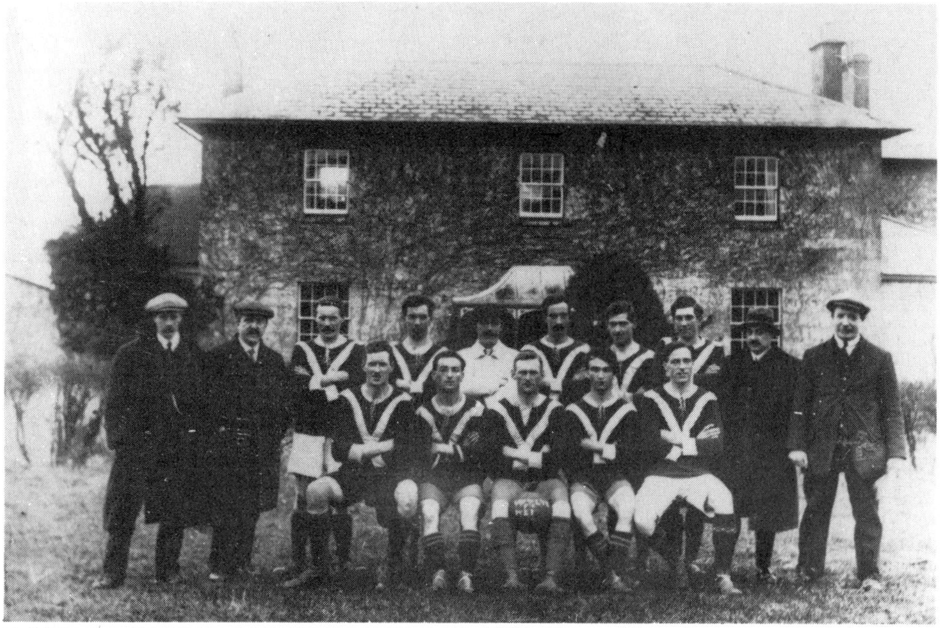

PLAYERS AND OFFICIALS OF WYLYE FOOTBALL CLUB, 1921. Many of the players were employees at Wylye railway station.

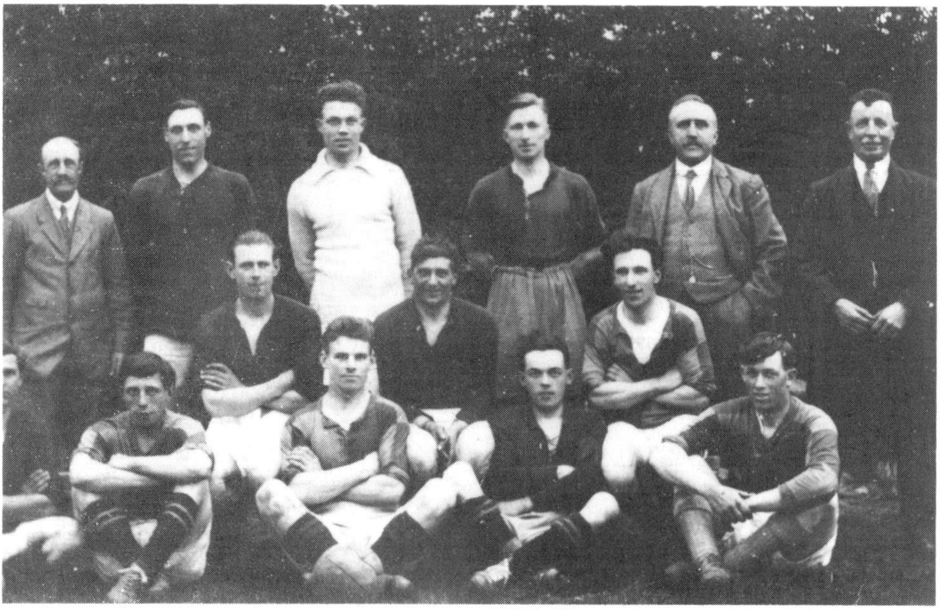

PLAYERS AND OFFICIALS OF WYLYE FOOTBALL CLUB, 1926. The mainstays of the club during the 1920s were Mr Lush, Percy Harvey, Lance Lovet, Mr Chapman and Mr Miles.